ONE MORE MOUNTAIN

ONE MORE
MOUNTAIN

CAROLINE FROST

Matador
9 Priory Business Park,
Wistow Road, Kibworth Beauchamp,
Leicestershire. LE8 0RX
Tel: 0116 279 2299
Email: books@troubador.co.uk
Web: www.troubador.co.uk/matador
Twitter: @matadorbooks

ISBN 978 183859 251 6

British Library Cataloguing in Publication Data.
A catalogue record for this book is available from the British Library.

Printed and bound by CPI Group (UK) Ltd, Croydon, CR0 4YY
Typeset by Troubador Publishing Ltd in 11pt Minion Pro

Matador is an imprint of Troubador Publishing Ltd

For Allister: you are my best friend, my inspiration and my world. Thank you for believing in me.

CONTENTS

PROLOGUE

What inspires us to pack up our lives, put a rucksack on our backs, read *Lonely Planet* travel guides and head into the unknown? I can't speak for everyone but what I can do is tell you what inspired me and my husband, Allister, to do just that.

At the time of boarding our flight from Heathrow in July 2010 we had been married nineteen years. These were nineteen great years, but they were not without their challenges. Everyone faces difficult times at some point in their lives and if you never have then you belong to a small and lucky group. You often hear said that the challenges we face help shape our lives. This was true for Allister and me as our own challenges ultimately gave us the desire and drive to take that 'gap year for grown-ups'.

June 2011 saw us return from our travels and the years that have followed have no doubt been influenced by this amazing experience. For me, travelling was the inspiration I needed to fulfil my dream to write. Moving back and forth across our life together, this book explores the emotions of facing a future without being able to have children, the impact of cancer on our lives and how these experiences built up to and ultimately concluded with us taking a fantastic year away from everything we knew.

You may read this book sat on your sofa, travelling on a train or lazing in the sun. Wherever you read it, I hope you enjoy it.

Maybe you will cry with me, maybe you will laugh with me, and maybe, just maybe, you will be inspired to see the world from a tent, campervan, cabin, apartment, hotel and hostel!

ONE

COUNTDOWN COVENT GARDEN

NOVEMBER 2009

'WHERE DO YOU WANT TO GO ON HOLIDAY NEXT YEAR?' Allister grinned at me. I looked at my husband and giggled. The annual debate was about to start.

'How about going to the Maldives?' I asked.

'There aren't any mountains there,' was all he could say, 'so what am I going to do all day? I will be bored sitting on the beach with nothing to do.' I suggested snorkelling at this point, but I knew already we weren't going to decide before the theatre. We were going to see the musical *Oliver*, not that this has any relevance, and we were enjoying a glass of wine and a meal in Covent Garden beforehand.

You see, our problem, and in fairness it is not really a problem, is that we enjoy lots of different things and the ideal holiday would incorporate all of them. Alas, the mountains of Scotland, the golden beaches of the Maldives, the wildlife of Africa and the food of Thailand cannot all be found in the same two-week holiday.

'You know what?' Allister was grinning at me again.

'What?' I said, hoping that Al, as I often prefer to call him, was about to decide for me.

'Let's go to the Maldives,' he said. It was clear he hadn't wanted to think about it too much as he had settled for my first suggestion. Now, I won't bore you with the endless back-and-forth chat that now ensued as we debated islands, cost, the number of nights and so on. The most salient point was that we only wanted to stay in a top resort. Now, this could be considered excessive, but we concluded, or rather defended to ourselves, that we would probably only go once and it's a stunning place and we should spoil ourselves. My husband then rambled on for quite a while about it being a good idea to go there soon. He explained that with the tides rising the islands were probably not going to be there for very much longer. Long enough in reality but he reads a lot of *National Geographic* magazines and I get to share in all the best bits, frequently. Anyway, this moment proved to be pivotal in shaping the next eighteen months of our life.

Allow me to go back a little bit in time to 2003. This was not the best year in the Frost house, and I will come back to this later, but as the year faded away and we moved forward we started to talk about going travelling. Now, how many of us have done that? I bet you have sat round a dinner table with friends or stood at the bar with a mate and said, 'You know what? One day I would like to pack all this in and just go, see the world.' Well, we did this a lot and we really believed we would do it. Well, one day! When does 'one day' come, though? For us we did get as far as thinking about it and talking about it and trying to work out when we might be able to afford to do it and thought

2011 seemed like a plan. So, the years drifted by, we saved a bit of money but every year we kept going on the annual holiday and basically spending a fair bit of what we saved.

Back in Covent Garden, and with hindsight I think perhaps it was the wine talking, I uttered the words that were about to change everything.

'If we keep going on these nice holidays every year we are never going to go travelling. No one thinks we will go anyway so are we or not?'

'You're right,' said my husband. 'Let's just do it, let's go next year.'

'Yes, yes, yes, let's go,' I said, banging the table. We then noticed the time and realised *Oliver* was soon to start so a quick conclusion was needed. Al announced he would talk to work tomorrow and I told him this was fantastic. I was so ready to pack up my entire life and go off around the world with a rucksack containing all I needed. Yes, it was definitely the wine talking.

It is strange how the euphoria of a great night out can make you feel that you can do anything and when you awake the next morning those threads of self-doubt re-emerge. This was so true for me the next morning. The big problem was that when I awoke Al had already left for work. This left me drinking my morning tea wondering if Al really would 'talk to work' about taking a year off. Was I ready? Did I really want to go? Would I ever want to go? Could we afford it? How would our parents react? Would we miss everyone too much? What about my home? What about all my stuff? Could I cope with not knowing where I would be the next day and the day after that? I am sure you get the picture.

I feel I must point out that we Frosts did have one small advantage in the whole 'give up your jobs and clear off for a year' plan. Al works for Sainsbury's and they offer a great scheme to employees. As an employee, after so many years of service, you can apply for what is called a career break. There is quite a bit to it, but the gist is you get up to a year off and then return on the same grade, pay and benefits. You must apply for it, and it may not be granted and there is not a 100% guarantee that you will get your job back, but history shows this does not happen often.

The phone rang, disrupting my musings. This was probably a good thing.

'I've done it,' said Al. I am not sure what happened to the 'hello and how are you' bit. Now, we all get that feeling when you know exactly what someone means but you must check just in case you are wrong.

'Done what?' I therefore replied.

Al laughed. 'I've applied for the career break. There is no going back now, Kitten.' Do I want you to know my husband calls me Kitten? Probably best to get it out of the way, and, given that I am going to talk very openly about our life together, my pet name does seem trivial.

My husband had work to do and left me to spend the day thinking about this. It is true that I thought about little else for that day. Lucky it was my day off. The only solution really to handle this shock was to clean. What better way to work off some serious anxiety than to clean with an unbridled enthusiasm that should really be kept for more exciting pastimes? You may not agree with this but let me tell you our house was gleaming by the end of the day. At least we were able to sit in very pleasant surroundings that evening when we discussed again our idea for disappearing for a year.

This time the conversation had a more practical vibe, as twenty-four hours of contemplation had passed, but basically the deed was done and now we just had to wait to see if the year off would be granted. At this point I must confess there was a part of me that was hopeful that it wouldn't be.

Two

Travelling
Karijini National Park

August 2010

I will never forget 17TH August 2010. This was the day that I can honestly say I felt completely content with my life and myself.

If you are reading this book and you are someone close to me then you will know that I have never been one to take risks. I worry about failure, and this has indeed held me back in my working life and in the past has stopped me doing things that I would probably have been good at. I also love my home comforts and for things to be clean, tidy and well ordered. We were in Karijini National Park in the north-west of Australia and had been travelling for about four weeks. We were living out of the back of a car, sleeping in a very small two-man tent and sharing toilets and washing facilities with random strangers and a range of small Australian critters. I hate camping, I hate bugs, I hate mess and I was facing many more months of it. So why was I so happy?

A sense of achievement was foremost in my mind. Despite six crazy months in the build-up to the trip, and all those doubts that came along with that, we had done it. We were in Australia, we were travelling and our life in England was neatly packed away in a storage container, on what had once been a pig farm, somewhere in the Meon Valley.

I mustn't forget the utter beauty that surrounded me at this point, either. Allister took a picture that really encapsulated the moment. We had hiked down a steep-sided gorge where at the bottom we were alone, dwarfed by the cliffs and surrounded by pools that were a stunning bright-green colour in the sun. This was Joffre Gorge. I sat and stared upward, and this was the moment. This was what it was all about. It was why we came and why we were going to make the most of the next year. Allister took a picture when I wasn't looking, always the best kind, and when I look back on it now it reminds me that if you put your mind to something and work hard at it you can achieve it.

It would be wrong of me, though, to tell you that travelling is endless months of great fun, no bad days, meeting great people all the time and breezing easily through every moment. It would be wrong, because quite frankly it is not true.

Our arrival at the Karijini National Park was not as idealistic as my description of the cliffs and green pool portrays. The problem with the north-west of Australia is that there is not much there and after driving for hours and hours we arrived at our destination tired. Karijini National Park is orange, all of it, and we soon discovered that most of its roads are unsealed. This is the Australian terminology for roads not covered in nice smooth tarmac. Our car was certainly not four-wheel drive and I am not sure that it benefited well from the thirty-kilometre trip across the park to our campsite. Being shaken to bits, the car and us, was a tad wearing but the scenery was spectacular, and I was hopeful for an idyllic camping spot. The guidebook indicated it was so, and despite the remote wilderness location it did boast that hot showers were available.

We arrived, paid for our camping pitch and drove to the designated spot. It was a beautiful wilderness – this was not in question – but for some reason I expected there to be a break in the orange rock and find a lush piece of thick green grass on which we could erect our tent. This was not the case, and I am afraid I did have a small mood swing.

We bought a small two-man tent as it was lightweight and could be carried in Allister's rucksack (not in mine, obviously, as I needed to carry shoes). It was a high-quality tent and over the months ahead the fact we had invested wisely before leaving England proved to be one of our better decisions. It had one very big disadvantage. It narrowed at the end where your feet go, and this rendered it unsuitable for an airbed. This left us sleeping on sleep mats. If you have ever slept on these, you will know they are called mats for a reason. They are thin and allow you to fully appreciate the earth beneath you. I am all for being at one with nature – it was after all part of the reason we had decided to undertake this trip – but a girl needs a comfortable night's sleep. Sleeping on orange rock for three nights (oh, yes, we had booked three nights before checking the site) did cause me to lose sight of the stunning location we were in.

Allister is a very mild-natured and patient man and is one of those 'glass is half full' people. In the early days of our trip he needed these skills quite a bit as I moaned about campsites, kitchen facilities and above all toilets and showers. This was one of those days.

Allister's happy mood wavered a little when he realised that hammering tent pegs in hard orange rock is not easy. It probably didn't help that wise Australian campers were arriving with cordless power drills that meant holes were created, pegs were inserted, and tents were fully erected, whilst Allister was still trying to find a slightly softer rock.

Needing some time out, I left him alone to complete his challenge. I was certain he would get on better without me and so I decided to go in search of a toilet. This proved to be a mistake and did not help my mood. The toilets and 'hot showers' were in the middle of the orange rock campsite in corrugated iron huts. As the echo of my call of nature reverberated around, I had to assume that every single camper was listening. I looked at the spider staring up at me from between my feet and I knew it was going to be an interesting three days.

I headed back to my lovely husband and decided I was being a little difficult. I painted on my 'yes, honey, this place is amazing' face and offered my assistance in putting up our current home. This was my next mistake.

The guidebooks don't tell you that the orange rock dust lasts for all eternity. There should be advice that tells you to wear clothes on arrival that you hate and will never wear again. We left England with all our belongings in rucksacks, and thus, due to the space limitation, clothing was minimal. At this point the few clothes we did have were in quite good condition as we had only been travelling for a few weeks. A white T-shirt was a mistake. This went orange, my hair went orange, my skin went orange and my trainers went orange. They remained orange for the entire trip; well, my hair and skin faded but the clothes did not. The lesson was learnt quickly, though, and we decided to wear the same clothes for the next three days so that we didn't ruin anything else. Ladies do not be alarmed: we did splash out on fresh undies.

The tent finally stood proud in the orange landscape and we congratulated ourselves by making the obligatory cup of afternoon tea. I must confess that sometimes during our travels this was replaced with a celebratory beer but being English an afternoon cuppa was a habit that was tough to break. The day petered out and ended on a high note as we had a barbecue under the stars and looked forward to a few good days hiking. It was an early night, as the temperature plummeted after sunset. I don't think we were in our sleeping bags any later than 8.30pm on all three nights.

The first morning saw me up and about not long after sunrise. This was I am sure due to having been in bed so early the night before, and probably because the hard rock did not make me yearn for a lie-in. I decided, as it was quiet all around, to take advantage of an empty shower. There was a very good reason why no one was using the shower. I learnt the hard way that when a shower is solar powered it warms up nicely during the day, but when temperatures are freezing cold at night all the heat disappears. The good news about my icy shower was that it woke me up and I refused to let my blue fingers and toes dampen my mood. Following my advice, Allister skipped the morning shower and we set off for our first day of hiking.

I was right not to let a freezing-cold night and a freezing-cold shower make me all grumpy again, as it was this day that we hiked down Joffre Gorge and a day that proved to be one of the most enjoyable of our trip. That evening, following our fantastic hike, we enjoyed a few beers, some good food and some great company from our fellow campers. It had been a pretty perfect day and it defined what travelling was all about.

THREE

LIFE CHANGES
GETTING THAT CALL

MAY 2003

NO ONE CAN EVER REALLY EXPLAIN TO YOU HOW THAT moment feels when you hear the word cancer. Somehow, everything else in the sentence is lost. When Allister told me he had cancer, it is true that I cannot recall anything else he said to me. All I knew was that he had cancer and it was not what I wanted to hear.

I had to go and pick Allister up from the hospital. He had phoned me and given me this news from his hospital bed. I thought he was phoning me to come and pick him up as I was expecting him to be discharged. He still would be, but now he had an outpatient's appointment to see an oncologist. Sitting in my lounge and taking a moment before going to collect him was the calm before the storm. I wasn't to know that. At that moment it was the worst I can ever recall feeling, but I would feel much worse over the months ahead. In situations like this there is only really one thing to do and that is to phone your mum. Of course, she wasn't expecting me to say what I did, but I think she often wondered if Allister would get cancer again. He had been unwell for some months, so signs were there, but I just chose never to believe that it would be the case. Anyway, my mum calmed me, as mums do; I got in the car and headed to the hospital.

I think I maybe need to go back a little to explain how we got to this point. Allister Frost, aged only fifteen, was diagnosed with Hodgkin's lymphoma. His mum, a hairdresser, was washing his hair when she found a lump in his neck. She was of course extremely concerned. Allister always tells me he knew it wasn't good news from the beginning. First of all, his mum and dad took him to see his GP regarding the newly discovered lump. Allister tells me his GP took some blood and looked concerned.

'This does not bode well,' young Allister thought. He had to go into hospital to have the lump removed, and then wait for the biopsy results. When Allister went back to the hospital with his parents to get the results, he had to wait outside a long time whilst the doctor spoke to his parents. His anxiety reached its peak when the door opened for him to see that the reason for the delay was that his parents had needed some time to compose themselves.

'This definitely is not good news,' young Allister concluded.

It must have been an immeasurable level of stress that Allister and his parents went through over the following months. He had surgery to have his spleen removed and undertook chemotherapy. He also studied for his O levels, passed them – except French – and recovered. He was a lucky boy as the treatment he had was quite new, and, who knows, diagnosed a year or so earlier and I may never have had the opportunity to meet and marry this wonderful man. Meet and marry him I did, and I never really thought too much about the cancer he'd had. I knew all about it, of course, but I didn't know him then and it was part of his past. It wouldn't come back now, would it? No, of course it wouldn't. I didn't even get worried when he used to go for his annual check-ups. He would tell me he was fine, and I would say, 'Yes, of course you are.'

It did come back though, this time as non-Hodgkin's or a non-classic Hodgkin's lymphoma. I'm not sure anyone ever really got to the bottom of that one but come back it did. What followed in the months following that day in May at times was horrendous; I can think of no other word. We both can look back now and reflect and even laugh at some of the situations that happened. They were indeed funny, but they certainly did not feel so at the time.

I arrived at the hospital, and as I walked onto the ward, I felt like I was looking at a child when I saw my husband sitting on the bed waiting for me. It was in that moment that everything changed between Allister and me. He was to become so utterly reliant on me that it would be many months into his recovery before I saw my strong and independent husband re-emerge. There are no words that you can say to anyone who has been told they have cancer that are going to make them feel better. I therefore held his hand, gave him a hug and said, 'Let's go home.'

I think we noticed Allister was not really right on our holiday to Florida in September 2002. Allister had been diagnosed with Crohn's disease in 1988, when we were students at Plymouth Polytechnic. It had, for the most part, been reasonably under control and I guess we had just kind of got used to Allister needing to visit the bathroom more frequently than an average twenty-something guy. Florida was different, though, but I don't think we thought it was odd at the time. He was always tired and lethargic, and I spent a lot of time on my own because he was otherwise occupied in the bathroom. Once we got back home from Florida things did not improve, and in fact they gradually worsened over the following few months.

At Christmas it was clear Allister couldn't continue as he was. It was concluded his Crohn's disease needed steroid treatment in hospital to get it back under control. In January 2003 Allister went into hospital for a week. He wasn't feeling ill. He was bored and moaning about his accommodation and fellow guests. The patient lighting a cigarette in the middle of the night whilst leaning against the oxygen bottle he had to aid his breathing didn't make my husband feel particularly relaxed! He was keen to have his treatment and get out of there. After about a week treatment was complete, and home he came.

He should have been going back to work, but it was only a short time before he started to feel quite unwell. A fever started, a fever that was to last almost continually until July. A real period of helplessness followed as Allister got worse. He seemed to rarely leave the bathroom; he had a constant fever and was losing weight rapidly. Visits to our GP revealed he was now also anaemic, and the conclusion was he needed further hospital treatment for his Crohn's disease. Allister was readmitted to hospital.

Looking back, it seems unbelievable that it took from September 2002 until May 2003 for lymphoma to be diagnosed. Even this diagnosis had to be proven further before chemotherapy could be started, but that's for a later chapter. In simple terms, his Crohn's disease masked the lymphoma, as the symptoms Allister had, were consistent with Crohn's disease. Underneath he had cancer, but no one knew, and I watched my husband deteriorate.

It was early February 2003 and X-rays showed around 20cm of Crohn's disease in the lower colon. Options were surgery or a drug treatment called Infliximab. This drug had a proven history of inducing and maintaining remission in Crohn's disease, so this seemed like a good plan. Side effects were many, as is always the case with these things, and alarm bells rang when we were told that one of them was the increased risk of lymphoma. Please consider we thought at this stage we were dealing only with Crohn's disease and it had been twenty years since Allister had been diagnosed with lymphoma. Was this an acceptable risk? We thought so.

Allister started his treatment on 26th February 2003. We were told that Infliximab was developed in mice and Allister has referred to it affectionately ever since as mouse pee. Now, I didn't really care what he called it if it worked. This treatment would be given over a few weeks and so we were told he could go home. He would get more rest at home and receive his treatment as an outpatient. We were told we should expect to see a gradual improvement as the treatment progressed. This all seemed to make sense, so, armed with supplements to aid in building Allister up again, steroids to assist in the treatment of the Crohn's and an appointment for the next dose of mouse pee, we headed home.

Further Infliximab treatment followed and, while we may have been trying to deny it, I think we both knew he was getting worse. How much worse was revealed when I took him to the outpatient's department for a follow up appointment with his consultant. He was weak, thin and feverish, and a noticeable cough had now developed. Again, in hindsight I think it had been there a while and the significance of this was not to be obvious until sometime later. Allister collapsed mid-appointment. He was heading back to hospital immediately.

There are moments in your life when someone demonstrates that the world is full of good and kind people. Allister's consultant called an ambulance. It was a late appointment on a Friday, and we were at a clinic that the consultant held in the small local hospital in Petersfield, where we lived. He needed to be admitted to the main Portsmouth Hospital. One of the nurses agreed to wait with us. My husband slept and the nurse made me a cup of tea. This was an ambulance transfer and not classed as an emergency. We waited for four hours and this nurse stayed with us the whole time. I thanked her and said goodbye.

As we left, I overheard someone say, 'I thought you were finishing early today to travel north to see your family.'

'I was,' she said, 'but they needed me.' Sometime later I wrote to that lovely lady and thanked her. She was someone who demonstrated what working in the medical profession should be about. My husband was a person with feelings, and I was an upset and worried wife. She cared and I will always remember her.

Allister needed surgery. This is what we were told once he was back in hospital. He was to undertake an operation called Hartmann's procedure. I remember sitting at home in a daze after this was agreed to be the next course of action. Allister was to have the affected section of his colon removed and would need to have a colostomy. When telling family and friends it was like I was talking about someone else. How could this be happening to my thirty-four-year-old husband? I think the hope, and what became a belief that it had to be the case, was the possibility that it could be temporary. A successful operation would mean the colostomy would be needed only to rest the colon and eventually could be reversed. I know Allister never let himself believe it would be anything else. At the time of the surgery he was so unwell that I don't think the reality of what a life change it would be sank in, but later it would, and he would cope with it unbelievably well. Would he have done so well if he thought it was to be permanent? I rather think he would, but the belief that it wouldn't be helped immensely.

The day of the surgery came amidst concern as to whether he was well enough to go into the operating theatre. He was very weak by this stage and was enduring a constant fever. The operation was indeed cancelled as it was found he was potassium deficient. I have no doubts he was deficient in many nutrients by this stage, as the little he was eating was going straight through. Potassium tablets were given in volume; Allister tells me they were disgusting, and the operation took place on 9th April 2003.

He was discharged ten days later, on 19th April, and readmitted ten days after that, on 29th April. Why didn't he feel better and why did he still have a temperature? Further investigation was needed.

On 1st May 2003 Allister made that call from his hospital bed telling me he had cancer. The surgeon who had removed part of his colon believed what he was seeing was not just Crohn's disease and he had decided to order a biopsy. Those results came back on this day. Allister was discharged, again. His symptoms were explained now, or so we thought. There was no reason for him not to go home, with his appointment in place to see the oncologist in the outpatient's department a few days later. Going home seemed to be the right decision.

I look back and so regret that. I truly believed he would be better off at home rather than sitting on a busy and noisy hospital ward. I was wrong.

We got home, sat on our sofa and held each other.

'I'm scared,' Allister said, looking at me like he was lost.

'It will be ok,' I said, as scared as he was, but saying it like I really believed it would be. I am not sure he was convinced.

FOUR

COUNTDOWN DEFINITELY GOING

JANUARY 2010

AFTER AL PUT HIS APPLICATION INTO WORK FOR THE career break a strange period followed in our household. We were in that limbo state where we'd made the decision for Al to apply for a year off but were waiting to find out if it would be granted. In this period, we decided not to tell anyone what we were planning. If it was turned down and we decided not to go, then there would be way too many conversations of 'what a shame', 'you must be disappointed', 'what are you going to do now?'. As we had no idea ourselves what we would do if the career break application was turned down, it seemed best to have our own heads clear first. It is important to remember as well that at this point there were a lot of doubts and questions in our heads – well, in fairness, those were in mine – Allister's mind was made up: he was going!

We expected that Al would have to meet his regional manager and discuss the application before a decision would be given. This was indeed the case, and a meeting was arranged. What now followed was a catalogue of events that prevented the meeting from taking place and seemed to indicate we were not destined to go.

First up, Al had a dose of swine flu, well, suspected swine flu, but regardless of whether it was real or not he was not particularly well and said meeting had to be postponed.

Next up, it was the lead-up to Christmas. For anyone reading this book who works in retail, you will know the festive period is not a time for meetings and chats about your future goals and ambitions. It is a time for cramming the shelves with yummy foods and gifts to tempt the masses into parting with their hard-earned cash, and in Sainsbury's it's a time for Christmas lines, co-ordinating turkeys, sprouts and Christmas puddings to ensure maximum sales are achieved. The meeting was postponed.

Next up, it was the weather. The meeting had been rearranged for early January and then it snowed. It wasn't just a few flurries that prevented my man from reaching his destination. He was also without a car, as it had been abandoned somewhere on the A272 the night before in his valiant attempt to get home from work in a blizzard. Boy Scout that he was, though, meant the boot was packed with rucksack, hiking boots and extra clothing, so he just hiked home the last five miles. Our car was not going anywhere, though, for a good few days, and so the meeting had to be postponed.

This meant Allister and I still did not know if we were going on our trip, and remember this monumental decision was taken in a pub in Covent Garden in November. This delay, however, turned out to be the best thing that could have happened. As time passed by, I somehow managed to convince myself that the career break wouldn't be granted. There was no basis for this. Obviously, I had no experience in these kinds of things, but I somehow just knew. I then found myself feeling so very disappointed. 'Odd,' I thought, given that I wasn't sure if I wanted to go. By the time the meeting came around in mid-January, I was on edge all day waiting for Al to phone me to tell me if it had been agreed. There was no doubt at all I now wanted to go, and Al had never had any doubts anyway. If they said no, well, we would just have to find another way. We didn't have to, though. The application was agreed. Al confirmed his six months, and a bit, notice and on 25th June 2010 he would be leaving work for a year.

Now what?

FIVE

COUNTDOWN
GETTING ORGANISED

JANUARY 2010

I THOUGHT THE HARD PART WAS MAKING THE DECISION to take our year out. It turned out that telling all our family and friends we were going to be away for nearly a year was a lot harder.

It seemed right to tell our parents first. My parents don't live nearby so I phoned them, and my mum answered. I decided the 'launch straight in approach' was best and announced, 'Hi, Mum, got some news, good news, don't worry, Allister and I are going travelling for a year and we leave in July.' I think it's fair to say there was quite a pause; naturally my mum needed to digest this piece of information. I think I won the 'who has the most news this week?' competition. I can understand the silence, as this would have been surprise and shock. Allister and

I had started talking about wanting to go travelling towards the end of 2003 and, at first, we had talked about it a lot. We did stop talking about it, though. When you have some doubts yourself, it is important to iron these out. We did this rather suddenly in Covent Garden, and I guess most people thought it had just been an idea after Allister was ill that had gone away once normal life resumed. It hadn't; it was just quietly simmering until ready. The silence was broken, and my mum made all the right sounds. She was happy for us, we deserved it, and she hoped we would have a wonderful time, but of course she would miss us terribly. What more can you ask for from your mum? This conversation was not quite as hard as I thought it would be. I had expected this one to be the worst. My brother and his girlfriend had gone travelling ten years earlier and as the daughter back at home I did appreciate that my mum did count down the days, every day, until the prodigal son returned from his adventures. Poor woman, now her other child was also clearing off for a year. The telephone call had gone well, though, and the bonus was that Dad was out and Mum would therefore break the news to him when he got back. I could only hope she took a gentler approach than I did.

Next up were Allister's parents. They live locally so we opted for the face-to-face approach. We walked round to their place and when we were all nicely settled on the sofa, with coffee and yummy biscuits, Allister gave them our good news. We got an excited yelp from Al's mum and a blank look from Al's dad as he hadn't heard what we said properly. We ran through it again at a louder volume and the reaction we got from them both was the same as my mum's. They were happy for us, we deserved it, and they hoped we would have a wonderful time, but of course they would miss us terribly.

Telling our siblings was easy. I knew my brother would think it was great. Both he and his girlfriend had spent the previous seven years doing their best to convince us to go. They loved it when they went travelling and wanted us to do the same. Al's sister was likewise enthusiastic to hear about us going. I think this was because she thought we had given up on the idea and she thought that was a shame.

Telling friends was a mixed bag of treats overall. I have a wonderful group of girlfriends. They don't all know each other, and I have met them through different parts of my life, including school, polytechnic, family, neighbours and work. All my girlfriends thought it was great news, as did their other halves, and the best bit was that we would have to plan lots of farewell drinks, meals, nights out etc. before we left. Our social calendar was set to be the busiest it had ever been over the months ahead. It is important, though, that you know and understand your audience. When I phoned my friend Julie and told her our exciting plans, she said, 'Well, that's not good news.' This could have been interpreted as a slightly negative response, but I know my wonderful friend well and I had no doubts that she was very happy for me and the comment was indeed probably the biggest compliment I had. She was simply saying that a year without me in her life was not good news. It's not what people say, after all; it's what they really mean.

Travelling for a year would mean leaving our home and we had no hesitation in deciding to rent it out. This process did not prove to be that straightforward and there will be more, much more, on this later. This did mean, though, that we needed to add our neighbours to our list of people that we had to break our news to. We were lucky to have lovely neighbours but if you ever rent out your house it is important to communicate with your neighbours. Just because you are happy to have random people live in your house for a year does not mean your neighbours will be as happy. They may like having you next door; you are perhaps very quiet, cause no problems and put their bin back if they are out on collection day. I am not sure our neighbours were thrilled at the news; after all, they could be about to get the kind of neighbours for a year that make excellent material for BBC documentaries on living next door to people who make your life a living hell. However, they seemed genuinely happy for us to be embarking on such an adventure, whilst behind closed doors they were no doubt keeping everything crossed for some nice and upstanding 'temporary' neighbours.

I also needed to inform the company I worked for. I only had to give one month's notice and given it was only January I felt it a little soon to be resigning. After all, a lot can go wrong in six months! I decided I would give extended notice to the company, though. I had a good boss and wanted to give him ample time to deal with my departure. In my head I settled on three months' notice and made a note to resign in March with a view to leaving the company in June.

Several things now seemed very real, once the cat was out of the bag and people were asking us a lot of questions about our jobs, home, possessions and of course travel plans. We soon realised we couldn't answer any of them, because, apart from knowing we would rent out our house and leave in July, sometime, we knew nothing else. We hadn't done this before, and we weren't exactly sure where we wanted to go! Some serious planning was needed, so there was only one thing to do: go to the pub! We had what is commonly referred to as a brainstorming session. This resulted in a random list of tasks with one or both of our names marked against them. My name seemed to feature more heavily than Al's and I put this down to me visiting the loo and leaving him with the list. We decided we would fly off mid-July, the 13th to be precise. This would give us both some time at home after leaving our jobs, allowing us to pack up our house, move out and spend some time with family and friends before going. We had always said that, if we went travelling, the main part of the trip would be to tour Australia. We chatted about this and decided we hadn't changed our minds so we would fly to Australia via somewhere and then fly home via somewhere and maybe somewhere else. We weren't very sure, as you can probably tell.

Allister and I are 'list people' so the creation of our 'travel file' was very exciting. Naturally we purchased colour dividers and decorated the front cover of the A4 ring binder with pictures from previous holiday adventures to ensure we stayed focussed on why we were doing this. We decided the best approach to rectify the random task list we currently had was to break it down into the six months we had before we left. We now had a divided section for each month from January to June, and even one for July for the last-minute stuff we would no doubt need to do! I will share the highlights from our task lists with you over the coming chapters, and I hope that, should you ever decide to rent out your home, leave the life you are so plugged into and disappear for a year, you will benefit from having some handy hints.

As it was January and we now had a January task list it seemed a good idea to get cracking. Deciding on the rest of our destinations was on our minds, as we wanted to book our flights, but it was important to make sure we could get into Australia first, and for that we needed visas. It was a sad day when we saw in black and white that we were too old for the working visa and therefore only qualified for the tourist visa, allowing us to stay in Australia for a year. Once we got over our realisation that we weren't in our twenties anymore, we went ahead and applied online for our visas. We thought this process would take a while, and this was our first mistake. Our applications were processed and accepted within about three days, but our additional notes in a covering email were obviously not taken into consideration. We had requested our visas to commence from July; unfortunately, they were valid as soon as our applications were accepted, so we would have to be out of Australia by 13th January the following year. We were thinking of spending Christmas and New Year in Sydney and leaving Australia sometime after that. It seemed the exact date for leaving had now been decided for us. All we had to do now was decide where else we wanted to go.

Six

Travelling Starting With A Singapore Sling

July 2010

Tuesday 13ᵗʜ July 2010 was departure day and we were flying to Singapore. It was day one of our trip. The night before we left, we had slept, in our almost empty house, on an airbed. We had moved out the previous day and all our belongings were safely stored in our metal container. I did think that night that it was to be the first of many on an airbed. Little did I know then what luxury this was, given an airbed was not going to fit in our two-man tent. My mum and dad were taking us to Heathrow, but the flight wasn't until 10pm so we had the day to fill. This proved not to be a problem. We had lunch out, took a final trip to our storage container to deposit some remaining items and delivered our car to our brother-in-law, who was going to be driving it whilst we were away.

When you are leaving friends and family for an extended period there is an extended period of goodbyes. For us this meant a lot of fun. We went to pubs and restaurants, went to friends for dinner, had friends stay over and, well, you get the picture. The downside is how many times you say goodbye. This can be emotional for your friends and family, and indeed many tears were shed. In the interest of my sanity I maintained a reasonable level with my waterworks, shedding odd tears but no full-on blubbers. The wall broke when I stood at departures and said goodbye to my parents. I did put this down to weeks of farewells, all building up into one big finale. Whatever the reason, I cried all the way through departures and so Allister steered me to the bar for a calming drink. This seemed to work, but tears were replaced by a wave of complete exhaustion. The thing about waiting for the flight was that there was nothing to do. This was the first time there had been nothing to do for six months. Anything that we might have forgotten would stay forgotten. We both realised we were already detached from our life. This was an amazing feeling that seemed to make me want a nap.

I hate flying, so the prospect of a twelve-hour flight would usually fill me with dread. Take-off typically causes me to get a bit sweaty and attempt to break Allister's hand as I hang on to him in the belief that if there was a crash, he would of course save me. I fell asleep on our flight to Singapore before take-off. I awoke to the sound of food being served and the knowledge there were only a couple of hours left. The best flight I have ever had. Al had also slept, although I think he took about an hour longer than me to nod off. There were big advantages to this as we were ready to party. Well, we don't really party very hard but as we landed at 6pm local time we were certainly up for discovering the nightlife of Singapore.

When we started to plan our trip, one excellent piece of advice we were given was to book your first night's accommodation before you arrive. Generally, you arrive tired and jet-lagged and may well be in a country that is not English-speaking. We took this advice and extended it a bit and I can say it was one of the best decisions we made for our trip. We were on our way to Australia for the main part of our adventure but wanted to enjoy some time in Singapore, so we booked six nights in advance at a small, modestly priced hotel. We had an added advantage that Allister's cousin lives in Perth, Australia, and she was keen to have us stay, so we arranged a week there to follow on from Singapore. A week would give us time to buy a car and then we would head off into the unplanned stuff. Now, this ended up being nearly two weeks in Perth as there was a car incident, but I shall come back to that.

Landing in Singapore we were a long way from that seasoned traveller feeling where you easily work out public transport, directions and currency in the blink of an eye, so we did what any normal holidaymaker would do, and we hailed a cab to our hotel. This was the one and only time we did this. From that day forward it was with our own wheels or public transport. It was important to feel like a proper traveller, after all.

I feel no need to compete with *Rough Guide* or *Lonely Planet* in writing a travel book that tells you every detail about a place you are visiting. I do recommend their use, however, so if you are planning a trip invest in at least one of them. They are great for hints and tips, and certainly if you have no idea what you want to do then they will give you plenty of ideas. As our trip progressed, though, we realised sometimes it is better not to know what the 'top ten things to do' are. I am not saying we didn't do a lot of them, but some of the best days we had were stumbling across a deserted beach or hiking up a remote mountain that wasn't in the guidebook.

I do want to share with you, though, some travel hints and tips and of course highlights and tales from the places we visited. I therefore must give you some best bits from Singapore. Food: you will never leave Singapore lighter than when you got there, really all I need to say. Tiger beer washes the food down well and is better than being convinced by your husband that he simply must have real ale and what better bar than Nick Leeson's old haunt? Tiger beer we could get for about four dollars, Allister's Old Speckled Hen was about fourteen dollars. He only got to have one of those! Beach life in Singapore: don't bother. You, Sentosa Island, a view of a thousand cargo ships and watching planes from Indonesia, as they display their military prowess, leaves you wondering why you got covered in sand. Ladies, when travelling to Singapore, be wary of high humidity. Perhaps your hair would not be affected like mine, but my hair grew in volume resulting in a very 1980s big hair look. Thank goodness I packed a selection of hair accessories to tie my hair back, a state that was necessary through the high humidity of northern Australia too. Singapore Zoo was a good day out, although for us the day was longer than it should have been as we forgot to get off the bus on the way back to the hotel and ended up very lost. The evening only added to the feelings of displacement as we visited 'Little India' only to discover it was the day when the women stay at home. As a blonde female I did stand out in the crowd somewhat. The newly opened Marina Bay Sands hotel only left us feeling less than enthusiastic about our upcoming camping arrangements, but the infinity pool was worth a look as it afforded amazing views over the Singapore skyline. Finally, no trip to Singapore is complete without a visit to Raffles Bar and a Singapore sling cocktail. We simply could not miss that, and we made the most of the free monkey nuts, adding considerably to the piles of shells that covered the floor. Never miss a chance for 'free stuff' when you are travelling!

The time to leave and catch a flight to Perth soon arrived. This meant the time had come to be proper travellers and get to the airport using public transport. Singapore's MRT (mass rapid transport) is a dream so in fairness not that tricky, but credit where credit is due. I did walk the streets to the station with my rucksack on my back, and please do consider this was holding all my belongings. Allister was carrying his too, which was a little heavier than mine. It did after all contain the tent. He was also carrying the day bags as well as his camera, but I was happy to play the 'I am a woman and not as strong as you' card at this point. We boarded our flight, which Al very much enjoyed, as he entertained himself counting the volcanoes that were pushing through the clouds. As we disembarked, I was told that there were thirteen of them.

Being in Perth was great. It was lovely to spend time with Al's cousin and her boys, and not forgetting Max the dog. It was winter and so it was a lot cooler than Singapore and my hair recovered well. We had a mission, though, and this was to tackle the second-hand car dealers in a place called Wanneroo in the hope we could get ourselves a bargain. Holdens and Fords are the traveller's choice of cars, so we went in search with our limited budget. The first day proved unsuccessful as a number of heaps were presented to us with a sales pitch of 'it's a real good runner, mate, full service history and I know I have the log book somewhere, just needs a new battery and it will start first time, no worries; you won't get a better deal anywhere else' and so on and so on. Not to be disheartened, we hit the dealers again the next day, and this time landed ourselves a Holden Commodore 3.8 V6. It is often said that travellers prefer to buy wagons (estate cars) rather than sedans (saloon cars). The reason that wagons are preferred is that you can sleep in them with comfort. I beg to differ on that point, and, as I had no intention of sleeping in my car, a sedan was just fine. The advantage also is that a sedan has a big boot where all your belongings can be locked out of sight. A wagon tends to say, 'come rob me'. A wagon tends to say, 'come rob me'.

We needed to get the money from the bank to pay for the car, so we arranged to collect it after the weekend. We had organised ourselves an Australian bank account. More about the financials of travelling later, and although this sounds boring, I hope to offer some good advice on managing your money abroad for an extended period.

On Sunday 25th July 2010 we saw our first kangaroo. This has no real relevance in this chapter, but I felt I needed to say it. It is strange how this great excitement soon disappears. Spending five months in Australia means you see a lot of kangaroos and wallabies. You can always tell the new travellers by their manic picture-taking; the more seasoned traveller simply ignores them.

We picked up our new car, which of course needed a new battery, and then headed to Big W, a kind of cheap and cheerful all-encompassing department store. We had a tent and sleeping bags with us, but no other camping gear and the plan was to drive and camp our way around Australia. Never go to a camping shop to kit out your car when you are a traveller on a budget. Big W is an oasis of stuff, and if you can't get it there then you probably can't get it anywhere. For a very modest sum of money we bought sleep mats, cool box, ice packs, large water containers, chairs, pillows and cases, cutlery, pans, plates, mugs, bowls, clothes pegs, battery-operated tent light, torch and batteries, large plastic container to store all our food and not forgetting some chocolate because we had missed lunch. We did have to buy a stove from the camping store but that was it. Later in our trip we did meet fellow travellers who were regretting the day they did not visit Big W.

Plan A was to head north from Perth up the west coast of Australia. We decided instead to opt for Plan B and head south first, to explore the south-west corner of the country. This area is less visited by the travelling set and was highly recommended by Al's cousin. So, we packed up and headed off, planning to spend four or five days down there, head back to Perth for a night and then north we would go.

Travelling teaches you things don't always go to plan, as we were about to find out.

SEVEN

TRAVELLING SOUTH-WEST AUSTRALIA

JULY 2010

LEAVING PERTH TO HEAD SOUTH WAS AN EXCITING day. It was our first day on the open road in our new car. Our car was packed with all our new camping gear, plenty of food and water and the *Rough Guide to Australia* was in the glove box. What could go wrong for us? Nothing at all; after all, 'planning' was our middle name. Planning does not include the weather; it was winter in Australia, but I am not sure that we expected it to be quite so wet and cold. We ditched the camping idea straight away; we were, after all, going to be heading north into the hot tropics soon and we had a good five months ahead of us, so best to camp when it was warm and dry. This is how we defended our decision anyway.

First stop was Busselton Jetty. Guidebooks will tell you it stretches 1.8 kilometres across Geographe Bay and is the longest timber piled jetty in the Southern Hemisphere. It has a spectacular underwater observatory, jetty train and other great stuff. It was closed when we got there. Our walk to the end of the jetty and back was not going to happen. It was tipping down with rain by now, so we headed to a place called Dunsborough. We found a reasonably priced motel and then sat in a lovely little bar called the Malt House. We drank a beer, ate a burger and thought about where to head the next day and what to do given the terrible weather.

We awoke the next morning to some sun. I hit the shower and Al made a cuppa; he became very good at this on our travels as he soon learnt it was the only way to get me going in the morning, particularly after those grumpy tent nights! As I dried off Al was still sitting in bed drinking tea. From the bathroom I heard an engine start and, before I heard the smash, I knew it was coming. It was a real sixth sense. Hearing the smash, I also knew it was our car before I even looked. Any temptation the driver had to make a quick getaway was soon removed as Allister yanked open the door, and with only a hat covering his dignity shouted, 'Don't you move.' There were two men in a truck, and I think they were so alarmed at the naked man in the doorway they froze. This got worse for them – or better, depending on your point of view – as I got really flustered, grabbed a pen and paper and dashed outside. I had forgotten I had not yet put my jeans on and soon realised I was standing outside in my underwear. We both decided to get dressed at this point. I don't think we expected two Irish builders to drive their truck into the side of our car on this particular morning, but you are supposed to be prepared for anything when you travel. I also don't think we expected problems quite so soon, but it had happened and now we had to deal with it. The driver's door had a lovely big dent in it and wouldn't open; there were other dents and scratches down the driver's side and the indicator light was in pieces on the floor. We got the builders' details, spoke to their office and then decided we may as well take it to a garage back in Perth. We weren't sure how long it would take to get repaired, so we were better placed back at Al's cousins. We rang her and headed back north. It seemed the tour of south-west Australia would have to wait for another time.

Arriving back in Perth, we headed to a body shop to get a quote for the repairs and then sent the information to the building firm for them to give the go ahead. It seemed it would be straightforward, and we hoped it would only be a few days' delay in Perth. This of course was not the case. We hadn't factored in the recent hailstorm in Perth. This had caused a huge amount of vehicle damage and the body shops were very busy. 'There is a three-month waiting list for repairs' busy. Obviously, we couldn't wait for the repairs and we explained this to the guy at the garage but there was nothing he could do. The car was safe to drive, no hidden damage, just dents, no indicator and a driver's door that couldn't open. The very nice guy at the garage took a big pipe and jimmied the driver's door. It creaked but now it opened. This was better. Our problem was that we had planned to sell the car at the end of our Australian tour, giving us money for New Zealand. It had depreciated rather a lot in the six days since we bought it. Allister made some running repairs, T-cutting the paint work and supergluing the indicator light back together; he had the foresight to pick up all the bits from the motel car park. We were good to go but out of pocket. Sometimes things work out better than you expect and a phone call to the building firm again revealed that the driver shouldn't have been driving, the other builder was the insured driver: oops! We were never sure that they meant to let this slip, but they did and a little chat between Allister and the managing director was needed.

We spent a weekend waiting for the outcome of this call. It turned out to be a great weekend, though. On Saturday we headed to a place called Walyunga National Park, for a walk and some kangaroo spotting. We were rewarded with lots of them hopping around the park, and like all new travellers we spent a long time following them and taking pictures. Sunday saw us spend a typical day in Perth. We strolled around Kings Park in the morning – worth a visit if you make it to Perth – and in the afternoon we watched Aussie rules football, not that I can explain the rules to you. It was a big game, a local derby between the Fremantle Dockers and the West Coast Eagles. I can't remember who won. We then fired up the BBQ to cook some snags and these were washed down with a few tinnies. Please note the fluent use of the Australian language.

Monday morning arrived and we waited anxiously to hear back from the building firm. Allister's little chat resulted in us receiving a cheque to the value of the quote for the repairs. These repairs were never going to be done now as we couldn't wait three months, and after all we could get in the driver's side now and superglue had fixed the indicator light. We had recovered 60% of what we had spent on the car, and even if we sold it for loose change in five months' time we were covered. We decided this was an excellent result and treated Al's cousin and the boys to a pizza to celebrate.

It was time to leave Perth, this time for good. We were keen to head north, mainly because it would be warmer. Our plan for Australia was to drive from Perth to Sydney across the top. We would detour down to the middle, but we aimed to be in Sydney for New Year's Eve. We would be leaving Sydney on 13th January and moving on to New Zealand for two months. As we were now a couple of weeks behind schedule, we decided to give the south-west a miss. We hadn't been away from home that long and still had a schedule mentality. This would soon go, and as such our planned Australian route would change a lot. This is the fun part of travelling and it is better not to plan too much. The spontaneous stuff is more fun, and you can never predict accurately the places you will drive quickly through and those you will stay a while simply because you like it.

On 3rd August 2010 we waved goodbye to Al's cousin, the boys and the dog and headed north up the west coast of Australia. Now we were really travelling!

EIGHT

THE EARLY YEARS
GETTING TO KNOW ALLISTER

1987 TO 1990

ALLISTER AND I MET AS STUDENTS. WE WENT TO Plymouth Polytechnic and we were on the same course, studying biological sciences. We moved in different circles during our first year but the start of the second year saw us thrown together on a biology field trip in Swanage. Is there a better environment in which to meet your future husband than wading through freezing-cold streams during the day and sitting in a pub all night to warm up? I doubt there is. We were also lucky enough to sleep in dormitories in a ramshackle house where the night-time activity involved drinking, pillow fights and organising a rota system to go and find one of our fellow students who took to wandering around Swanage barefoot after a few too many ciders.

Our main obstacle in Cupid's quest to put us together for all eternity was that we were both interested in other people. For me it was a guy already in a long-term relationship and unaware of my existence, but a girl can dream. For Allister it was my friend, the life and soul of the party and so never going to be interested in my future husband. The signs were there, though, that Cupid would succeed. I think it started during the nightly 'girls versus boys' pillow bashing when Allister got a bit over-competitive and I ended up with my head crashing against the wall. He was so concerned, and he looked really worried. He thought he had knocked me out. Allister is very competitive and taking the time out to see if I was ok, which could have resulted in a serious loss of points, was a big thing for him. I thought he was sweet, but nineteen-year-old student girls don't want sweet, do we? Perhaps there had been a small spark ignited for him, though, as the next night we all descended on the pub and I found the sweet curly-haired Allister sitting next to me. I don't think he was ever really what you would call a natural flirt with the girls, and I did feel a bit sorry for him when his opening line was shot down in flames by his mate.

'Are you new on the course, as I haven't seen you before?' Allister asked me.

'Nice one, Al,' said his mate. 'Caroline has been on the course as long as you. Lines like that aren't going to get you anywhere.' I don't know why I felt sorry for him, though, as he thought this was hilarious. I guess he was still in pursuit of my friend and was just being friendly.

Returning from our field trip, a night out was planned to celebrate our return to hot showers, private sleeping arrangements and our new-found 'friends for life' mentality that only field trips can achieve. We headed to the Barbican in Plymouth and as I reached for my purse, to chip into the kitty, I realised there was no purse. It was of course sitting on my desk back in my flat. I decided to go home and get it, as it wasn't too far, and from the rabble I heard a voice say, 'Would you like me to walk back with you as it is getting dark?' It was Allister, still being friendly. I accepted this chivalrous offer and noted that all the other guys were far too interested in their pints to even consider such an offer. A small thought was forming in my head that Allister was rather nice, and in addition I did rather love his curly hair. He wasn't the smooth one with the chat-up lines, for sure, but somehow that added a bit of charm and his attempts when we walked back from the flat had me hooked. I was wearing some Impulse spray at the time. The advertising on television for this showed young men smitten with ladies who were wearing Impulse and giving them flowers. Allister picked me flowers from the floral display in the town centre and made a joke about Impulse. He did make me laugh and has been doing so ever since.

Our social life now was very much in the same circles. The second year brought together different groups and we were all having a great time. Allister and I dodged around the obvious fact that we really liked each other and spent many evenings just chatting. There was not really any flirting because neither of us was very good at that. Finally, with a drop or two of beer courage inside him, he followed me out of the student union one night and asked me if I wanted to come over to his place one evening for something to eat. I said yes without hesitation; he then kissed me, albeit a peck on the cheek, and blushed and we made a date.

I had to admire Allister for his attempts to impress on that first evening of alone time. He lived in a shared house and only one of his housemates was at home. I couldn't help but notice how good-looking and charming this housemate was, but he made himself scarce, allowing me to focus on Allister, who was cooking for me and had opened a bottle of wine. Wine was a rare thing in those days for us poor students, unless it was cheap Lambrusco, so I was impressed. Cooking had a different sort of meaning to us as students in the late 1980s than it does to us now. Now we take pleasure in digging out a Jamie Oliver cookbook and transforming our dinner table into a fabulous display of multiple courses of sheer pleasure for our friends and family to enjoy. Back then, well, it was beans on toast, Super Noodles and peanut butter. Allister had really tried, though, and pizza and chips were cooking in the oven. I should have known then that cooking was never going to be Allister's thing. He did get his timings a little wrong and the chips had black edges and the pizza was still a bit frozen in the middle. Lucky for him I had drunk quite a lot of the wine by this point and it was a good icebreaker. I got a much better kiss after that!

It was safe to say we were an item and young love blossomed in the autumn term of 1987. It wasn't without some competition for the affections of my man. Al often jokes now about how his first year at Plymouth saw little interest from the opposite sex but once he had a serious girlfriend, then, to use that common phrase, 'like buses, all the girls came along at once.' I did have to make sure on several occasions that these girls were shown the error of their ways and knew Allister was not available! And then there was Allister's very good friend and housemate, who he spent a lot of time with during the first year. She was the only girl in a house of boys and getting through the door past her wasn't always easy. Not that she wanted Allister for herself – she had a boyfriend – but Allister was spending less and less time in the house and this meant less and less time with her. I think I stole her mate. We overcame this little hurdle, became very good friends and have remained so ever since.

Our second year flew by and suddenly we had been together for a year. Don't you just love those first few months together, the getting-to-know-you and that initial excitement? We spent many nights out with friends and then headed back to his place or mine where we would sit and chat until the sun came up. Even on the nights I didn't plan to see him, and he was out elsewhere, it wasn't uncommon for Allister to arrive on my doorstop at 2am, a little on the tipsy side, saying he missed me. He says now, if anyone asks, that I just lived nearer to the nightclubs than he did, so it was less far to walk home. I prefer the original version, I must say.

We took the plunge at the start of our third year and moved into a shared house. As it was a shared house, we had our own rooms, but this was probably unnecessary by this stage. Still, at least it was an escape sometimes. Our housemates were a mixed bunch, more friends of mine really, but it seemed like it would work out. It didn't. Allister was, still is and no doubt always will be a bit of a torment. If something irritates you, never let on to Allister. He so likes to wind people up and several of our friends have enjoyed his antics in the past. Most people have a good sense of humour; one of our housemates did not. She had a hot date one night and was keen to get into the bathroom to pamper herself accordingly. Not before cleaning it, though, of course. When a girl needs quality bathroom time then the facilities in a shared student house aren't always the best. She scrubbed it and scrubbed it and scrubbed it and no one was allowed in. There was only one bathroom and Allister soon got very annoyed. She refused entry until her work was done and locked Allister out. When she had finally finished cleaning, and Allister had taken his turn, she got ready for her night out emerging from the bedroom dressed in her best going out gear, made up beautifully with her hair done to perfection. As she walked down the stairs Allister sprayed her with hair mousse. We moved out.

We found a nice little flat in an old converted house. It had a kitchen/lounge combined, shower room and bedroom. What more did we need? There was one small problem and that was we hadn't told our parents. I wasn't sure them hearing about us living together – properly, so to speak, rather than in a shared house – was going to be taken all that well. Sharing a love nest, living in sin, and shacked up together were words I thought best avoided when I phoned my mum. She didn't say much. She just said, 'I will tell your father.' I never did find out what he said. I can't remember what Allister's parents said; maybe Allister never told them.

Our third year flew by and suddenly we were taking finals. Allister handled this better than me. Strict forty-minute revising sessions in the library were followed by twenty-minute gaming sessions spent playing Asteroids in the student union. I considered this to be a way too relaxed approach. I preferred to lock myself into a cubicle in the library for eight hours straight, panic, absorb nothing and reach such high stress levels that Al decided to call my parents down to Plymouth to calm me down. It all worked out well in the end. We both achieved BSc honours grade 2:2, referred to, we heard, as the 'party students' grade'. I prefer to think of it as the grade you get when you also gain valuable life experiences, meet great people and have a good time as well as a bit of study. We both had a wonderful three years and gained friends we still have today. The problem was we didn't really want to leave, so we didn't, well, at least not straight away. What else is there to do with a biology degree other than spend your summer in Devon, on the beach? Allister had a motorbike by this time and so we even had transport. We needed some cash to fund this summer of fun, though, so I got a job as a waitress in a hotel; this also funded driving lessons, and Allister worked on the frozen food department in Sainsbury's. Our parents were thrilled that their investment in our education had paid off. We weren't in a hurry to join the grown-up world and did think in passing of going travelling for a year. The reality was, though, that we had no money and probably more significantly not enough confidence to take the plunge. I had only been abroad twice in my life at this point. The first was a two-week camping holiday in France with my parents when I was fourteen. The second came shortly afterwards and was an educational cruise around the Mediterranean with the school. Interestingly this was on a ship called the SS *Uganda*. It was newly refurbished, having just returned from service in the Falklands as a hospital ship.

Eventually the grown-up world was calling and so we planned our strategy. We decided, as we were coming up to two years together, that we kind of liked it and so the best option would be that we would both continue with our job-hunting and whoever got the first job would determine our future location. Allister won and joined the Sainsbury's Graduate Trainee Management Scheme. He was to start in Guildford, so we left out flat and headed to Surrey. During this transitional period, I had shelved the idea of becoming a teacher, my original intention when doing my degree, and I got myself a job as a recruitment consultant.

It was a strange few months in the lead-up to Christmas 1989. Allister was in a hotel, courtesy of Sainsbury's as he was working at a store opening ahead of commencing his training scheme, and I was renting a room in a house. Strange is a gentler way of saying I hated every minute of it. To go from three years of studying, being surrounded by loads of friends and having a wonderful time to working five days a week and living in a room in house shared with an old, albeit very lovely, lady was quite an anticlimax. I would drive to see Allister a couple of nights a week and we spent weekends at either his parents or mine. It was a time when both of us were very unsure where we would end up. I quit my job after the owner of the company met Allister and told me he wasn't ambitious enough and would hold me back in life. I was never very good at taking advice.

Allister started his job as a trainee manager, I got a temporary job at another Sainsbury's nearby and we found ourselves a flat in Guildford town centre. It was in a great location, modern, split-level with a master bedroom in the loft space and a spare bedroom, handy for friend stopovers after a night out. This was all good and we enjoyed our life in Guildford. Whilst working at Sainsbury's and trying to decide what to do with my life, I realised I quite liked retail. I was in a new superstore, which was great fun. Sainsbury's was recruiting a lot of trainee managers at the time and as I already had a foot in the door my application went without a hitch. I even got to stay in the same store and was soon enjoying a great social life and a new career. Both working as trainee managers in different stores had its disadvantages, of course. We talked shop a lot, pardon the pun, and retail isn't the best of working hours. In those days, a trainee manager worked long days; after all, you weren't committed to the cause unless you put in a good twelve hours a day. This meant we didn't have the time together we were used to, but at least we were working, had our own place and were going in the right direction. I guess we had finally settled into the grown-up world.

NINE

LIFE CHANGES
WHERE DID MY HUSBAND GO?

MAY 2003

AT 1AM ON WEDNESDAY 7TH MAY 2003 I CALLED AN ambulance for my husband. He would not come home again until Monday 11th August. There were many times during those summer months when I had to fight against the thought that he might not come home at all.

In May I was due to take Allister to his first outpatient's appointment with his oncologist. After receiving the awful news that he had lymphoma I watched Allister deteriorate rapidly. We had spent what was the bank holiday weekend at home. We had family visit after we had told them all the news and I watched, in only a few days, my husband change. He went from feeling a bit unwell to needing an ambulance.

I kept a diary during Allister's illness. This started as a few notes to make sure I understood and remembered what the doctors said to me. It became a daily record of every detail of his condition, his treatment, what information I was given and the results of every single test. Stress does many things to you, and one of them for me was the feeling my brain was overloaded with information. May 2003 was a complicated month and the notes I wrote down helped me understand what was going on, ensured I could have meaningful dialogue with the medical staff and enabled me to understand his care. I asked his parents to do the same, and when I did leave his bedside during this month, they kept the diary up to date. Reading back now I can say for sure that their handwriting was better than mine.

Sitting here on my sofa writing this book is the first time I have read this diary since 2004. It has made me cry, which is not ideal as this book is supposed to be more funny than sad. The sad stuff in life, though, does make the good stuff even better, so, as tears of sadness change to tears of joy, laughter follows, and this has certainly been the case in my life with Allister.

There is no denying that A&E in Portsmouth is not an ideal choice of venues for the end of a bank holiday weekend. It was, however, the preferred destination of those who had overindulged during the extended break and in the world we live in those who have drunk too much, taken too many drugs or got into a serious fight do get priority if their condition is deemed to be more serious than a man who has cancer and, although seriously ill, is stable. This meant about twelve hours sitting by my husband's side, as he lay scared with only a curtain separating us from the swearing drunk who we were lucky enough to have as our neighbour.

The Oncology Department at Portsmouth was at the time on a different site to where we were and so it was eventually decided to transfer him to the Oncology Ward, where he could be seen and assessed by his oncologist. Back in an ambulance again and Allister was moved across town.

It is difficult to decide how much detail to now put into this chapter. It was a huge struggle at the time to understand fully what happened over the following few weeks, but I will do my best to give an accurate account.

Allister had undergone surgery in April to remove part of his colon, and it was this that led to his cancer diagnosis. The reason Allister felt so unwell at this stage, though, was put down to a postoperative infection and not the cancer. He had a high fever and was showing signs of confusion. He had blood tests and a scan. This revealed a shadow on his liver. At this stage it was deemed it was unlikely this was lymphoma as the scan showed no other visibly affected areas. This was where the complication really started because for lymphoma to be detected in the colon, it was strange for it not to be found elsewhere. For chemotherapy to start he needed to be clear of infection, and the oncologist needed to be sure that lymphoma was present. Given that no lumps were seen on the scan, this was a difficult call to make.

The oncologist wanted him transferred to the main hospital for investigation into the shadow on his liver and to hopefully get his infection under control. Back in an ambulance again, and Allister was moved back across town.

Allister went onto a general ward, but he was not in the right place. It took two weeks and several really difficult situations before he was finally moved into the High Dependency Unit.

It was a truly dreadful and heart-breaking two weeks. I adore my husband, and I helplessly watched the man I love become a stranger.

To start with his fever was not going and his confusion was increasing. The hard thing about convincing people that your husband is behaving in a bizarre and irrational way is that you are talking to people who don't know what your husband is really like.

At this stage he was primarily still under the care of his gastroenterologist; this was the consultant who looked after his Crohn's disease and had admitted him for his surgery. I remember one morning that Allister was smiling, polite and answering questions sensibly to anyone that asked. I knew he was somewhere else in his head. He had a vacant look and to me seemed like a total stranger. His consultant thought he sounded a little better. My tears of frustration had an effect and he sat down and asked Allister lots of questions. He asked him his name and age; did he know where he was, what he did for a living and, oddly, the date of the Second World War. Allister got them all wrong, well apart from the date of the Second World War. I particularly liked the fact that Allister inflated what he did for a living and instead of being a deputy store manager for Sainsbury's he said he was a director of the company. Ambition, even from his hospital bed! Allister at least did me a favour here, as his consultant did agree that he was behaving oddly.

He had a lumbar puncture to check his spinal fluid for infection, as his mental deterioration at this stage was not easily explained. This was clear of infection but would be examined further for signs of lymphoma. This would take a few days so it was decided he would remain on antibiotics and his liver would be scanned again. He now also had a blood clot and his blood results showed he was deficient in potassium, phosphates and calcium. This could have been adding to his confused state, but was it causing it? He was given supplements to boost these levels plus build-up drinks. He was eating little and he was painfully thin by this stage.

Allister's fever, confusion and anxiety continued. He told me stories sometime after he was ill of experiences he had during this time. One day I sat by his bed and kissed his cheek. I remember he got really agitated, but I never knew the reason in his head. He told me it felt like I got stuck to him, even though it was a quick peck on the cheek. He told me that the kiss felt comforting and then everything stopped; it seemed nothing was moving, and I was stuck to him. He thought he was dead. On another occasion I put up some get-well cards on some string at the end of his bed. He ripped them down after I left. To Allister the lion on one of the cards was moving and its eyes were following him around the room.

Some of his distress was more obvious. I had spent a long day by his bed and about 10pm the nurse on duty convinced me to go home. Allister had been so low all day and hadn't wanted me to leave at all and I wanted to stay. He was asleep, finally, and the nurse promised she would call if he needed me, so I went home for some rest.

I went home completely drained and trying hard to suppress my feelings of complete despair. I managed to get some sleep as exhaustion overtook me, but I was back at the hospital by 7.30 the next morning. Allister was sitting in a chair by his bed with a nurse trying to get him to eat some cereal. It was one of those many moments where I just felt so sad for my husband. He looked terrible and added to his overall ill health was a great big gash over his eye. When I asked what had happened, it seemed Allister had a busy night after I left. He awoke to find me gone and got out of bed in search of me. There was some logic in this, albeit a little unrealistic. As I was a woman, he decided I must be in the women's ward and Allister was found checking all the ladies' beds asking the occupiers in the dark if they were his 'kitten'.

Allister was retrieved and returned to bed, where the sidebars were raised, the idea being he wouldn't get out again. Alas, this did not deter him from finding me and he took a dive over the top, landing in a heap on the floor. Allister tells me that he does remember being on the floor. At the time he remembers thinking it was cold and then the floor got warmer – this was his blood – so he decided to stay put. He still has a small scar over his eye today, a reminder of that night. I did feel so upset; after all, I went home confident that he would be looked after, and the man in the opposite bed telling me he was left on the floor in a pool of blood for half an hour didn't help, not that I know whether that was true or not. I couldn't help but be a little sceptical about what he was saying. It didn't stop my feelings of guilt, though. In my heart I knew I could not be at the hospital twenty-four hours a day but seeing the dreadful state my poor husband was in made me want to be by his side all the time. Allister needed full-time care by this stage; it was clear a general ward was the not the place for that.

Each day as we waited for blood results, scan results and histology he just got worse. His behaviour was increasingly odd. He took to wearing his sunglasses as he said the room was too bright and took instructions very literally. I gave him a toothbrush one morning and he sat up in bed to clean his teeth. I gave him a glass and told him to spit. I assumed, of course, that he would spit in the glass, but I didn't say those words, so he just spat toothpaste across the room. We laugh now when we talk about it, but at the time he realised he had made a mistake, and this just upset him further. He was confused but not so confused he didn't understand he was confused, if you know what I mean. He told me time was disjointed. He would look at the clock and see it was 3pm. He would look again and see the hands of the clock moving fast and then it would be 4pm. He was seeing fragments, but they appeared as sped-up movements of the clock face. His agitation increased and culminated in a full-blown panic attack on 14th May. He was so overwrought he had to be sedated. It calmed him and he fell asleep. I cannot put into words how I felt at this point. I held his hand and watched him sleep. The sedative had a calming effect on me too as I got a quiet few hours.

The next day he had a seizure. No lasting damage from that, we are pleased to say. His potassium levels and phosphates were still very low and the most likely cause. His fever was improving, though. He was prescribed diazepam to keep him calm and I went home that night wondering what would happen next. My dearest friend Julie was staying with me at the time. She took a week's holiday to stay with me and arrived with a casserole from her mum. My friend didn't really cook at the time, so her mum stepped in. I didn't mind that my friend wasn't a great cook. A friend that will give up a week's holiday just to stay with you to show support doesn't need any other skills. That evening we sat on the sofa and chatted, and I relaxed just a fraction. I didn't want my husband taking diazepam, but I knew it meant he was calm and resting, and at this point this is what he needed. At midnight we were still sitting on the sofa chatting when the phone rang. I don't know fully what I thought but I do know I thought the worst. Allister's consultant, the gastroenterologist, was on the other end of the phone. It was a split second between me hearing his voice and him saying the words, 'Caroline, it's me, don't panic, Allister is ok. I am phoning to tell you I am having him moved to the High Dependency Unit. We need to give him food intravenously because he isn't eating. He has been taking steroids, as you know, and these can suppress lymphoma activity and reduce fever. We still need to ascertain if the lymphoma has spread to his liver. His potassium levels are so low now that he needs a high dose, and this cannot be given on the ward.' He went on to tell me that he was going away for a week and, in his absence, he wanted to be sure Allister got the full-time care he currently needed.

I had such mixed emotions that night. It was the saddest I can ever remember feeling. I was so upset that my poor husband had got so sick he now needed to be in the High Dependency Unit, and yet at the same time I was so relieved because he would now get specialist nurse care and monitoring twenty-four hours a day.

The next few days gave me some respite too. I was able to go home in the knowledge he was being looked after, and I did at least get some sleep for a few nights.

I met his gastroenterology consultant the following week and we discussed what was going to happen next. Allister was to have another scan. He told me that Allister's oncologist had confirmed that the biopsy that was taken from the part of the colon that was removed during surgery showed only a small number of cells with lymphoma. It was therefore still likely that what was being seen in his liver was an infection. It was very important to be sure. If lymphoma was not present in the liver, then it was better to wait until Allister was stronger before commencing chemotherapy. If lymphoma was present in the liver then it would have to be a different strategy, and therefore we had to wait. All of this made sense, but everything just seemed to take so long, and I couldn't help but think that if Allister had lymphoma then surely it was better to get on with the chemotherapy sooner rather than later. The next couple of days did see some improvement in Allister. He was behaving like my husband again and this change coincided with his potassium, phosphate and calcium levels increasing. It is quite incredible, really, that these chemicals have such an impact on behaviour.

It was FA Cup weekend whilst he was in the High Dependency Unit. Allister has been a fan of Southampton Football Club since he was a small boy. It was to be Southampton versus Arsenal in the final. We were members of Southampton Football Club, and members who had attended six games or more during the season would qualify for tickets. We had not been to many games for obvious reasons, and at the time Southampton got through to the final I was unaware that my husband would become so ill. I had written to the club at this time and requested tickets for Allister, explaining his Crohn's disease and surgery. I got offered tickets. I didn't think telling Allister whilst he was in the High Dependency Unit was the best time, so I kept that to myself and arranged instead to get a television taken in for him so he could watch the match. His mum and dad got him a flag and a football shirt, and we sat/stood around his bed with a couple of nurses and watched it together. It was interesting to see Allister's heart rate monitor fluctuate with the highs and lows of the game. In the end they lost 1–0. I don't think this improved Allister's overall mood.

As Allister was behaving more normally there was talk of transferring him back to the general ward. I was not happy about this as I felt without the close monitoring the High Dependency Unit was providing, he would deteriorate again. His blood was showing a high sugar level, so he was given insulin, and subsequent tests revealed a drop in his potassium levels again. It was decided that a renal consultant would look at Allister's outputs and kidney function as, with high doses of potassium being given, the reason for the loss still wasn't clear. The view was that he could still be transferred back to the general ward, as his outputs could be monitored from there and the liver scan result had come back clear. I sat with Allister and became aware that he was sounding confused again. I got really anxious at the thought of him going back to the general ward and discussed this with the consultant on duty. He spoke to Allister, and, not knowing him at all, concluded that he did not need High Dependency Unit care and should be on a general ward. Allister's mum arrived and I needed a coffee to calm down, so I left her to sit with Allister. I did not witness what happened next, but my husband did me a huge favour.

I returned to the High Dependency Unit after about half an hour to find my husband sleeping peacefully and my mother-in-law looking a little overwrought. It transpired that after my departure Allister got very agitated and confused and it would seem a little bit lustful. He started to swing his pulse monitor cable around his head and any nurse that approached to take it off him had the benefit of Allister's lustful thoughts. He seemed only to find swear words to use and he was behaving like a completely different person. His poor mum was trying to tell everyone what a lovely boy her son was whilst Allister was shouting abuse at everyone in the High Dependency Unit. He finally threw up everywhere and then went to sleep. It later transpired he had complained of feeling sick earlier and had been given an anti-sickness pill. He wouldn't be given that pill again! The good news was that the consultant who I had spoken to earlier came over to me as soon as I returned. He was gracious enough to concede that I was right, and my husband needed closer care than a general ward could offer. I had no idea why he thought this at this stage, as all I could see was my husband sleeping, but I was pleased with the news all the same. Allister would move to the Renal Unit as his kidneys appeared not to be working properly and his potassium loss could be monitored closely.

Allister now settled into his next location at Portsmouth Hospital. He still had low levels of potassium as well as phosphates, magnesium and calcium. His fever was still high, and a cough that had been around on and off for months seemed to be getting worse. A chest X-ray was ordered, but this showed normal. Given the disappearing lesion in the liver, another scan was ordered to look at that. It was a never-ending round of tests that concluded nothing, and I was mentally exhausted and beginning to wonder if chemotherapy would ever happen. All his scans were to be reviewed as there were no signs of infection in his blood or urine, and yet he still had a fever.

The end of this awful month resulted in the conclusion that the lesion on the liver was still visible and a biopsy would be attempted. Fluid was building around Allister's heart now as well, just to add a little something extra to the ever-growing list of problems he was having, and a final challenge was the detection of MRSA. There was good news. His blood clot was thinning. As you can imagine, this did not make a huge difference to my level of concern at this stage. May had been a terrible time. I was exhausted and scared, so very afraid for what lay ahead.

What would June bring?

TEN

COUNTDOWN
THE TASK LIST

JANUARY 2010

IT WAS JANUARY 2010 AND OUR LIFE WOULD BE dominated for the next six months by our newly created travel file and our monthly task lists. Without a doubt this was the best thing we did in preparation for our trip. Our initial brainstorm list provided the starting point, but the list of things to do increased more and more as time went by. We would be having dinner or be out with friends and suddenly think of more things we needed to do. The travel file was never far away, and we updated it as soon as we could. This might sound boring, but, trust me, if you ever decide to go travelling then being well prepared makes for a much smoother trip. Our monthly task lists meant we left the UK on 13th July with almost everything done. We weren't perfect and one or two things did get missed and go wrong; after all, you can't plan for the unpredictable, but we left happy that we covered all that we could. So, where did we start?

The first thing we wanted to do was finalise where we wanted to go. Deciding this took us a little longer than we thought it would. To put it simply, we just kept changing our minds and then, when we thought we had it sussed, we realised we were travelling to Thailand in the wet season and Tahiti in the cyclone season. We settled on heading to Australia, stopping off in Singapore for about a week. From Australia we would go to New Zealand: logical choice and a place we had always longed to visit. Next we decided we would visit some of the Hawaiian Islands. Allister had a desire to see active volcanoes and the night skies from the 13,790-foot Mauna Kea. Measured from its base at the bottom of the Pacific Ocean, this is the highest mountain in the world and reported to have some of the best night skies in the world. You can even see the curvature of the earth from the summit. Allister had read about all this stuff in his *National Geographic* magazines, so this is where we were headed. The fact that it would be hot and has a fair few nice beaches also helped make our decision. It made sense to head back to the UK via the USA from Hawaii, but we had visited the USA a lot in the past. We settled on ten days only, flying into San Francisco and heading north to explore an area we had not been to before.

We felt January had been a successful month. We knew where we were going, we had our visas for Australia, Al's cousin who lives in Perth knew we were coming to stay in July and most importantly our loft was empty of fourteen years' worth of accumulated rubbish. We eased into February with a confidence that this was going to be easy.

ELEVEN

TRAVELLING THE OPEN ROAD, WESTERN AUSTRALIA

AUGUST 2010

I MANAGED TO DELAY THE INEVITABLE DAY WHEN I would have to start camping in Australia. When we left Perth, in our recently dented new car with our boot full of camping kit and food, camping was the plan. The problem, as I saw it, was that it was still winter in Australia. I admit this is not quite like a winter in the UK, but it was chilly and wet. We headed north up the west coast, visiting first the Pinnacles desert in Nambung National Park. It is well worth a visit, although a very good idea to avoid the mid-day coach tour invasion. The Pinnacles are three-metre-high limestone columns that were formed underground but have risen as the sand has eroded away. The place is a little eerie when quiet and fantastic for the photograph enthusiast. Someone once told me that tradition declares you should run naked around the Pinnacles. We remained clothed and this did not detract from our enjoyment.

We stayed – in a motel, thank goodness – in a place called Kalbarri. A visit to Finlay's Fish BBQ was recommended and it certainly was a unique place. You pick your fish from a huge range and this is then cooked for you on the BBQ whilst you sit around a campfire in a kind of indoor/outdoor shack. I am not sure if it was Finlay doing the cooking, but we had a fun night and really got to appreciate for the first time the friendly Australian way. A couple of guys on a fishing trip welcomed us to their table, drank us under the table and willingly told us their life histories. On leaving we got invited to visit if we made it to Adelaide. All these things do not come naturally to us slightly more reserved English folk, but as our Australian tour developed, we became used to the Australians wanting to know all about us. This was of course always followed by them telling us everything about themselves. Our notebook was soon full of names and addresses of places at which we were welcome to stay. I think this was the strangest thing for me. The friendliness of Australians was great; we had some fun, sociable nights along the way, but I would not invite people I had met only once to come and stay with me if they happened to be passing through my hometown. If this had been the odd person then I would not have thought anything of it, but it did at times seem to be the normal way. In fact, after a while if a chatty Australian didn't ask me to stay, I would wonder what I had done to offend them.

A visit to Kalbarri National Park allowed us to enjoy a fantastic hike and our car experienced its first trip along one of the many unsealed roads in Australia. One big road will take you all around Australia and in-between there is a lot of dirt road where your car takes a serious pounding as it bounces along gravel and corrugated tracks. A 4×4 is much needed if you plan to do a lot of this, and indeed many roads were unsuitable for our car. A 4×4 was a budget step too far for us, but not to be deterred, many a bouncy road was taken, sometimes intentionally and sometimes not. Some loose plastic on the bumper and losing a few screws from places unknown was a small price to pay.

Arrival in Shark Bay signalled the start of camping and our first few nights were relatively easy. I think it was a novelty and staying in a resort-style place to start with helped; there was even a bar. I think Monkey Mia, as it was called, would be different in peak season, as no doubt it would be packed. Its main attraction is the dolphins making their way to shore early morning to be fed. We were not in peak season; it was not overly busy, and we were lucky enough to feed the dolphins ourselves: a lovely experience. The Shark Bay area is a World Heritage-listed site and certainly is very pretty. Tourism descends in such places, and for me it lacked the feeling of remoteness that it should have had. At the time I didn't think about this but as we headed into more desolate parts of Australia, I realised it did feel a little like a theme park. I would still say, though, that it is worth a visit if you are ever in that area.

When we look back, I know Allister and I would say that the weeks we spent in Western Australia were some of the most memorable of our trip. We drove up the west coast, reaching the Cape Range National Park and Ningaloo Marine Park. We set up our tent in a place called Yardie Homestead. I think it was at this point that I started to describe campsites as rustic. This place had a certain amount of charm, but clean and modern it was not. We did enjoy our time there, although it was a shame that it was so cold. This did not deter us from snorkelling, though, and it was worth the cold dip. Once we got through the pain barrier and kicked hard for several minutes, we were able to enjoy beautiful fish. In fact, we stayed on the beach so long it was dusk as we headed back to the car. That evening was our first and last drive in the near dark. We experienced an onslaught of wallabies seemingly attracted to car headlights and lacking any real road sense. As many of them attempted to throw themselves into the path of our car – or, better still, into the side of it – we realised the error of our ways. A ten-minute drive must have taken us a very slow and cautious hour. We always made sure in future that we reached our camping destination in the daylight.

Moving on from the Cape Range National Park took us to the Karijini National Park. From there we headed to a place called 80 Mile Beach. This really just serves as a stopover on the way to Broome. Given that it was seven hundred kilometres of nothing just to get to 80 Mile Beach, it is fair to say Broome was not reachable in a day. Before visiting Australia, we both had an image of the outback. Our drive from the Karijini to 80 Mile Beach went some way to consolidate this view. It was an endless drive of nothing for the eye to see, apart from the oasis that is an Australian roadhouse. On this drive we shared our roadhouse stop with bikers on Harleys. I think these were the only people and vehicles we saw all day. One of the things we noticed that day is how safe and comfortable you feel in your car. The radio was on and we were eating up the miles.

Driving all day means changing driver, and when we pulled over for the first time to do this it was quite a strange experience. With the engine off, the only sounds were insects and all we could see was the endless road and Australian bush. We suddenly felt very isolated, probably for the first time on our trip. This area didn't even have mobile phone reception and I think we got a real sense of vulnerability. What if the car wouldn't start? What if another car arrived containing a violent killer? What if wild animals suddenly attacked? Natural thoughts to have, of course! Getting back into the safe haven that was our Holden

Commodore meant all these thoughts vanished and a relaxing drive resumed.

We would have no doubt been fine in the event of a breakdown, aside from violent killers, of course, as our car was very well stocked. We certainly had plenty of food and most importantly a lot of water. I would recommend carrying large water containers. We did not break down on this road, but our car was not reliable for the whole trip. We were lucky enough to break down in populated areas, but we might not have been so fortunate, and you can go a long time without seeing another car in some areas.

We had our stopover at the aptly named 80 Mile Beach, did our laundry, and spent an afternoon drinking coffee and chatting to a great couple from New Zealand. We were lucky enough to stay in touch and some months later we visited them at their home whilst we were on the New Zealand leg of our tour. Travelling is great for meeting new and interesting people and Allister and I were thrilled to meet our New Zealand friends. We certainly hope our paths will cross again.

We moved on and headed to Broome, where we joined every other Australian from the south keen to escape the chilly south in wintertime and enjoy the hot and sunny north. Now, my first impression of Broome was not one of wild enthusiasm. It seemed over busy and overrated, but places grow on you and we ended up staying quite a few days, as the weather was great, the beach was lovely and there were plenty of bars to enjoy. Our faith was put to the test as we ventured into the sea within the area marked 'There Are No Crocodiles in This Section'. It was like a leap of faith as we prayed that those underwater nets do work. I can confirm, though, that we arrived back in the UK with all our limbs, so on this occasion the system was successful.

One of the highlights of our stay in Broome was our trip to the open-air cinema. Bug repellent is a must, but an experience worth undertaking as you sit in what feels like deckchairs, underneath the night sky, watching the film. We kept it traditional and watched a film about a man travelling to Broome from Perth. It seemed apt, and as some of it was filmed in the cinema we were sitting in, we felt it couldn't get more real. Well, we thought that until a plane flew right overhead just as there was an explosion in the film. That got the heart rate up, I can tell you.

Moving on from Broome, the Kimberley area was a real highlight for us. En route we visited a place called Geike Gorge, taking a boat trip to see our first crocodiles. These were freshwater ones that generally don't eat people, so we felt quite safe as we viewed them from the modest safety of our very open and low boat. Our days now were very much at one with wildlife. We shared our time not only with crocodiles but lots of flies, a range of insects and arachnids, bats the size of eagles and not forgetting a collection of lizards in varying shapes and sizes.

We were truly in the outback and proper travellers now. To be honest, I was not enjoying every single moment of our wildlife experience. As I lay in my tent, on the first of two nights spent in this area, I was plagued by the sensation of something crawling over me. Several complaints to Al and a look around with the torch revealed nothing and only created tension in our small home. Finally, the sensation spread to Al, and closer inspection revealed our tent to be full of ants. These ants were so small they had got in through the seams of our tent and their size meant that they were not easy to see. It was the mass movement that finally caught our eye. It was a very long night as we battled to get them out, and then painstakingly we sprayed every seam with insect repellent.

The following evening only added to our wildlife adventure as we made our way to the outdoor kitchen. As the floor started to move, we soon became aware that it was covered in ants. Unlike the previous night, these were a much larger variety and the crunching underfoot did not do much for our appetites and we decided our second night would be an early one. We were confident that our newly fully insect repellent-treated tent would keep us safe. The morning greeted us with intense itching and, as we got out of the tent and watched the bright-green spider follow us, we realised we had not spent the night alone. Given that we were still breathing, we assumed it was not one of the very poisonous ones and were happy to endure the itching for a few days. Al scratched his back whilst I scratched my butt.

I would go back to this area – hard to believe, I know, given we were nearly eaten alive by bugs – but it would be with a four-wheel drive. Our access into the Kimberley was limited because of our vehicle, but we still put this part of our trip on our highlights. We based ourselves in a place called Kununurra for a few days and treated ourselves to a day trip to the Bungle Bungle range in the World Heritage-listed Purnululu National Park. This involved an hour's flight in a light aircraft taking us over Lake Argyle and views of the diamond mine, with a day spent travelling in a four-wheel drive and walking through gorges that are millions of years old. The Bungle Bungle range is truly awesome. Walking through the black-and-orange striped sandstone structures, which look like giant beehive domes, is a unique and fascinating experience. The early-morning flight did cause a small amount of air sickness but fortunately we landed in the nick of time. We both decided ten minutes more and the pilot would have shared a little more with us than we would have liked. I was lucky enough to sit in the front with the pilot, which made for some great views but did cause extra stress as

I wondered at what point I was going to be sick all over him. I wasn't, though, and the flight home was much calmer, ending a truly fabulous day. I would recommend this trip if you make it to the area.

Next stop for us was the border from Western Australia into the Northern Territory and the land of the infamous seven-metre saltwater crocodiles. They do eat humans!

TWELVE

TRAVELLING LIFE IN A TENT

SEPTEMBER 2010

REACHING THE BORDER OF WESTERN AUSTRALIA signified some serious time on the road, and the realisation that I had got used to camping and the way of life.

The tent was now put up in a precision operation lasting approximately thirty minutes. Allister led the way in style, with me holding whatever I was instructed to hold. I had even reached a standard where Allister felt I could be given the responsibility of assembling poles. I took this task very seriously and felt I was achieving a high standard.

With our tent in place and able to withstand cyclone-force winds, we would sit in our bargain camping chairs for the obligatory post-tent-erecting beer. If no Australians were watching us, then this would obviously be a lovely cup of tea.

Our drink was always followed by Allister's health and safety chat. This was in simple terms an instruction for me not to forget that a tent has guy ropes. Unfortunately, I did not always listen to Allister, and even if I did then this didn't mean that I took any notice. As I fell over the guy ropes one evening, my big toe got very firmly snagged and twisted, and I then recalled that chat. The pain, swelling and lack of movement suggested a small crack. Al said it would mend and indeed it did, eventually.

We soon learnt the best spots to pitch a tent. Make sure you have plenty of space around you; your zone can be marked with camping chairs and other camp items. Ensure you pitch away from bird-filled trees because the occupants like nothing better than to decorate your tent, and at all costs avoid dips that fill with water in the night. The trouble is, not everyone thinks the same way as you and I recall one evening when, after the tent-erecting process was complete, we headed to the BBQ to cook our sausages. On return the loudest family in the campsite had pitched their tent next to ours. Now, I say next to ours but what I really mean is on top. There was a vast expanse of grass with a few trees and some parrots, and yet only a two-millimetre gap was visible between our tent and theirs. We headed to bed around 9.30pm – remember, we are party people – but our neighbours chose to retire sometime later. We shared in full their late-night conversations and other bedtime activities!

Do not forget in this camping experience that we were sleeping on sleep mats. These are wafer-thin devices that require a degree of skill in getting comfortable. My husband decided that for him this was ensuring that he had maximum points of contact. This meant lying on his back. He was happy with this strategy and so at night he lay down; six seconds elapsed, and he was asleep. Alas, sleeping on his back meant only one thing: snoring. For me it was sleeping in the recovery position that limited my pain, but Allister had to be stopped. A good prod, he

Time to go travelling!
Tuesday 13th July 2010.

Monkey nuts! Raffles Bar, Singapore.

Early morning, chasing parrots!

Our Australian wheels and a lot of rock and dust.

OPPOSITE: *Contentment in Joffre Gorge. Karijini National Park,
Western Australia, August 2010.*

A break from travel planning. Polperro, Cornwall, February 2010.

*Camping in comfort? Not this time. Karijini National Park,
Western Australia, August 2010.*

Broome Life.

Love a kangaroo. Mount Kosciusko Mountain Retreat, New South Wales, Australia, November 2011.

Bad shirts and curls. Allister, the early years.

The real-world beckons. Graduation, Plymouth, 1989.

So far from everything. 80 Mile Beach,
Western Australia, August 2010.

moaned and rolled, and peace descended in our little tent. This routine took us all around Australia.

I certainly had a few issues with camping and 3am was one of them. I say 3am and it may have been a little earlier or later, but the result was the same. When you sleep at home in your own bed, in your own comfortable house, ask yourself how many times a week, a month or even a year, you get up in the night for a bathroom visit. When you camp this is a very regular event. I cannot explain why night after night I would waste fifteen to thirty minutes debating with myself whether to get dressed and walk to the toilets. I never could wait and so always got up eventually. I would return to find my husband had not moved. He never did.

Next up was the 6am parrot chorus. The sunrise was early in the north, and with it came the birds, which were very colourful and appealing during the day but somehow less so at 6am. They would squawk and chatter for about half an hour and then, once confident all campers were awake, would fly off. Some good news, though: that noisy family that kept us awake all night were so irritated with the parrot chorus they packed up and left very early.

Camping does not mean you have to miss out on all of life's pleasures and I made sure I tried not to. A daily shower, ideally hot, was one of these. The morning after the neighbours from hell I decided to ease my grumpiness and headed off to the shower, armed with herbal shower gel, age-defying face wash and fruit fusion shampoo. I ignored the rust, faulty lock, sand and cracked floor and stepped into a surprisingly hot and powerful shower. It was all going so well until someone flushed a toilet. Boiling-hot water hit me. Handwashing followed the flush and ice-cold water was all I got. So, the shower ended, and I stepped out onto my thongs. Please note the use of Australian language. In the UK these are better known as flip-flops. Thongs or flip-flops are a vital item in the camp showers as they mean that floor contact can be avoided, and this is very important.

Back at the tent, on this rather unimpressive night of camping, my husband had made an extremely bad error of judgement. He was chasing parrots, which were back, and my cup of tea was nowhere to be seen. My mood did not improve.

The good news was we had camped on grass. After the hard rock and red dust of the Karijini National Park this soft and dustless environment was real luxury.

Al just loved camping. He had only one small complaint: tent nose in the morning!

One other thing I must add to my discovery of the great outdoors of Australia is the 'bush loo'. If you ever travel down under you will soon learn that these come in a variety of styles. The main problem is that you often come across them when you have been driving for five hours and have seen nothing. A sign for a rest area appears and you will find yourself eagerly pulling in. Given it has taken five hours to spot this oasis, you would think it would cross your mind that cleaners probably don't stop by very often. It does not. The loo style can be the composting, the hybrid and, my personal favourite, the classic. This one came with instructions on its use, chemicals to use before and after the event and strict rules on the lid being put down on completion. We were told they were good for the environment, but I had a different opinion on that one. All I could ever see was the lid up, chemical bucket still full of chemicals and just a sense that very little cleaning attention had been given to it lately. It was a common occurrence for us to get back in the car and stop by the side of the road five minutes later. The great outdoors was much more inviting!

Please don't think that this period of getting used to living at one with nature in any way impaired my enjoyment of our trip. It was amazing, and I did have a fantastic time, but it was not luxury. This is all part of the experience, though, and by far the best way to really get away from all that you are used to and fully appreciate the country, its people, its scenery, its wildlife and its weather.

It really didn't take long to adapt to the traveller's way of life. I went several days without make-up, my undies would dry on the back shelf of the car, my towel would dry on a tree, I stopped nagging Al to shave, and I got very excited when I saw a laundry. I even went through a phase of wearing jewellery on bits of leather or rope. It is truly amazing how adaptable we are.

Thirteen

The Early Years
The Big Question

1990 to 1991

'Will you marry me?' Allister stood grinning in front of me.

I threw myself at him and said, 'Yes.' It wasn't a very difficult decision because we had already been out and bought the ring. Allister had even done the honourable thing and asked my dad's permission. It took him the whole weekend to pluck up the courage; in fact, it was the second weekend he had attempted it as he failed miserably to find the words the first time. I have no idea why this was the case. My dad is a big softy and Allister scored huge future-son-in-law points with his very traditional approach to asking for my hand. All this meant, of course, that Allister and I had chatted about and decided to get married over dinner one night, so the proposal didn't exactly take me by surprise. Allister wanted to pop the question, though, so after the ring was purchased and my dad was on board, he hid the ring and I was told he would ask when he was ready. I was rather hoping for a moonlit beach or candlelit dinner, but I guess coming down the stairs in my sweatpants had to suffice.

We were engaged and this was very exciting and keeping with the traditional theme we decided to embark on our quest to buy our first home. We were living in a rented flat in Guildford and didn't really have any money but in the early 1990s this didn't really matter. One hundred per cent mortgages were there for the taking for us first-time buyers and we wanted to get on that property ladder as soon as we could. We were so headed for the semi-detached, walking the dog after work, washing the car on a Sunday and of course the obligatory two children, one of each, naturally.

We spread our wings in our quest to find our perfect first home, as it seemed Guildford was out of our price range unless we wanted to live in a studio where the bed would come out of the wall of the lounge at night. I hoped we could afford something with a proper bedroom. We achieved our dream when we made it to Farnham. It seemed that heading a bit further west made house prices a little bit cheaper. We put in an offer for a one-bedroom starter home, which was currently being built in a new development just outside Farnham. It all seemed great as the homebuilder even helped organise the mortgage; a 95% mortgage with a 5% home loan as we didn't have a deposit. I think the word I would use now is naïve. You know the expression that if something is too good to be true then it probably is; well, this was the case, but it was going to be six years later when we would finally realise that.

All was well in the Mr Frost and soon-to-be Mrs Frost household. Jobs were going ok, house was progressing, we were happily picking carpets and curtains for our new abode, and Mum and Dad seemed to have the wedding day plans under control. We were to get married in the village I grew up in. This is a place called Codsall. It is in Staffordshire and therefore not a quick trip from Guildford. We would visit at weekends to view venues, talk to the vicar and discuss the guest list, but Mum and Dad had the advantage of being local and thus handled the fine detail. We were more than happy with this. They were paying after all.

There is always the odd glitch along the way, and this firstly came in the shape of me having a 'funny turn' one night in the flat. Allister was watching television and I was coming down the stairs to join him. About halfway down I got a ringing in my ears and then all this fog descended around me. I didn't faint but I couldn't see a thing, and everything sounded muffled. I shouted for Al, who led me to our bed and put a flannel on my head. We still don't really know why he did that; I guess he had no idea what else to do. Sound and vision returned, but I was naturally concerned so I popped along to see my GP. My blood pressure was extremely high. Please note I was twenty-two, not overweight and reasonably fit. It was odd and attributed to the contraceptive pill. I was to come off it immediately. Now, as a newly engaged and soon-to-be-married girl this was not good news. My GP wanted to monitor my blood pressure for a while and it was likely I would remain off the contraceptive pill for some time, if not forever. Allister headed for the chemist to buy us an alternative contraception method and we had some extremely grumpy sex over the following weeks. My blood pressure went back to normal very quickly, and has remained so ever since, but the pill was to be avoided and I was advised it was to be avoided indefinitely.

It was important not to let this stand in the way of the perfect wedding day and honeymoon. We had booked and paid for an all-inclusive holiday to the Dominican Republic, and, given my lack of world travel to date, I was very excited. The second glitch duly arrived. The holiday company went into administration. Should we have been concerned that we hadn't heard of them before we booked? I think yes. We were determined not to be deflated by this news, and we had no problem getting our money back, so we booked two weeks in Gran Canaria and patted ourselves on the back for having the right insurance.

Our house was finished, and we were keen to complete before we got married and headed off to the Canaries. This wasn't to be the case, and completion would land whilst we were away. We didn't want to delay and then have to pay extra rent, so what to do? Easy: get your husband's parents to move you out of the flat and into your new home whilst you lie on the beach. We made sure this was sorted.

We had about a month to go until we got married. The big day was 29th June 1991 and at 12.30pm I would become Mrs Caroline Frost. Everything was sorted: the church, reception venue, guests, cars, flowers – our best man, Allister's long-time friend from school, was prepped and planning the stag night – and the bridesmaids had been fitted into the classic meringue-style dresses that I wouldn't make them wear now. Most importantly, of course, I had my dress and a variety of hen nights were in the pipeline. I recall I had three. A night out in Codsall with all my school friends, a night out in London with all my polytechnic friends and a night out at the Chippendales with my soon-to-be mother-in-law and various other female Frost family members.

The third glitch, and really it was so much more than a glitch, was some life-changing news. Allister had an appointment at Southampton General Hospital. Having had Hodgkin's lymphoma when he was fifteen, he was still having annual check-ups. I didn't go with him; he always told me it was more for statistics as he was one of the first patients to survive after receiving a very new treatment at the time. I got home from work on that day and Allister was sitting on the sofa. I thought at the time he looked nervous.

'You'd better sit down,' he said. Considering where he had been that day, this was not a good choice of words. I really expected the worst. I sat down and waited for him to tell me the cancer was back. The room seemed silent for a very long time and then came the words that would absolutely change our life together forever.

'It looks like I won't be able to have children,' said Allister.

'Oh,' I replied. This was all that I said. I think it was because it was a relief. Not being able to have children is significantly less stressful than dealing with cancer. Well, that was my thought at that moment. My relief that he did not have cancer was so great that the news about not being able to have children was somewhat lost on me.

'Do you still want to marry me?' he suddenly said. Well – what a ridiculous question, was all I could think to that. I was twenty-two, in love with Allister and a long way from wanting children. I did of course realise that this was not an ideal situation but somehow it didn't seem to matter too much that day. Allister didn't have cancer; we were getting married, and the rest? Well, the rest we could think about later.

Allister went on to tell me about his appointment. It had certainly taken an odd turn when the baby bombshell was dropped. His doctor was chatting to him about his upcoming wedding and he casually asked, 'How do you and your future wife feel about not being able to have children?' It was probably good that I wasn't there. The doctor was naturally horrified when Allister asked him what he was talking about. It transpired that the new treatment that Allister had been given when he was fifteen had a potential side effect: sterility. Allister did not know this. Why was this not discussed with Allister when he had his treatment at fifteen? We will never know for sure. The doctor did not forget that appointment. Many years later our paths would cross again, and he would indeed talk about the day that was forever etched in his memory. On the day of the appointment he recovered the situation well, but he could not change the reality that Allister would probably not be able to have children.

Being young and about to get married and go on our honeymoon, our first thought naturally fell to our current contraceptive issue. I was no longer taking the contraceptive pill and we couldn't see the point of using another, less enjoyable method of contraception if we didn't need it. These things always need confirming, though, so off Allister went, back to the hospital, to leave a small deposit for analysis. The results came back, and, having had to tell Allister that he probably couldn't have children, the doctor now had to tell Allister that he definitely couldn't have children. At least we could throw our contraceptives in the bin before our honeymoon, and I would never have to worry about whether to go on the pill again. We adopted the glass half full approach and concentrated on looking forward to our wedding.

We thought we ought to tell our parents. I think they were more upset than we were. I suppose they had the wisdom that comes with age and the foresight to predict that further down the marital track we were probably going to be far less relaxed about this news. My mum reminded me that in the early days of getting to know Allister she had commented on whether his treatment would have affected his ability to have children. This conversation came back to me in that instant and I recall that I told her she was a bit ahead of herself as he was just my new boyfriend and she didn't need to buy a hat just yet. Seems my mum was rather wise, and perhaps knew she was meeting her future son-in-law. I had forgotten all about her words until that point. It wouldn't have changed a thing, though, and it never would. I knew for certain: I loved Allister and I was marrying him.

FOURTEEN

LIFE CHANGES
SUMMER WITH GRAHAM

JUNE AND JULY 2003

MY TIMINGS MAY NOT BE SPOT ON, BUT I THINK MY love for Graham Norton started in June 2003.

My husband was not in a good place. The first few days of June saw him have a blood transfusion as his haemoglobin levels were so low, a heart echocardiogram to look at fluid build-up around his heart, and a liver biopsy to examine the lesion that was in there.

My life developed into a routine that I think, looking back, kept me sane. I was working but I had reduced my hours. I was working a four-day week, Monday to Thursday, and on these days, I started early so I was able to finish around 4pm. This allowed me to spend the rest of the day and evening at the hospital with Al, and not working Friday gave me a longer weekend to spend more time with him. I didn't want to be working, I wanted to be with him all the time, but work was a good thing. It meant I had to think about something other than Al and for a few hours a day I could talk about something non-medical. It was also important, of course, for getting paid. It was looking like we were in this for the long haul and Allister's sick pay was not going to continue for ever. Unfortunately, being ill does not mean that you don't have to pay your mortgage and bills.

After my day at work and hospital visit, I would normally get home around 9pm. There were usually phone calls to make, Al's washing to do – boy did he get through a lot of pyjamas – odd things needing my attention and of course I needed to eat. I would always ensure, though, that I was sitting down in front of the television by 10pm. My one hour a day of relaxation, occasionally washed down with a small glass of red wine. Only very small, mind you, in case of the need for a trip to the hospital. Weird to think now that I lived my days always with that thought.

This hour of television joy kicked off with the half-hour highlight show of *Big Brother*. Now, I am not a fan of *Big Brother*, but that summer watching the totally meaningless activities undertaken by a bunch of random strangers, their relationships and of course their entertaining rows seemed so strangely normal that I found it great to watch. It was nothing, though, compared to the pleasure of watching Graham's half-hour show that followed at 10.30pm. This show was more outrageous than his rather tamer show that is on BBC 1 these days, which I still love, of course, but his Channel 4 show will always have an extra special place in my heart. I would always go to bed feeling a little better after watching Graham. I did so look forward to my nightly date with him; he was indeed the only person to make me laugh that summer. Thank you, Graham, for everything!

I sense I may be talking about Graham a little too much, so let me recall more of the long, hot summer, and it certainly was a hot summer: there hasn't been one like it since that I can think of.

It felt like a time of routine. When I read back the diary that I kept, I feel quite overwhelmed at the amount of time that elapsed around endless tests and waiting for results. It is quite hard to summarise what happened during those summer months. Al was in hospital, getting worse and being tested for every disease known to man; well, that is how it felt, anyway.

The key problem was the need for conclusive proof that lymphoma was present in the liver or indeed anywhere else. If his fevers and ill health were being caused by something else, then chemotherapy was not the right approach, given how weak he now was. I found myself hoping that the liver biopsy would come back positive for lymphoma so that chemotherapy would start. This must sound awful, but remember lymphoma was diagnosed following his bowel surgery back in April. To me there was no doubt and this delay could not be good. As each day passed, I watched my husband deteriorate, and the man I knew and loved seemed not to be there anymore. As far as I was concerned, chemotherapy was the only thing that might make him better. I was frustrated and scared. June was the worst month that I recall and was the month that the thought that my husband might never come home sometimes crept into my head. I even found myself thinking about what I would do if he died. I concluded that I would go abroad for a year and do voluntary work. I thought this would take me away from my memories and the pain. What was I thinking? I did not allow these thoughts to stay for long, and I would always quickly find something to distract myself from such negativity. In my head I had to be strong, and I think looking back Al became a project I could not fail at. I planned my hospital strategy, delivered my husband the best care I could, managed my time with precision and hounded the medical staff for every detail to ensure nothing was missed. I look back and realise that it was my subconscious way of coping with such a huge amount of stress. It was almost a feeling of detachment, but not quite. I didn't cry much over those summer months; if the tears came, I would stop myself. Now that can't have been good and many months later, I certainly felt the effects of that.

The sixteenth of June was Allister's birthday. I took him in a cake. It was a bright-green frog. I don't know why I did this. Perhaps I wanted him to laugh, as he didn't do this anymore; perhaps I wanted him to enjoy some food: he didn't do this anymore; perhaps I wanted us to feel normal, and we certainly didn't feel like that anymore. I got a watery grin and then he fell asleep. I spent every evening that week eating green cake whilst I watched Graham Norton!

As June progressed Allister continued with a permanent high fever and the doctors continued their tests. He had a persistent cough; he was weak, thin and exhausted. Towards the end of June my poor husband was very low: this I think was not a surprise.

I spoke with his gastroenterology consultant on 25th June. This day was a turning point, although it did not feel like it at the time. I think it was probably because most logical avenues of investigation had been done, time was moving on and Allister was getting worse. He confirmed the problem in Allister's liver, classed as non-specific changes, was also evident in his lungs. All the antibiotics and anti-fungal drugs he had been given had not had any effect. Due to the problems with his chest he was now to be given a course of anti-TB therapy. Overall medical opinion was that lymphoma was the likely cause of his symptoms, but at this time chemotherapy was not going to be started as the oncology consultant felt it was important to obtain the evidence.

Starting chemotherapy if not required was not something she was prepared to risk. Further CT scans and X-rays would be done.

The twenty-ninth of June arrived, and it is a day I remember very well. It was our wedding anniversary. Allister did not remember this, and this was to be expected. His mum did, though, and she gave me a bunch of flowers and a framed photograph of Allister. It was a photo that she had of him in a top hat and tails at his sister's wedding and a photo she knew I loved. I went to bed holding that picture that night. It showed him laughing and enjoying himself and it was a memory of him that seemed a long time ago. That kind and thoughtful gesture from my mother-in-law triggered a lot of emotions. The worst was the thoughts creeping into my head that Allister might never come home. It was a hard night as I fought the emotions of missing him by my side in bed with the awful thoughts that he may never lie there again. I started to think about his funeral, which was simply horrendous. I hadn't allowed myself to think that way and when I did the tears did come. It was the loneliest I had ever felt that night and the most scared. I knew, though, that I couldn't let myself dissolve because Al needed me so much. I put the photograph down and convinced myself he was going to get through this. I will never know for sure how I did that, but those thoughts were not allowed to come back. The next day I felt stronger and more determined than ever that he would recover and come home to me.

The challenges kept coming, though, and the following week Al needed another blood transfusion and he continued to be as hot as a boiling kettle.

I met with Allister's oncology consultant on 30th June and she talked to me at length about what was happening and why. During the next two weeks they would continue with the anti-TB therapy. Following the surgery, he'd had in April, where lymphoma was identified in the bowel, the normal course of action would have been to start chemotherapy straight away. Allister's health deteriorated quickly, and he simply wasn't strong enough to start it. There was then no further evidence for the disease, and in someone so ill this was unexpected. This meant it was important to be sure that something else wasn't causing the symptoms. She advised she would wait for CT scan results and consider an MRI scan to look again at the bone marrow; however, the liver was the most important result and another biopsy was a possibility. She expected that chemotherapy would start in two to three weeks' time.

As we moved into July Allister continued with a permanent high fever and the doctors continued their tests. On 7th July it was confirmed lymphoma had been identified in Allister's liver. He also needed to have fluid that had built up around his heart drained as soon as possible. This fluid build-up could be down to his long-term fever and ill health, but it too would be tested for lymphoma. Allister went into the Cardiac Unit overnight; it had, after all, been a while since he had visited a new location in the hospital. He seemed very confused and muddled again, which caused me much alarm, but this lasted only overnight. There was some good news!

The ninth of July was my birthday. Allister moved back to the general ward and had another X-ray. My brother and his girlfriend cooked me a meal and bought me pamper gifts to cheer me up. It was a lovely gesture, and when I look back, I remember it was always the little things that people did that helped the most. A text message, a card or simply making me a cup of tea was all I needed. There was nothing anyone could do to make me feel better, but my brother and his girlfriend gave it their best shot that evening and it really helped. It was a hot evening and we spent a nice evening on the patio. It really needed a couple of glasses of a nice chilled white wine to wash it all down, but I had to drive, and I had my one ear on the phone as always. The evening was rounded off of course with Graham Norton!

On 11th July Allister was transferred back to the Oncology Ward at the other Portsmouth Hospital site. He had been there before, in May, and it was hard to believe two months had elapsed. He was to start chemotherapy but needed some maintenance first. He had very low protein levels, so he was given a feed tube to try to build him up a bit; he was looking a little skeletal by this point. Some drugs to improve his white blood cell count were given, anti-TB therapy was stopped; he didn't have TB. He was still taking potassium and needed sodium as well and just for good measure some anti-sickness pills to ensure he could tolerate the feed intake. Allister was very down at this time, and it was an impossible task to change this. All I could do was be there. Unfortunately, most of the time he was asleep and when he was awake, he generally bit my head off. He couldn't help this, and it wasn't my husband lying in the hospital bed. He had been ill for months and this changes a person. I knew he was still there inside and when he got better – and he would – I would get my Al back again.

Allister was to have a combined chemotherapy treatment for Hodgkin's lymphoma, as indicators in the cells showed this, and for non-Hodgkin's lymphoma as he was showing this too. I did say he was complicated! He would be scanned after four weeks to look at the liver and his fevers would be monitored, as would his blood. Hair loss would be expected after about ten days. In fairness he was thinning far more than he liked to admit so this wasn't too much of a concern in the old grand scheme of things.

The sixteenth of July 2003 was Allister's first day of chemotherapy.

FIFTEEN

COUNTDOWN
THE TASK LIST

FEBRUARY 2010

WITH JANUARY BEHIND US AND AN AIR OF INNER CALM settling around the Frost household, we perused our February task list. We were not leaving on our trip until July so a slightly 'not real' feeling was still hanging around and no doubt adding to the confident swagger we were exhibiting.

Our task list was still fairly light. The trouble is that a lot of the stuff you need to do when you are leaving the country for the best part of a year needs to be done at the last minute. We were yet to appreciate how crazy June and July would be, hence the swagger. So, what did we achieve in February? We talked for the most part, mainly about how great we were for planning this trip, but we did manage a few other things.

It did seem that there were a few too many 'Carry forward

to March' entries in our task list. This was not alarming at this stage, after all there were months left yet!

The most important thing was that my mum and dad's loft was to be the destination for all our paperwork. We were of course not going to be able to put the entire contents of our house in their loft, a shame, I know, but we had laid the foundations that would be added to with further valuable items. They did not know this yet, and in fact would not fully appreciate the scale of additions until we loaded my dad's car on moving out day, declaring, 'This is all way too valuable for our storage container!' I am not sure how long it took my parents to get all our stuff in their loft, but we were on a flight to Singapore and not worrying about it too much!

I must also recommend shredding to anyone packing up their house into a small box. It is very therapeutic, closely followed by selling all your junk to unsuspecting strangers at car boot sales. We were building a nice pile of things for this purpose. We had only touched the surface of clearing out our house, but it was to be a task we would enjoy greatly over the months ahead. What you find, though, is that, despite how much you throw out, when you come back a year later you find yourself wondering why you still have so much accumulated junk. When you live without most of your material possessions for a year you realise how little you actually need. As I write this book today our garage still has a corner full of stuff designated for a car boot sale. This will take place once it gets a little warmer; I am not one for winter car booties!

I was disappointed we had not yet organised our flights, but time was on our side.

I had very successfully avoided decorating our bathroom. My argument for delaying this task was that the bathroom would be smarter for the tenants that we hoped to get into our house whilst away.

So, February went ok. We even managed a week in Cornwall; all this planning was very tiring!

SIXTEEN

TRAVELLING THE OUTBACK AND BEYOND

SEPTEMBER 2010

CROSSING THE BORDER FROM WESTERN AUSTRALIA into the Northern Territory heralded the start of what would be one of our best months in Australia. It was the land of Australia that we visualise when we think of the Outback. It was endless red dusty roads, miles of nothing but flies, heat and wildlife that can eat you.

Our first stop was a place called Nitmiluk National Park, situated near a small town called Katherine. From here we planned to head south to the middle, but first we wanted to spend some time at the 'top end'.

The hottest camping we ever experienced followed. The only thing that saved it was that camping in the National Park meant the wildlife came to us. Our tent was surrounded by wallabies, and that was great. These little beasts came with a catch, though. Campers meant food and anything left in the open would soon be eaten. In fact, the mere smell of something yummy would see a wallaby happily ravage a tent. We were of course very sensible, and all foodstuffs were left safely locked in the car.

One of the highlights of Nitmiluk National Park was Katherine Gorge. Canoeing was a popular pastime in the gorge and, given the heat, the thought of being on, in or just near water was very appealing. The Northern Territory is land of the crocodiles, both the less harmful and smaller freshwater variety and the more harmful, human-eating, larger saltwater version. The gorge was a fresh water-filled beauty spot and we set forth, with much enthusiasm, to hire a canoe. The warnings given by the company with said canoes were moderate and consisted of advice about staying off the banks as the freshwater crocodiles were nesting and this could cause aggression. They could not 100% guarantee that a saltwater crocodile wasn't present in the river, but of course they do check regularly (yeah, right!) as the salties can wander their way into the freshwater areas. Surprisingly, our desire to canoe and get in the water outweighed our fear, although I decided not to go for a swim and always kept my arms inside the canoe.

On sighting some swimmers as we made our way up the stunning gorge, we had a moment where we just simply couldn't help ourselves. Two young Irish lads were swimming their way across from the edge of the gorge, where they had walked, over to the lovely sandy bank on the far side. As they reached the middle, where our canoe was passing, they noticed a sign on the far bank they couldn't quite read. We knew it was the words 'Nesting Crocodiles – Stay off the Bank' and they asked us for clarification. Now, at this point we were very honest and advised of the warning. For reasons we can't be sure of, they seemed unconvinced that crocs were in those waters and continued their swim. As the sign came into their view, they experienced a degree of panic. I know we should have calmed them by advising that only freshwater crocodiles were in the water and if they stayed clear of the bank, they should be fine. Somehow, we instead uttered the words, 'Yes, there are crocodiles in the water, and they are aggressive as they are nesting. You need to get out of the water.' This seemed so much more fun, especially as in their panic they started swimming in circles! I think we simply felt they should have believed us in the first place. Anyway, rest assured they swam back to their friends, no crocodiles appeared, and we paddled smugly and with somewhat hysterical laughter further up the gorge.

The rest of our stay in Nitmiluk involved nights drenched in sweat, days of walking drenched in sweat and pointless cold showers that left us drenched in sweat. As the cold and rain hit us later in our trip, we found ourselves yearning for this hot, sticky weather.

A trip to Darwin followed and, although the heat remained, the sun did not for the first couple of days. Torrential rain saw us abandon our tent to the respite of a small cabin and we watched from our window as other campers' tents filled with water or simply collapsed under the strain. The best bit about the cabin in Darwin was that it had a bathroom. A couple of days of private ablutions were simply heaven. We liked Darwin. As a place to live it wouldn't hold much appeal: the extreme climate, humidity and isolation would not suit everyone, but as a place to visit it is great. There is something for everyone, and certainly for the young backpacker Mitchell Street holds a deluge of hostels and bars that provide work and entertainment, tempting the traveller to stay longer than planned. A case in point is the son of a very dear friend of mine who set off travelling in February 2010. He found his way to Darwin, and at the time of writing this book is still there. We spent a couple of good evenings with him on

Mitchell Street, and a phone call to my friend, his mum, after quite a few beers, led to a very emotional half an hour.

Heading out of Darwin our tent was pitched again in Kakadu National Park. This is a World Heritage Site and really became known to the world when it was used as the location for the filming of *Crocodile Dundee*. It is managed by the Bininj/Mungguy people and the Department of Environment and Heritage and it is certainly a unique and interesting area. It borders Arnhem Land. This 91,000-square-kilometre area became an Aboriginal reserve in 1931 and has remained so until today. You cannot visit Arnhem Land without a permit, but Kakadu itself provides much insight into the fascinating Aboriginal history through rock art sites and burial grounds, and of course an excellent visitor centre. As a short visit Kakadu is informative, but a sense of real wilderness is hard to find as you are directed around designated walking routes and you can find yourself moving from car park to car park without really getting a true feel. Boat tours or, even better, hiring a four-wheel drive would be a good idea and something we missed out on doing. Even so our short visit was worthwhile and gave us a memorable highlight as we chanced upon a large group of saltwater crocodiles.

Saltwater, or estuarine, crocodiles are the world's biggest reptile and can grow as large as six metres long and weigh up to 1,000kg. They have changed little since dinosaurs walked the earth, although they are a little smaller nowadays, and with no natural predators they are indeed as menacing to look at as they sound. The East Alligator River area of Kakadu, although oddly named, provided us with a view of what is called Cahill's Crossing. Our timing was perfect as the incoming tide flowing upriver provided a time in the day when the saltwater crocodiles gather to await an influx of Barramundi fish. Looking down on the river from a safe vantage point, we watched in amazement as the crocodiles took to surfing the waters to catch the fish, turning the water around them blood red. The noise of the crunching fish only added to what was both a macabre and fascinating sight. Excitement mounted as trucks and four-wheel drive vehicles attempted to drive across the causeway; this road was clear at low tide but soon covered in fast-flowing water as the tide came in.

We watched with alarm as a truck stopped, having underestimated the speed of the flow, and the salties swam around. Fortunately, the driver had the sense not to get out and was able to reverse his truck back from where he had started. There are many warnings in Kakadu about the dangers of crocodiles, but this has not prevented many people losing their lives by ignoring these warnings. Whilst I could cope with the obliteration of Barramundi fish, I was not keen to see the truck driver meet the same fate. Lunch was soon over, and the crocs gradually disappeared. We happened to walk around the same area later in the day and calm waters and no crocodiles were all we could see. A chance walk in the morning had given us a unique and memorable view of these magnificent creatures in the wild. Visits to the zoos and boat trips to watch 'croc jumping' do not come close to witnessing the brutality of nature up close. I was yet to see a koala in Australia, and, excited as I was by finding this cute, furry creature in the wild, I sensed it would not be giving me quite the same experience.

It was time to leave Kakadu and head south to the middle and a stop at Alice Springs. Our first stop en route was camping at a place called Edith Falls. It was still very hot, and the lure of swimming in freshwater pools that were high up on top of the cliffs and guaranteed free of crocodiles was a temptation we could not resist. Beautiful pools and waterfalls awaited, but of course you must walk up to get there. We were hot before we started the climb, but on arrival I don't think either of us has ever got undressed and into water so fast. The relief was amazing. It was a beautiful spot and we spent quite a while enjoying the scenery and swimming in crystal-clear waters and waterfalls. It was worth the hike, and at least going down was easier.

We then popped down the road to Alice Springs. Popping down the road meant driving 1,200 kilometres of relatively deserted landscape over two days. An overnight campsite provided some light relief in a place called Wycliffe Well. I say the word 'place' loosely because it was just a campsite, but it provided a small bar and oddly a Chinese restaurant. The oddest was its claim to be the UFO capital of Australia, and quite some time was spent supping a cold beer as we viewed the artefacts, memorabilia and newspaper reports. We did of course spend the night watching the skies for the next visit, but, alas, the sound of a braying donkey, very drunk local Aborigine folk and the odd police siren were all that kept us awake. The only other memorable event was the change of temperature. It was cooler, and our expectation of the red-hot centre of Australia was not being met. Pleasant relief it was, though, and, while we tried very hard not to let weather dominate our thoughts on our travels, it was not always easy. Our home was, after all, just a small amount of canvas, mother earth in all its forms and the back of a Holden Commodore car.

Our plan was initially to drive through Alice Springs to the West MacDonnell ranges. Our trusted guidebook told us of a campsite at the end nestling in the mountains, which sounded wonderful. It was already quite late as we reached Alice Springs and the sensible option would have been to stop and camp and carry on the next morning. Alice Springs is a functional town and not that pretty, so we thought, let's carry on. A lengthy drive was met with the news that the campsite was full due to a motorbike convention and not a space was to be had. We drove back to Alice Springs and arrived late, finding the G'Day Camping and Caravan Park had space. As we pitched our tent, darkness descended, and we spent quite some time trying not to blame each other for our lack of judgement. We spent the next day in Alice Springs doing what I would call functional stuff. When travelling you must shop for food, wash your clothes, get on the internet to check your finances, send emails, and in our case update our blog with photos and fascinating tales of our travels to entertain our friends and family. And sometimes you just need a break from your break!

With a car full of food and clean underwear we headed to Kings Canyon. This was a relatively short distance from Uluru, formerly known as Ayers Rock, and an excellent stopping point. Great weather meant great hiking, and Kings Canyon is a stunning area not to be missed. After an enjoyable couple of days, we were excited that our next stop was Uluru. It was hard not to call it Ayers Rock, but Uluru was now its name, so Uluru it was. We awoke to heavy rain and packing the tent up was always a challenge in such conditions. We got going and hoped that by the time we reached Uluru the awful weather would have passed. It did not, and it did not pass for another week, giving us a very different experience to that which we had dreamed about.

The Uluru–Kata Tjuta National Park is made up of Uluru and Kata Tjuta, previously called the Olgas. This area is the most visited in Australia, and despite the obvious commercialism it is a place not to be missed. Uluru is truly impressive. It is a monolith, which is a single piece of rock. Its colours and textures vary dramatically at different times of the day. This effect is the result of the earth's atmosphere filtering the sun's incoming rays. It can remove the bluer light, allowing the redder light through at different times. Reflections from the rock and clouds in the sky enhance further the vivid colours. Uluru is what we think of when we picture Australia; well, this and the Sydney Opera House, of course!

I would love to say that as we approached the National Park area Uluru loomed over the horizon, glowing red against brilliant blue skies. Alas, this was not the case, and, we almost drove into it as we failed to see it in the gloom of rain and mist. We drove to the campsite and pitched our tent in what can only be described as torrential rain. A handy picnic shelter enabled us to somehow assemble the inside with little leaking, and somehow, we got the tent up with the inside completely dry. My husband really was a Boy Scout! We stayed for five days in the wet and cold in the belief that the next day the weather would change. It was supposed to be hot and sunny, surely. The only advantage we had was that in an area notorious for its flies there was not one to be found. It was too cold for them. We used our time well, making sure we hiked all the trails around Uluru. The weather meant the climb up the rock was closed and this was disappointing, but we did get to see Uluru with waterfalls pouring off it. We were told many, many times that this sight was rare, so we tried to enjoy the moment.

Uluru has a resort-style area, and this could have been a real blot on such a remote and beautiful place, but it has been well designed. In fact, we were extremely grateful to use the coffee shop as a place for relief from the wet and cold. Al even managed a visit to the resident hairdresser for his first visit to a hairdresser ever. As a boy growing up and thereafter, when your mum is a hairdresser, why do you need to go anywhere else? I am not sure if he really wanted a haircut or if it was just some time spent in the warmth, but he came away very proud of his new neat and tidy head.

Our reason for persevering with our stay at Uluru was our desire to see both the sunrise and sunset over it. Our patience paid off. On the fifth morning we awoke at about 5am due to the absolute freezing temperature that had descended overnight. Al put his head out and declared that the skies were clear, and the sun would be rising soon. There was no need to stay in the ice box any longer, so, after scalding hot showers to thaw out all parts of our bodies, we drove the short distance to the rock. I was reluctant to leave the warm and cosy heated-up car, but we needed to walk to get the best view of Uluru at sunrise. It was a stunning sight, and we added to the experience by returning at the end of the day to watch the sunset. We had finally been able to witness the remarkable colour changes of Uluru, as the sun appeared in the morning and as it disappeared in the evening. It is awe-inspiring and somehow it invokes an emotional response. We were left feeling calm and content with our world.

This heralded the end of our stay at Uluru, and we planned to leave bright and early the next morning. We decided to celebrate our day with a treat at the pizza restaurant in the resort area. Not used to eating large meals, we significantly over-ordered and decided to request takeaway boxes so that we could enjoy the pleasure that is cold pizza for lunch the next day. We were politely told that this was not the restaurant's policy as due to the Something or Other Food Act they could not guarantee how we would store said left-over pizza and as such we could get food poisoning and sue them. The fact that they were also a pizza takeaway and customers were marching past us with their lovely takeaway orders had no bearing on this request. Apparently, this was covered by a different Something or Other Food Act. Despite our very lengthy protestations the restaurant manager (yes, we obviously called the manager) would not be swayed. Allister and I had no choice. Being on a tight budget, we could not leave food to go to waste, so the only thing to do was to eat it all. As we forced down every last cheesy mouthful, we did question our decision and this we did even more so as we lay in the tent that night, feeling a tad unwell. We were victorious, though, and had walked out of the restaurant with a sense that we had won the battle. Clearly the restaurant manager couldn't care less whether we ate the pizza or not, but we were telling ourselves the contrary.

Departing Uluru, the next morning, having skipped breakfast and sucking on indigestion tablets instead, we headed back to Alice Springs for an overnight stop and to do some more laundry. Over a week had passed since we had last been there and this had been a week of hiking, rain, mud and wearing lots of layers to keep warm. This resulted in us not having very many clean clothes left, and so washing was much needed before we carried on. Boys and girls really are very different, and laundry day always reminded me of this case in point.

En route to the laundry, I asked Al, 'Do you have anything else that needs washing?'

'No,' he replied.

'Didn't you sleep in those trousers you are wearing for five nights in Uluru?' I asked.

'Oh, yes, best wash those,' he replied.

'And what about that T-shirt?' I commented. 'How many days have you had that on?' He duly stripped off what he was wearing and dropped it into the laundry bag. As no one appeared to be around I decided to add my T-shirt to the already very large bag and pop on a clean one. I did not look around enough, and as my flesh was on show the owner of the campsite hollered across that I could stay at his campsite anytime I liked. Such good news! At least I enjoyed some peace and quiet with a magazine as our washing went around, and I pondered how I was to increase diligence in my lovely husband. One pair of his socks in the washing seemed wrong on so many levels. Boys!

Moving on from Alice Springs we arrived again at the UFO capital of Australia. This time the only unwanted being at night was in the form of a dingo, which, attracted by the enticing aroma of Allister's trainers conveniently placed in the outer tent, decided it wanted to inspect a little closer. It managed to get its paws in and drag out the trainer before we were awoken, but Al's yelling was enough for it to drop the trainer and run off. Mind you, it didn't disappear before leaving us a little present up the side of the tent, as we discovered in the morning. Al had to wash the tent thoroughly before we packed up to leave. Camping really was such a huge pleasure.

Heading north from UFO/dingo town we stopped at a place called Devils Marbles. These are huge rock formations, many of which look like giant marbles with cracks through them, and in truth the only interesting thing on a long and boring drive. At least Al had some play time as he clambered over the rocks. My time there was a little less relaxing. I wandered aimlessly around only to find myself face to face with a very large python. As I dodged its slithering form, I was aware my heart rate had increased rather a lot. Al was too busy climbing rocks to notice my look of panic and breathlessness.

Heading into Queensland, we had an overnight stop in the town of Mount Isa. This is a very characterless place with few highlights. Let me correct that: there are no highlights. I recall being grumpy and going to bed early; it had been a long day with a wet and dreary ending!

Mood and weather improved as we arrived on the north coast at a place called Kurumba, on the Gulf of Carpentaria. It was lovely to see the ocean again and it was hot and sunny. This area is popular with Australians for a holiday, particularly for those that fish. We enjoyed the bar overlooking the sea, but the noisy Bucks night – Australian speak for a stag night – did not make for a peaceful camping experience. We certainly did not expect to hear a huge group of twenty-year-old lads singing Bruce

Springsteen all night. With their unique chorus of 'Oy Oy Oy' alongside the yapping dog backing singers, it was certainly a long night. We encountered our first cane toads to add to the list of unpleasant wildlife. One of these landing on your foot will make you jump, as Al found out to his cost when I screamed, jumped out of my seat and accidentally head-butted him.

If you ever venture to this part of Australia, then I would recommend a trip to the Undara Lava Tubes. These tubes were created some 190,000 years ago by lava flowing from the now-extinct Undara volcano. The lava flowed north-west towards the gulf and the surface of the rivers of lava that were formed hardened, forming insulated tubes that allowed the lava inside to keep flowing. This has left behind a mass of tunnels below the surface, which are today completely covered in vegetation. The tubes stretch for around 160 kilometres and most weren't even uncovered until the 1980s. Interestingly there are tool sites around the cave mouths that show the Aborigines had knowledge of this place a long time ago. The place is of course a real tourist attraction, but even with the high number of visitors it attracts we enjoyed some great camping, with open fires and a sense of wilderness. You can't visit the tubes on your own and must join a tour. On our tour we were joined by the Frosts from Birdsville – what were the chances, eh?

We drove from here across an area called the Atherton Tablelands. It was very pretty, with rolling green hills interspersed with mature woodlands. Our drive culminated in our arrival at a place called Yungaburra. This was a lovely town to wander around, with its attractive buildings, interesting shops and a real sense that it was well looked after. It was a town with real character, but our appreciation of it was cut short when Allister announced he was not feeling 100% and demanded a motel for the night. Obviously I was desperate to pitch the tent as normal, and so it was with much reluctance that I found us a lovely motel room with a huge bathroom, rain-head shower, a selection of aromatic beauty products, tea, coffee and of course a lovely selection of shortbread biscuits. I was not happy having to put up with this, I can tell you!

Still complaining the next morning, Al with stomach-ache and me with having to put up with the huge king-size bed and fluffy pillows, we landed in a place called Granite Gorge. I say landed because it was not in the *Rough Guide* and we happened upon a leaflet about it. A place that demonstrates well the advantage of not always following religiously the routes mapped out in your guidebook, whichever one it may be. The campsite I would describe as rustic, but great to have a campfire again. I was keen to move the large axe that was leaning against a nearby tree before going to sleep, and my encounter with cane toads, cockroaches and the huge campsite dog in the 'no working locks' ladies' toilets meant my bathroom visits were minimal. This all aside, the area had some great walking trails and was home to wild rock wallabies. You can feed them, and we spent a lovely time sitting on the rocks with the wallabies feeding out of our hands. They can be a bit greedy, as Al discovered as they hung onto his shorts, and then having overeaten threw up on him. Australian wildlife never gets boring.

September ended as we reached Daintree Rainforest and Cape Tribulation on the north coast of Queensland. We pitched our tent on a campsite that was of such a poor standard that after our first night everyone else left, leaving us all alone. We persevered a second night so we could at least explore the area. The rainforest is the oldest in the world, and the biodiversity that has been established over 160 million years is incredible. The large concentration of ancient, rare, primitive and endemic species that you can see amongst fan palms and rainforest giants can be astonishing. The rich emerald green rainforest stopping as it reaches the golden sandy shoreline only enhances further the stunning beauty of the place. We enjoyed a wonderful walk along Cape Tribulation beach in the morning and for most of it we were all alone. The significance of the area was rightfully recognised in 1988 when it was added to the World Heritage list.

We aimed to be in this area of Australia in the dry season, but it was easy to think we had mistimed it. The night was met with torrential downpours that resulted in the top of the tent reaching our noses as the weight of water pulled it down. It did not leak but constantly pushing off the rain all night meant little sleep was had. This weather, along with the deluge of bugs seemingly resistant to 100% Deet spray and enjoying significant flesh nibbling, and a level of humidity that was causing the start of personality disorders, meant that we decided one day was enough.

We headed out of Daintree and were left with a parting view of everything that epitomises the grungy traveller. Three girls were getting out of a campervan, the entire mess inside followed them out onto the roadside, and then they started cleaning their teeth. I suppose we should have been grateful for the small demonstration of personal hygiene, but alas they spat it across the pavement. What was wrong with using the toilet facility next to where they were parked, I will never know. We both discussed the somewhat disgusting habits of our fellow travellers but somehow Al's distaste dissipated as they started kissing. It made him smile all day, and at least they were minty fresh, I suppose.

SEVENTEEN

THE EARLY YEARS MARRIED LIFE

1991 TO 1996

ON 29ᵀᴴ JUNE 1991 I BECAME MRS CAROLINE FROST. This was a good day. It was a great day. I do look back and realise how young we were, though. The photos and video are evidence of that. Being only twenty-two and twenty-four when we walked down the aisle, I often wonder how many people sat there on that day and thought that we were too young. I can conclude, of course, now that we weren't. We are still together and happier than ever. There is no greater proof than that.

If you look back on your own wedding day, do you find the moments you remember are fragmented snapshots of the day? Maybe it is the disjointed video that makes me remember it that way. I can remember Allister having hay fever for the first time. I can remember two of our friends wearing almost identical dresses. I can remember my grandma holding my hand as a photo was taken. I remember my chief bridesmaid had lost a lot of weight and I remember she cried for a lot of the day. I have a lot more memories, of course, and none more so than the moment we said our vows and became man and wife. This is of course my favourite memory. It was a shame that the video man caught on camera Al standing on my dress and me pushing him off. The most romantic of moments ending like a *Carry On* film.

Being young it did of course mean that the evening turned into a big party for us and for all our guests. It was such a big party I disappeared for a lie down at one point. The most concerning part of that was that Al didn't notice I was gone. He was having way too much fun being the centre of attention, with all the girls wanting to dance with him. Al can't dance. It is a real shame, as he so loves *Strictly Come Dancing*, but this night it didn't matter as he was the groom, so he could look as daft as he liked.

We had a wonderful day, and this became a wonderful honeymoon. We went to Gran Canaria, and at this time my experience of a holiday abroad was very limited. Quite ironic now when I think of all the countries I have since been lucky enough to explore. At that time, though, the excitement of going abroad was amazing, and it was this I think that made it such a great honeymoon. We just were not used to holidays like that. It wasn't anything plush or flash, but it was hot, sunny and very different from what we were used to doing. We could enjoy it even more knowing that Al's parents were working very hard, moving us out of our flat in Guildford to our newly purchased one-bedroom starter home in Farnham.

This was a task they completed well, and we arrived back in the UK to our new home. In all honesty the moving us into our new home wasn't a big job for Al's parents. We didn't own much – but let's not take anything away from all their hard work in our absence. They did allow our friends in, though, whilst we were away, so our house was filled with balloons when we got back home. They were everywhere, even in the toilet. It did make up for the fact we had no furniture, apart from a donated sofa and chair from Al's mum and dad's conservatory, an old chest of drawers of Al's from our student days, covered in motorbike stickers to add some class to it, and a television. Let us not forget the blow-up airbed that was to be our sleeping arrangement for some weeks whilst we waited for our new bed to arrive.

As young newlyweds we did not care about any of this. We had boxes full of wedding gifts that were yet to be opened. This was far more important. Who needs a bed when you have lots of new stuff to unwrap? There really is a lot to be said for getting married and setting up home at the same time. Your wedding list is a fantastic shopping list. We arranged the following weekend to have our parents visit and we held ourselves under control for a week waiting for the grand opening day. We had a wonderful time and were soon surrounded by fluffy bath towels, a kettle, toaster, plates, mugs, wine glasses, tea towels, picture frames, cutlery and much more. It was like watching an episode of the *Generation Game*!

We were very good to note down what everyone bought us so we could write our thank-you cards. Big mistake number one for us newlyweds followed. Having opened our lovely shiny new kettle, it was with a little disappointment that we opened another gift to find it was another kettle. Or so we thought. So sure were we that the content of the box was a kettle – it was a kettle box, after all – that we did not look inside. We did not experience any further duplication and were delighted with all our new stuff. Our new house was now looking much better equipped. We spent some time afterwards writing to all our guests, thanking them for sharing our special day with us and for their generous gifts. As we had been very good and had noted down with care what everyone had bought us, we were able to thank our friends and family with that personal touch by naming what they had bought. In the case of the duplicated kettle, this was to be our undoing!

We got a reply to our thank-you letter from the duplicate kettle friends. They informed us, quite politely, that they had actually bought us a handcrafted teapot. We naturally went to find the kettle box and there inside was a very nice teapot. To this day we always make sure we open fully any gifts we receive. It was a lesson learnt, but alas we never saw those friends again!

After the excitement of getting married, a honeymoon, lots of gifts and the joy of the arrival of our new bed, married life settled down to I suppose what could be described as normal routines. Having completed the Sainsbury's Trainee Management Programme, we were both now department managers. Allister was a produce manager. He looked after the fruit and veg, for those of you unsure of the terminology, and I was in customer service. We didn't have much money in those early years and so we didn't go out much. We went to work, visited friends and family when we could and spent a lot of quiet nights in.

Our friends soon started following in our footsteps, and very soon new homes were being bought and weddings were being planned. The great thing about those early years was that it was the same for all of us and we did attend a lot of great weddings.

I did at times find my new life in Farnham a bit lonely. I had grown up in Codsall, Staffordshire, and my family and closest friends were still there. Our student friends from Plymouth were spread all over the country and so keeping in touch and seeing people was not always easy. It was a time when we didn't have mobile phones, the internet, or free weekend and evening phone calls, and Skype could not have been dreamed of! On Saturday nights in Codsall our friends would get together at someone's house and we could only enjoy that from time to time when we headed north. Starting a new life together was wonderful for Allister and me, so don't get me wrong, but I missed having friends nearby and it takes time to develop new relationships. Sainsbury's was good for that, though. Allister and I were working hard as department managers, but the social side was good too and we started to go to parties and have nights out. Al also started to play pool for a pub league, so we began to get to know people and feel a bit more settled.

What Sainsbury's wasn't good for at the time was the old work/life balance. With both of us working for the company at different stores, our hours were not always compatible. Not only were they not compatible but also weekend working made it hard to have time to travel to see friends and family regularly, and long working days made us feel that all we did was work. Al took this in his stride; the laid-back approach he has to life now was always in place, although I think over the years Sainsbury's may have thought him a little too laid back. However, he seemed to suit retail and overall was quite happy.

It wasn't quite training with the RAF to be a pilot, which was his unfulfilled dream, but it would do. Sainsbury's didn't care that Allister had suffered cancer at the age of fifteen; unfortunately, the RAF did, and he didn't pass the health assessment at Biggin Hill. What I think was so tough for him was that he first spoke to the RAF at a career's day at his school and he told them all about his cancer. They said he should still apply. He applied, attended the assessment centre and undertook many varied tests over a few days. Only three out of sixty passed the assessment and Al was one of them.

He then had a full medical and was then told he wouldn't be able to join the RAF because of his history of cancer. So much better to be told at the start, don't you think? Imagine the disappointment, and it was obviously significant as we still watch a lot of programmes about aeroplanes today! Had Allister been successful, he would never have gone to Plymouth Polytechnic, as he would have joined the RAF at eighteen. I always said to him that the good thing to come out of his disappointment at not being able to become a pilot was that he met me. No Plymouth, no Caroline! Probably one of the most romantic things he has ever said to me was that we would have met whatever had happened. Close to where I grew up in Codsall is an RAF base, and Al says he would have been stationed there, he would have been out having a drink and I would have walked into the pub with my friends. How very *Top Gun*! Tom Cruise he is not, but from time to time he does have the lines!

Whilst Allister was being all relaxed and getting on with his new career, my life at Sainsbury's was becoming much less enjoyable. It seemed retail and management combined was rather stressful – well, it was for me – and I felt it was not the right path for me anymore. It was time to consider my options, and a life outside of the stores beckoned. I was lucky enough to find a job within the company that suited me well. I joined the area systems installation team and spent a great year travelling across the south of England visiting stores to assist them with the setting up of new systems and to train the staff and management. These systems varied from new temperature control devices for a store's many fridges and freezers to new telephone systems, through to a completely new ordering system. It was my first taste of the world of IT and provided me with the knowledge that I was good at training people. Both these things would serve me well many years later when I would finally find the career that was right for me.

The expression 'if something isn't broken then don't fix it' is commonly used. At this time in my life, when I was young, ambitious and always looking for the next challenge, I did not pay much attention to this expression. Having only been on the systems installation team for a year, I moved to head office and joined a team responsible for the development and implementation of the new ordering system. It was in the early stages, so to be involved at the sharp end I thought would be great. The problem was that it turned out to be more of an administration role and I found it quite dull. I was far better off in the systems installation team, being involved with the new system hands on and training people how to use it. A transfer back to the installation team was no longer an option but I knew I could not stay at head office so back to the stores I went. I became an administration manager, and this was great for being involved in all the store's systems and for me far better than working on the shop floor, but I never really settled and by the end of 1993 I knew retail was never going to be for me. I felt constantly stressed and miserable and needed to make a dramatic change. I resigned and left Sainsbury's on Christmas Eve of 1993. I had no job to go to and no idea what I was going to do next, but whatever it was it wouldn't be working in retail.

Resigning from a good company with great career prospects seemed like a good idea at the time, but as 1994 arrived and moved from January to February I was still without a job and unsure of what I really wanted. There are times when things do work out for the best, though. I got a job working for a small electronics distribution company as their sales administrator. This was far removed from life in retail management, but what developed over the next five years was a wonderful career in a growing company that saw me learn everything about a small business from operations and accounts to sales and marketing. I progressed to managing a small team and was able to travel abroad for exhibitions and to support the French office. When the company bought a new business software solution, I was part of the implementation project team and responsible for staff training. Being involved in IT and training again was to eventually lead to my exit from the world of electronics distribution, but the five years were a fantastic experience and one I wouldn't change.

It seemed work was all sorted in the mid-nineties. Al was progressing well in retail management and I was enjoying electronics distribution more than you would think was possible. There was, I suppose, when I look back, a sense of conformity to our life. We had followed that so predictable pattern of go to school, move away from home to be a student, meet a girl or a boy, buy a house, get married, start a career and so on. This all felt great, and part of this was because our friends were doing the same things. Our lives were progressing together. The startling news we got before we were married that Allister couldn't have children was, with relative ease, put out of our minds in the early days of our married life. Suddenly, though, the friends we had, who had married, bought their first home and started their careers, just like us, announced they were moving on to the next step: babies. Over the next few years we would have to face up to the news we had received, and instead of putting it out of our minds we would have to deal with it. It was not going to be easy.

EIGHTEEN

COUNTDOWN THE TASK LIST

MARCH 2010

SHREDDING CONTINUED INTO MARCH. ANOTHER BIG event took place as Allister started clearing out our garage. The loft was done so the garage was the next space that we could attack. Our pile of stuff destined for a car boot sale was growing.

In March money dominated our task list. The list still did not look very long, but we were relaxed and happy that we were on track. We started to look closely at how we were going to access our money and budget effectively whilst we were overseas. We also realised that we needed to be saving every penny we could until we left. If you plan to go travelling, the question you will ask yourself is, 'How much money do I need?' I have been travelling and still do not have the answer to that question. Whatever you decide to take it will not be enough. The more you take, the more you spend. The less you take, the tighter you budget. My advice is that, if you have a figure in mind, double it.

The time spent researching the use of our current account and credit cards overseas proved to be some of the best time we spent before we went travelling. We were able to handle our finances with ease whilst away and got the best return we could from our savings whilst reducing bank and credit card charges as much as we could. The best advice I can give anyone travelling is invest the time in this. You will save money and it can make accessing your money overseas much easier than you think. Now, I say we sorted this, but I do mean me; Allister handed this task over very quickly.

Following a meeting with a lady from our bank, I quickly concluded we would not be using our current account outside the UK. The use of our debit cards in restaurants and shops and using them at cashpoint machines was of course perfectly fine. Well, it would be for the bank as the charges they would enjoy would seriously impact our budget. We needed a Plan B.

The use of a credit card provided much of this plan, and again research proved to be invaluable. Santander and the Post Office offered the best credit card for overseas travel. No exchange loading: this meant a fair reflection of the current exchange rate on all our transactions and no additional fees for using the card. Interest would be charged on any cash withdrawals, though, and the Post Office would also charge a flat fee for each time we did that. We had to find a better way of getting cash in our pockets, but for day-to-day expenses in shops, for accommodation, for fuel and so on we could use one of these credit cards. I could set up a direct debit from our current account to pay it off each month, so we were well on our way to being sorted. We ended up applying for the Santander credit card, which was soon cancelled in the fourteen-day cooling-off period. I shall say no more on that other than the Post Office was by far the better option.

The credit limit on the Post Office card was a limitation. For a new application it was £1,500 and there was no moving on this for the first year. However, given that we were supposed to be travelling on a tight budget and we were paying it off each month, this should suffice. We did develop into people who planned for the worst that could happen whilst away for a year, and thus felt a backup plan was needed. We decided to keep our existing credit card and we would take it with us on our trip. It had a £10,000 credit limit built up over the many, many years we had been using it. It would not be a good card to use overseas due to charges, but in the event of an emergency it would be ideal, and if we ran out of cash towards the end of the trip then we could just run up a bit of debt. So, credit cards – sorted! Well, I needed to set up the direct debit once I had the Post Office cards and online account activated but sorted in principle.

As we would be paying off our credit card by direct debit each month, we needed to ensure there was money in our current account to cover this. If you are away a long time, it is important to get the best you can out of the money you have. Putting all our savings into our current account was not sensible as the interest rate was non-existent, so we set up a new online savings account with the best interest we could find. We put all our savings into it and added to it as much as we could in the lead-up to leaving for our travels. Our current account also had a condition on it that meant £1,000 per month had to be paid into it. This was not a problem when we were working but we would not be doing so for a year. We hoped to rent out our house and rental money would cover some of that, but no guarantee. The solution was to set up a transfer from the savings account to the current account for £1,000 per month which would then in turn pay off the credit card by direct debit. We could access this online so could also move more money across if needed. So current and savings accounts – sorted! Well, I needed to set up the transfer and make sure all was working ok, but it was sorted in principle.

I was not finished yet, though. We had both set up an ISA and into these we placed the maximum we could: I think at the time this was about £3,800 each. I cannot recall the exact amount. Again, we could access these online, but the intention was not to. This was emergency cash for covering any house expenses in our absence. As we were going to rent out our house, what would we do if the roof fell in or the boiler exploded? It could happen. We ignored this money in our budget for our trip, but as it turned out the roof and boiler stayed intact, and we had only minor expenses on the house in our absence. We used this money on our return to pay off the credit card debt we swore we wouldn't have. Remember, whatever you think you will spend, you will spend more.

You would now think there was nothing more to do on the financial front, but you would be wrong. We were planning to be in Australia for about six months, and for that length of time the best option is to buy a car. Our plan was to sell my car in the UK and use the money from its sale to buy ourselves something cheap yet reliable when we got to Australia. For that length of time, hiring a campervan or other vehicle was out of the question. This was far too expensive. Much cheaper to buy a car, kit it out with camping goodies and then sell your car and what camping goodies you can when you leave. How to pay for this car, though? Our new Post Office credit card limit was not high enough and putting the money in our current account and paying by debit card was not an option. The debit card charges would double the price of the car. Well, maybe I am exaggerating a tad, but you get the idea. We would also need to be able to get cash and again, as I have already said, using our UK debit card in an overseas cashpoint machine was not an option. The solution, I felt, was that we needed an Australian bank account. How hard could that be?

In many cases and with many of the banks it was very hard. By hard I mean impossible. Whilst the internet provided me with the ultimate research tool, it did not easily give up the secret of setting up an Australian bank account when you are a UK resident. I was not to be beaten and finally the mystery unravelled, and I became a huge fan of the Commonwealth Bank. I appreciate they are getting some valuable advertising here, well, assuming this book has become a worldwide bestseller and it is not still sitting on my laptop having only been read by me and my next-door neighbour!

Anyway, here is the tip. The Commonwealth Bank in London enables you to set up something called a foreign exchange account. This is an account in sterling here in the UK. How does this work? It can be used in different ways, but the way it worked for us was that we transferred money into it from our UK current account. This money was then immediately used to buy Australian dollars, which were then forwarded to a designated Commonwealth Bank current account in Australia. Once we were approved for the foreign exchange account, the Commonwealth Bank in London set up this Australian current account on our behalf.

We designated the branch in Perth, as this was our first destination, and on arrival we had an appointment in the bank, set up before we left the UK. We arrived with our passports for identification, and a short meeting resulted in an activated account which we could use online and we were issued debit cards to get at our cash. Before leaving the UK, we had already transferred money from our UK current account to the foreign exchange account. When we arrived in Australia, this meant we had enough money in our new current account to buy a car and have some cash for the first few weeks. After that, every time we needed money in our Australian current account we simply went online, transferred money to the UK foreign exchange account and this was automatically converted to Australian dollars and deposited in this Australian account.

The other big plus was that we benefited from a commercial exchange rate. Put simply, you get more Australian dollar for your pound than if you buy your currency on the high street. It worked like a dream. Well, there was the odd problem, like no cashpoint machines in the outback and dodgy internet connections where we did not want to be accessing bank accounts, but, overall, a dream! Now, this wasn't all achieved in March, but I got as far as finding out we could do it. One thing at a time – the application could be sent in April.

March was all about the money. Not much else was achieved, but to this day I am so proud of what I achieved in the 'money management' task that Allister handed to me. It didn't end in March either. Oh no. Once you hit that open road and you are spending money on petrol, food, campsites and the odd 'adventure trip of a lifetime' it quickly becomes very hard to work out what you are spending and whether you are within your daily/weekly budget. The solution was naturally a spreadsheet, which I was able to set up within my Hotmail account. When internet access was available, we could feed in the data of our transfers, payments, withdrawals and let's not forget the all-important rental income. This allowed me to manage the funds with precision. I am sure you are expecting this meant we did not overspend. It did not. It just meant we knew that we had overspent and by how much!

I did resign in March as well. My boss took it well once he realised it was not his fault. I also gave him three months' notice instead of the one I was required to do. He was, and still is, I am sure, a nice guy, and I was keen to let everyone know what I was doing. Allister and I decided I would leave work five weeks before we set off. The sensible approach would have been to work up to a few days before to get as much money as possible, but we felt having the time to close down our life and spend time with friends and family was more important. It was the right decision, and, with Allister leaving work two weeks before our big departure day, we had time for some great send offs. We also needed every waking minute to get everything done. June and July's task lists got a bit out of control. We so should have done more in March!

NINETEEN

TRAVELLING WHEN RAIN DOMINATED

OCTOBER 2010

WE ARRIVED IN PORT DOUGLAS, NORTH OF CAIRNS ON the east coast of Australia, on Friday 1st October 2010. It was raining, as it had been for several days, and it signified the start of one of the wettest summers on record for the east coast of Australia. We were ahead of the floods that came towards the end of the year, and so retrospectively we were quite lucky. As we endlessly tried to dry out our tent and clothes on the back seat of our car, I don't think luck was foremost in our thoughts.

We did pitch the tent in Port Douglas, between rainstorms, but our stay was only long enough to buy some new T-shirts, have a few beers and wonder whether we would actually be able to go out on the Great Barrier Reef. It had been our intention to do this from Port Douglas, but the high winds, torrential rain and rather large swell on the ocean did not make us yearn to go snorkelling. It seemed that the tour operators felt the same, as most trips out to the reef were cancelled.

We headed to Cairns, where we hoped the weather would improve and we could get out on the reef. A soaking-wet tent on the back seat of the car, lashing rain and flooded campsites, not to mention our bad moods, meant we decided to rest up and dry out in a cabin for a couple of days. A couple of days turned into a week, but at least as we listened to the rain thundering on the roof, we could watch TV, eat nice food and enjoy a double bed and private bathroom. It was like having a holiday from our holiday – travelling is hard work, you know. I am not sure how Allister ever got me out of there to be honest. We did linger waiting for the weather to improve as we really wanted to get out onto the Great Barrier Reef, but I also think that being able to watch Ryder Cup golf on the TV meant that Allister wasn't in much of a hurry to leave anyway. We did venture out to visit a place called Kuranda. This is a rainforest village, and along with visiting some pretty water falls it made for a pleasant day. Mind you, the humidity was playing havoc with my hair again. I wore a hat a lot during this time to hide and flatten the overwhelming volume stretching out in all directions from the sides of my head.

We had to move on eventually. The bad weather never ceased in Cairns and so the Great Barrier Reef was missed. It was the only reason for going there for us. Many people enthuse about Cairns. It did nothing for us, just another town. The allure is clearly the reef, but as we never did that my memories are only the very fond ones I have of our cabin in the rain. We left hoping we could go out to the reef further down the coast, but we were aware we had missed out on probably the best places to go from. We landed on Mission Beach: deserted due to the weather, but a very basic cabin did us just fine and finally the sun came out. This was only during the day, and the night-times were very loud as heavy rain bounced off the corrugated hut that we were sleeping in.

A cruise out to a place called Normanby Island was a beautiful change from all the bad weather. It lies on the fringe of the Great Barrier Reef and so we did get to experience some good snorkelling. Lunch on the beach in the sun followed and helped remind us why we were in Australia. This had not been easy at times in the recent weeks as it had in fact rained every day since we had reached the east coast. An after-lunch walk around the island gave us a fantastic sighting of a manta ray flying out of the water as it was being chased by a shark. I was a little hesitant at getting back in the water for another snorkel after that, but Allister's nagging got me back in, although I didn't venture quite so far from the shore as I had done earlier in the day.

Carrying on down the east coast, the rain persisted and as we stopped in a place called Airlie Beach, we were acutely aware that we had not pitched our tent for quite a while. Staying in cabins in campsites was a lot more expensive than pitching a tent in them, and Australia was proving to be far more costly than we had anticipated. I think when we arrived in Airlie Beach Allister would probably have battled against the conditions and got the tent up, but I was less inclined. Instead I set about negotiating hard for a good deal on a cabin. There were a lot of campsites and they were not very full; the weather was impacting on the number of Australian holidaymakers, I assumed. Whatever it was, I succeeded in getting us a really good price. The cabin was small with just a bed and small kitchen area, but it was brand new and most importantly warm and dry. Following my successful negotiations, the sun came out; this figured I suppose, but it enticed us into the town, where an endless array of bars welcomed us. I will always recall Airlie Beach as the only place on our travels where we both did not remember the whole of a night out. One bar led to another; we forgot to eat and spent the whole of the next day in bed recovering. Ironically it was one of the driest, sunniest and hottest days we had seen for weeks and we missed most of it.

Once our hangovers subsided, we knew that we needed to get out to the Great Barrier Reef. We were running out of places to go from and we felt it was now or never. It was still very windy but at least it had stopped raining, so we booked a trip. Armed with a packet of Kwells, Australia's favourite seasickness pill, we boarded the boat with more a sense of trepidation than excitement. Complacency settled over us as we watched those who hadn't taken their Kwells decorating the side of the boat.

The Great Barrier Reef was not the calm and beautiful experience I had always dreamed about. The boat takes you out to a kind of floating entertainment centre, where you can dive, snorkel, go out in a glass-bottomed boat, eat lunch or just laze in the sun. It was more stable than the boat and so folks were all a little happier. I do now feel that the Great Barrier Reef is overrated, but I know that this view is probably unfair given that we snorkelled in a lot of choppy water. We did see some stunning coral and amazing fish but not enough of it, as we battled against the choppy water and somewhat murky conditions. For me it was incredibly hard work and as my mouth filled repeatedly with saltwater, I was very disappointed not to swim in the calm and crystal-clear waters I had hoped for. The centre did have a fantastic water slide, though, that launched us down a tube into the sea. As the afternoon progressed this became more fun than the snorkelling and kept me well entertained.

Airlie Beach is also the place to visit the Whitsundays from. Making the most of a sunny day, we booked a trip and cruised around these islands for the day. Daydream Island I did not think lived up to its name, but it was nice for an early-morning stroll and a coffee. The boat moved us onto Hook Island, and in-between being eaten by marsh flies we did get in some snorkelling. It was probably some of the best we had done and whilst we were aware that our guide was putting food in the water to entice the fish, we could only be grateful to finally see a lot of fish. There were so many – in fact they were bouncing off us – and a sighting of a huge Maori wrasse was a real highlight. The main reason a traveller cruises the Whitsundays was saved for the last visit of our day. We were dropped off on Whitehaven Beach. It is listed in the top ten beaches of the world and for a very good reason. Miles of endless powdery-white sand surrounded by turquoise waters greet you. It really is stunning. The downside, of course, is the number of boats anchored just off the shoreline, but it is well managed, and you can easily find a lot of space to walk along or sit on for the duration of your visit.

Moving on from Airlie Beach, the weather improved and returning to life under canvas could not be avoided any longer. We decided to stay at a place called Agnes Water. The campsite overlooked the beach and was really nice. Alas, when we booked our camping pitch, we were informed that tents had to be pitched at the back, crammed under a tree, and your car could not be parked nearby. I can only assume it was my absence from camping for quite a few nights that caused me to be so stroppy. There were empty pitches everywhere with a nice ocean view but to put our tent there we had to pay the price for a campervan or caravan because there was power. The owners could only offer a 'no comment' or 'we reserve the right' when we asked for one of these nice pitches, so we duly reserved our right and moved on. Shame, really, as it was a nice beach, but pride is far more important to maintain and sacrificing our own enjoyment of the area was clearly the thing to do.

I was obviously having some issues adjusting back to living in my tent as my temper did not improve at our next stop. We were in a very busy seaside town called Rainbow Beach. We intended to stay here and visit Fraser Island but, as our tent was pitched in a packed campsite in what felt like a corridor, I lost all reasoning on the purpose of our stay.

Looking back, it was a strange period of our trip. When you travel the east coast, it is easy to get caught up in the predictable route that travellers take, and your trip can become a bit of a list-ticking exercise. For us, our vision of the east coast had turned out to be far removed from what we envisaged: we had images of camping near the beach, hot, dry weather, BBQs in the evening and days spent lazing in the sun. The reality was far from this. We battled against the weather and got bored following the tourist trail, and the scenery was far removed from the spectacular north that we had so enjoyed. What this left us with was indecisiveness. We were struggling to get excited about anything, and in Rainbow Beach (night 100 of our travels) we had reached a point where we were not having that much fun.

The real plus side of travelling is that, if you don't like where you are, you simply leave and go somewhere else. We did just that and it seemed our time had come to find somewhere we liked. We arrived in Noosa, the sun came out and stayed out and we found a really nice place to pitch our little tent. Finally, we had some days on the beach, and we got ourselves back in the right frame of mind and visited Fraser Island. We were so glad we didn't miss out on this, and in fact our only regret is that we took a tour just for the day.

With more spare cash and being better organised it would have been a good idea to hire a four-wheel drive and camp on the island for a few nights. This is a place not to be missed. It is 123km in length and earns itself the title of the world's largest sand island, hence the need to drive a 4×4. The scenery varies incredibly, and we enjoyed all of it. We were able to walk through deep forests, explore unbelievably beautiful beaches and swim in the picturesque Lake McKenzie. The water was so pure it really had no taste, and I must say my hair and skin felt wonderful afterwards. Our tour was rounded off with a drive along the beach at speed in a 4×4 and managing to secure the front seats gave us the best views and experience for certain.

Noosa had a couple of other big moments. One was great and one signified the start of a long-lasting and exceptionally irritating problem. The great one was our first koala sighting. We hiked around Noosa Heads, where we had been informed that they roam in abundance. Abundance was not the right term, as we hiked for a very long time with no evidence of koalas, but it was a beautiful place to walk, and as we looked out over a place called Tea Tree Bay, we spotted our first koala above our heads. It was easy to understand why tourists got stiff necks when we joined a group of fellow spotters walking along with heads turned upwards in the quest to find more koalas hugging the tree branches,

As we sat later and ate a sandwich, I was reminded that not all of Australia's wildlife is quite so appealing. After only one small bite a bird that to me seemed the size of a pterodactyl swooped in and took the sandwich from my hand, inflicting a deep scratch and making me bleed in the process. Al assured me the bird was only the size of a crow (big enough, then) and my deep, almost fatal wound was in fact just a small scratch.

Our not-so-great moment was the morning that our car did not start. Being as thorough and indeed almost slightly obsessive about safety and having the right insurances, we had of course taken out breakdown cover. A very nice man from Australia's equivalent of the RAC told us we had a flat battery and we must have left the lights on overnight.

Now, this man clearly did not know Allister and me very well. If he did, he would have known that there was simply no way that we would have done this. We had a very strict checking and rechecking routine each night before crawling into our snug little canvas home. Anyway, there was little to be gained by arguing the point, so as the car got going again, we put it down to one of those things and put the incident out of our minds. The mystery of the workings of our car was going to challenge even the best mechanics over the coming weeks, but we were happy in our ignorance at this point.

Before dragging ourselves away from the very lovely Noosa we did make one final trip, and that was to the late Steve Irwin's Australia Zoo. I can take or leave a zoo – odd, really, given we went to Singapore's zoo as well – but I did very much enjoy this day. It was great fun, very educational and I got to see more koalas. Al was more interested in seeing crocodiles again and this very clear disparity in what we enjoyed only reiterates that boys and girls are very different.

Next we visited Brisbane. We drank a couple of lattes, moaned about the cost of parking and headed south. Brisbane is very nice, but we were keen to keep to the beaches. The Gold Coast seemed like the place to go. We stopped in a place called Surfers Paradise for some lunch and with a view to finding somewhere to camp. I must disagree strongly with the use of the word 'paradise': it so was not. To date it was the worst place we had visited: tacky shops, tower blocks, building sites and way too many people eating way too many burgers and chips. We headed out of town fast and just kept going. In fact, we kept driving until fading light and fatigue meant that we needed to pitch the tent. The place was called Kirra Beach and it was actually very nice. We had a lovely walk along the beach in the last of the light and then went for beer and pizza. We should have cooked, as eating out was not that affordable at this stage, but after the trauma of the Gold Coast we felt we needed it.

What we did conclude over pizza was that the sea and surf were losing their appeal and we needed a mountain. Australia is not known for its vast mountain ranges, but I must thank my brother for recommending a trip to a place called Mount Warning. This took us just into New South Wales and back to more rustic camping. This was great as we were able to light a fire and there really is nothing better than cooking your food in front of an open fire under the stars. Falling asleep in front of said fire was not such a good idea, as the very painful tick bite I found behind my ear the next morning proved. Fortunately, it was not the fatal kind and the pain gradually subsided. Mount Warning itself gave us a great day of hiking. It is the central plug for a huge shield volcano, and for added excitement it is not extinct. The caldera, which is a cauldron-like feature usually formed by the collapse of land following a volcanic eruption, is the second largest in the world. It is second only to Yellowstone National Park, but ad hoc facts aside it is worth a visit. It's a lovely walk and the views are worth the climb.

As we packed up our tent to leave Mount Warning our thoughts turned towards Sydney. Our drive down the east coast had always been about getting to this point. We had a few places to travel through on the way, but we were nearly there. We were both really looking forward to our city break and seeing all that Sydney had to offer. It was to be a real highlight.

TWENTY

LIFE CHANGES SUMMER WITH GRAHAM

JULY AND AUGUST 2003

ALLISTER'S RESPONSE TO CHEMOTHERAPY WAS dramatic. It took only five days for his temperature to return to normal. After high fevers for the best part of three months, fevers that sometimes reached over 40°C, this was an amazing moment. When the nurse wrote 'normal' on his chart I had to have it checked again.

This good news was the only good news at this stage, but at least there was some. Al was very stressed, and the chemotherapy was causing severe shakes. He was at this point on a ward with other patients and this was adding to his anxiety. His oncologist also went on holiday, and this made Al panic. All these feelings were a result of months of ill health and some of his strength to overcome hurdles slipping away. I got him moved to a private room and there he stayed until discharged. This helped him and it helped me. Having some privacy was hugely beneficial and started to help Al talk more about how he felt, instead of just snapping at me. This was good I can tell you!

The two days following the start of chemotherapy on 16th July were hard for other reasons too. In addition to the shakes, Al's temperature was still 40°C and his haemoglobin levels were so low that another blood transfusion was being considered. Al had a PIC line put in when the chemotherapy started. This is what is used for intravenous access over a prolonged period in instances such as chemotherapy being given. Al's PIC line site was very swollen and painful and looked infected. This needed testing. He had high fluid around his lungs, and this would be tested as well. No wonder he was stressed and bad tempered.

On 21st July Al had a normal temperature. It was a busy day, though. It was confirmed that the infection he had was MRSA – not good news. The fluid around his lungs was not showing lymphoma – good news – but would need draining off – not good news. His haemoglobin had dropped further so he would be having a blood transfusion – not good news. He would have to start two weeks of antibiotics for the MRSA, but this would not interfere with the chemotherapy – good news. Oddly, he was refusing to wash as well. Always something new to liven up my day!

It was a couple of days later that some positives started slowly creeping into our life. Al's temperature remained normal and this was helping him to feel better. Better enough that some much-needed physiotherapy was started. Al was painfully thin and with lack of use his muscles were non-existent. He could not walk without crutches and even with them could not stand for long. It was time to get him back on his feet, especially as his consultant was keen to get him home and for him to have his treatment as an outpatient. She wasn't the only one!

It was a couple of days later that Al had his next course of chemotherapy. He complained of a sore throat and the shakes started again. This was short-lived, which was great, and he continued with a normal temperature and his physiotherapy.

He really made my day when he asked me to help him have a shower. Weirdly, this caused me to think about my own shower problems at home. House maintenance is not something that is top of your agenda when you are spending all the waking hours you can at your husband's bedside. The screen for my shower was hanging off the wall and, although I could negotiate it well and avoid the bathroom floor flooding, I felt it was not a good thing for Al to be climbing around on his return. My parents were staying and were given a task to fix this. They needed something to keep them occupied as it was apparent that evenings spent watching Graham Norton were not enough for them. My parents had some light relief when my dad announced my bath was not straight, or the walls weren't, and, although he had fitted the screen – beautifully, of course – he was not confident that it wouldn't leak. The only solution was for my mum to take a shower whilst he tweaked the fitting to get it nice and snug. I am pleased to say I was not at home at this time and pleased to say that my mum and dad had a fun afternoon!

On the last day of July Al had another round of chemotherapy and his consultant told me he was doing well. A lot of the supplements he had been taking such as potassium, calcium and sodium were stopped. It was Allister's deficiency in these that had caused him to have a total personality meltdown back in May and June, so I was a little nervous, but I recognised it was good news. It was such good news in fact that his consultant told me that as soon as the intravenous antibiotics he was on for the MRSA were finished he could go home. Wow!

I went to see Robbie Williams at Knebworth at the start of August. A day out with friends was a rare event and I was very excited. Al was going to watch it on television as he made some excuse about feeling a bit off colour! It was blisteringly hot but sitting all day in the heat was worth it as I had a really good time. I managed to cry through Robbie's rendition of 'She's the One'. I thought my ability to cry in public had been lost forever as the year had turned me into someone who had subconsciously created a shield of detachment. It was this that enabled me to cope with the never-ending nagging doubt that my husband would not survive this. I didn't know this at the time, of course, but Al being a project I would not fail at helped us both. It helped me cope, and I believe it helped Al fight to survive.

Al's antibiotics finished, he had his blood transfusion, his potassium and sodium levels were holding their own and his white blood cell count was up. He came home for the weekend on Saturday 9th August. It was only for one night and it was unfortunately cut short as he had a massive nosebleed on Sunday morning, but still he was home. I can't remember what caused this nosebleed: something to do with his blood having been thinned for some reason. Anyway, whatever the cause, it was resolved on our return to the hospital.

On Monday 11th August 2003 Al's temperature was still normal. He had a blood test and his bloods were looking good; the hospital removed the feed tube that he had been given and told him to drink Fortisip build-up drinks instead to help get some meat back on his bones. It seemed he was moving in the right direction. There was a long way to go, but we started to see things improving instead of a constant worsening. Worsening and bad news were things we had become so used to, and positive news was not always easily believed.

On Monday 11th August 2003 Allister was discharged from hospital.

On Monday 11th August 2003 I took my husband home.

TWENTY-ONE

COUNTDOWN
THE TASK LIST

APRIL 2010

SHREDDING CONTINUED INTO APRIL. THE MONTH HAD arrived with the hint of spring in the air and the sense that we really did have quite a lot to do. The biggest priority in our April task list was to sort our travel insurance and book our flights.

Perhaps I should explain at this point that there were very good reasons why we waited until April to do these rather important things. Firstly, travel insurance was a little complicated. We had travel insurance with our current account. Al was fully covered for Crohn's disease but ironically, I had to pay a small annual premium as I had suffered in the past with occasional bouts of anaemia. Al was not covered for recurrence of lymphoma, but our theory was if this happened then we would just come home!

My small renewal premium was due around about April/ May and would last twelve months. It could not be renewed when out of the country, and thus we needed to make sure that we only renewed twelve months or less before we were due to come home from our trip, so I was covered for the duration. We also planned to travel for about a year, and this was not part of the standard policy. We could have a trip extension added to our policy when we renewed, and this would allow us to be out of the country for a designated number of consecutive days. This was approximately nine months. All of this meant that leaving in July 2010 meant we had to be home nine months later, April 2011. We therefore couldn't renew our travel insurance and apply for the trip extension until April 2010. Any earlier and we wouldn't be covered until the end of our trip. We could of course find other travel insurance, but we decided it would be too costly and too complicated! Well, more complicated than this was. Confused? We were!

The travel insurance dictated our travel plans. We could of course book our flights once insured. Not before, in case they got cancelled! Given flights could only be confirmed one year in advance, this made April the right time and a big month. We confirmed our travel insurance, paid my premium, paid for our trip extension cover and booked those flights. Flying back into the UK in April 2011 would not end our trip, though. Allister would not be due back at work until June, so we decided we would keep the house rented out until then and would tour Scotland on our return. We ended up going to France as well – handy when you have parents who have a house there!

It was a great feeling when we booked the flights. It made it all seem very real and very exciting. There was a sense that there was no going back.

The other important part of all this was that we did have to move out and we needed tenants to move in. We sorted out which rental agency to use during this month and concluded very quickly it would be an unfurnished property; I didn't want random strangers using my stuff, after all. It was better from an insurance point of view as we didn't have to worry about the fire hazard that beds and sofas might present. We had never rented out property before, and the agent was very good at sitting with us and giving us advice about all the things we would need to do. It seemed there were a lot more than we thought there would be. We decided it was best left until May. We would think about insurances, energy rating, electric and gas safety, utilities, TV and Sky, council tax, phone and broadband, post redirect and so on and so on next month. We had done enough in April, hadn't we?

We did ponder storage. Renting out our home as an unfurnished property did mean we had to find a storage unit. Plenty of those about, so we just needed to do some research and find the best deal we could. Al thought he had found the solution in April. He had not. A small wooden shack was not, in my opinion, adequate, even if they did deliver it to our house on a trailer so that we could fill it from our drive and then instruct the storage company to drive it away. Allister defended his idea on the basis we would not incur van hire costs and that we would only have to load once. Man logic said that if you hire a van you have to load it and then unload it again into the storage unit. I cannot argue with said logic, but, given that I felt we would need several of these wooden shacks, and it would increase the cost, then surely one single large, and non-wooden, container would be better. I was to be proven right, obviously.

It was onwards to May, then.

Twenty-Two

Travelling
In and Around Sydney

November 2010

I TENTATIVELY OPENED THE ZIPS ON OUR TENT AND stuck my head out. I knew from the sound on the canvas it was raining, and I could now see that swirling mist was adding to the overall ambience.

We were just outside Byron Bay, and when we had arrived the day before the sun had been shining, the campsite had been quiet, and we had enjoyed a nice afternoon on the beach. What a difference a day makes. At some point during the evening the school trip arrived. A deluge of minibuses unloaded a swarm of teenagers, and the campsite soon resembled *National Lampoon's Teenage Vacation*. As I peered out of our tent that morning, I was not surprised to see that the weather had not dampened the rampaging hormones of the young teenagers.

I was greeted with the sight of a young couple demonstrating this fact very well.

I sighed, poked Allister and suggested that he went and got me a cup of tea. Hormonal teenagers were no real issue: our return to rotten weather was. It is not easy when you plan a trip to camp for the summer in Australia, with an expectation that most days will be hot and sunny, to find yourself consistently cold and damp, and therefore having to adjust your thinking and your way of life. Reminding myself that it was all part of the experience and given that Al was not shifting out of his sleeping bag, I dragged myself in the direction of the camp kitchen. As it was the only dry place on the campsite it was very full of teachers and students attempting to cook breakfast for what seemed like hundreds, and I had a little difficulty getting to the hot water. I had certainly abandoned the idea of boiling our own kettle in the rain. Anyway, trying to smile, I made the tea and headed back to Allister. We had of course already paid for two nights, so packing up and moving on to somewhere else was not an option.

Luckily by the time we had showered the weather had improved so we visited Byron Bay lighthouse. This is the most easterly point of Australia so was interesting to see and the views were fabulous. There wasn't much else that appealed to us about Byron Bay, although it is a very popular stopping point for travellers. It was all a bit too surf shack and hippy love for us. We felt we should have been wearing tie-dye T-shirts and bits of leather around our wrists and displaying body piercing and a few tattoos to fit in properly!

From Byron Bay we headed away from the predictable travellers' trail and ended up in a place called South West Rocks. On the way we stopped at a place called Woolgoolga Headland. We stopped to look at the great view and we were lucky enough to see whales. As we looked out to sea, humpbacks with their calves were passing. When we were planning our trip to Australia, we thought a lot about the places we wanted to visit and the sites we wanted to see. We never gave any real thought to the wildlife, well, apart from the obvious expectation to see a kangaroo and a koala. One of the real revelations about our trip was how much we enjoyed experiencing the variety of wildlife that had come across our path. Beautiful birds, amazing sea life and land mammals never seen in the UK had really fascinated us and let us not forget experiencing crocodiles in the wild in the Northern Territory. It all made for some fantastic photography. I remember complaining to Allister when we packed for our trip about him taking his rather large and heavy Nikon digital SLR camera. I could not understand why our compact camera would not suffice. We did take this as well. As I look back now at some of the amazing photographs we have, I concede that Allister was right to pack fewer clothes and put his camera in his rucksack instead!

South West Rocks was another place that allowed us to enjoy the wildlife fully. We camped surrounded by kangaroos and spent our nights listening to them munch through the grass around our tent. The abundance of grass in this area did make the kangaroos a tad greedy and the high fibre intake did make for some interesting noises. There is nothing better than sleeping under canvas to the sound of kangaroos breaking wind all night! The Old Gaol, meaning Old Jail, made for an intriguing visit during the day. It might have been appealing as it looked more comfortable than camping; I cannot be certain.

Leaving South West Rocks, we had to decide what to do next. Our original plan when we were back in the UK, for what it was worth, was to spend Christmas and New Year in Sydney. Our trip down the east coast had passed a lot quicker than we thought, no doubt in part due to the terrible weather. It was early November and we would be arriving in Sydney in the next few days, well ahead of schedule. Our flight to New Zealand from Sydney was booked for early January so we had a lot of time to use between visiting Sydney and our leaving date. We were lucky to have a great solution offered to us by Al's cousin. We would continue from Sydney and drive along the south of Australia back to Perth. We would complete a full circuit of Australia and be rewarded at the end by spending Christmas with Al's family and their friends. A far better prospect than being in a tent on our own somewhere, and we would get to visit a lot of places on the way that we didn't think we would have time to see. We would have to book an internal flight from Perth back to Sydney in the New Year to get our connecting flight to New Zealand, but this cost would be worth the added experience we would gain.

With this all sorted in our heads and agreed with Al's cousin, we decided to detour to the wine region of Hunter Valley to sample a few glasses and have a look around. Lashing rain greeted us yet again and we were forced to check into a motel. A very nice, modern motel that was so nice I stayed in it from arrival at 5pm until 10am the next morning. Al went to the nearby bar all alone as I made the most of the walk-in shower and array of toiletries on offer. As a travelling girl it is important to make the most of lavish toilet facilities and by the time Allister returned, I was buffed, polished, conditioned, moisturised, manicured and positively glowing. It was complete heaven!

It turned out that the vineyard of one of Allister's favourite wines was in the Hunter Valley and so we breakfasted at Wyndhams. I am not sure Shiraz was the best choice of breakfast beverage for Allister but as I was driving, I wandered off, leaving him to the very nice lady who was offering him all sorts of samples. Early morning is quiet, and she was happy to entertain him, or maybe it was the other way around, who knows. What I do know is that wandering off and leaving him unattended was not my best decision. As a mellow contentment engulfed my husband, our hostess spotted her chance and sold him six bottles of Wyndhams' finest. This is not really in a traveller's budget and sensing my less-than-enthusiastic reaction she appeased me with some plastic Wyndhams-embossed wine glasses, hand cream and chocolates. Quite frankly, it rarely gets better than this when you are travelling, and I was soon smiling again. I did decide to ease Allister out of the door, though, and we moved on!

When Allister woke up, we were in Narabeen, on the northern beaches of Sydney. Our drive from Wyndhams had allowed him to sleep off his breakfast and as we pulled into the campsite later that day, I was confident a quick coffee would see him ready to undertake his duty as chief tent-erecting person. I was correct and we were soon pitched and looking forward to part one of our Sydney experience. We planned to camp in Narabeen for three nights, and then we would head to a hotel in the city for a further three nights. An advance Christmas monetary gift from Al's parents was paying for our hotel, and we were very excited about this.

It is all about priorities, though, and for me, much to Allister's amusement, this was to take a trip to Palm Beach. For those of you who do not know the significance of this venue, then shame on you. It is the location for the filming of that famous Australian soap *Home and Away*, and as such a prerequisite on the list of places we had to visit. We awoke to sunny weather and, despite having to endure Allister's sarcasm about our trip that day, he did concede afterwards that is was a very nice area. We had a lovely walk along the beach, and I enjoyed posing for photographs in all those famous spots. We had of course picked a day when no filming was taking place and so I was unable to gain myself an appearance as an extra, but I did not allow this to ruin my day.

From this point onwards it was all about Sydney, and the next day we got up with the sunrise and caught the bus to a place called Manley. From Manley we caught the ferry to Sydney. This was a truly fantastic way to see Sydney for the first time. The commuters on the ferry, who no doubt took this trip every day, did not seem quite as excited as we were as we rounded the headland and Sydney came into view. The sun had just come out, and as the Opera House and Harbour Bridge filled the skyline, we just grinned at each other. It was such an iconic view and arriving in Sydney by car would not have given us such a great entrance into the city. It certainly was a great way to dissolve the row we had just had. I cannot remember what it was about, but we had been certainly bickering on the ferry. All this vanished as we travelled into Sydney and docked at Circular Quay, a very short stroll from the Opera House. We had a truly memorable day. It was one of the most enjoyable days on our travels.

No trip to Australia is complete without seeing Sydney. There is something special about being so far from home and seeing a place that is so distinctive. We started our day sitting in the shadow of the Opera House, drinking coffee in the sun and looking out over the harbour: fabulous. It was really a day for wandering and soaking up the atmosphere, and the Botanic Gardens were a great place to do this. With wonderful views over the harbour, bridge and Opera House, we found the time just drifted by. We did find time to hop back on the ferry and tour around the harbour. The ticket we had bought in the morning was a day tripper ticket, giving a full day pass to ride the ferry, buses and trains. We made the most of it and sat on the ferry for the full duration of its route. It enabled us to get off across the other side of the harbour to enjoy the views back across the water, and the bonus was that it was very cheap. Sydney Harbour is full of luxurious boat companies offering you a cruise around the harbour. The government ferry may not be as plush and there is no champagne on offer, but the views are just the same. I would recommend using them to travellers on any budget.

We did not have to fit everything into this one day as we had our three-night stay in the hotel to look forward to, so it really was just about strolling round. The time flew by, though, and we were soon getting back on the ferry to head back across the harbour to Manley. The skies had darkened significantly and as we crossed the water the storm began. It was certainly very memorable to look back at the Sydney Harbour Bridge and watch the lightning striking overhead. As we got on the bus the other side we were always slightly ahead of the storm, but it was following us and as we got back to the campsite there were a lot of people walking around securing tents, campervans and caravans and urging people to get inside. We followed the advice, and as it was already quite late and had been a very long day, we were not perturbed about getting straight into our sleeping bags. Experiencing a violent thunderstorm in a tent in the middle of a field is quite something. How Allister managed to sleep through the whole thing I will never understand.

The next morning dawned and apart from some blown in litter and a sprinkling of tree branches it was as though the storm hadn't happened.

We were keen to get packed up and head to our hotel in the city. Having so much enjoyed the previous day we were really looking forward to spending some more time in Sydney, and of course looking forward to a hotel for a few nights. As seasoned travellers we had learnt that just because plans are made it does not mean they will be so. A case in point was this particular morning, when, for the second time, our car would not start. The RAC man this time declared our flat battery was due to our stereo draining our battery. We were very keen to get to Sydney, so we just agreed with him, unlikely as it sounded.

We got going and travelled into Sydney across the Harbour Bridge. It is a toll bridge, but paying the toll was a challenge. Cash, it seemed, was very old fashioned and we should have had a pass. Checking into our hotel, we knew that the bill for this would head to Al's cousin's house in Perth as this was the registered address of the vehicle. We would wait for her to shout and then send her the money. This seemed like a good plan.

We had a truly wonderful time in Sydney, doing everything a good tourist should do. We took a tour of the Opera House; it has a fascinating history and to fully appreciate its architecture it is worth seeing it both from the outside and from the inside. We walked miles to soak up the atmosphere and enjoy every part of the city. Like many great cities it is a place of contrasts. The modern Darling Harbour is a purpose-built development with all the attractions you would expect: a cinema, aquarium, gardens, exhibition centre, shops, bars and restaurants. Plenty to entertain – but head to the Rocks, beneath the bridge, to see the heart of historic Sydney. Like Darling Harbour, it has undertaken major redevelopment, but it is still worth exploring to understand more about the history of the city. If you like it lively then head to the Rocks on a Friday or Saturday night.

I could ramble for pages about every intricate detail of Sydney, but you can buy a good guidebook for that, should you ever visit. However, I will conclude my love of Sydney by saying: do go on the Bridge Climb if you ever do venture to these faraway shores. The company does a great job of making you feel like you are about to undertake a climb up Everest, but the build-up all adds to the experience and it is not as scary as you may think. You feel very safe and secure, and for views of the city nothing else comes close. Keep fluids to a minimum on the day, as you will be gone about three hours and there are no toilets at the top of the Harbour Bridge! Let's hope the day doesn't come when we see the golden arches of McDonald's shining on the top in the sun!

We left Sydney via Bondi Beach. Another iconic place that we felt we couldn't miss. It wasn't quite as awful as Surfers Paradise on the Gold Coast, but it did come a close second. To say you have visited allow one hour. This is ample.

Next stop was the Blue Mountains, where we stayed in a place called Katoomba. Day one was sunshine and great walking on the National Pass. This was a pretty area and worthy of a visit. Day two was heavy mist, followed by torrential rain, and it was freezing cold. We managed to spend almost the entire day in a coffee shop called Common Ground. It was a very quirky place run by tree huggers. Every man had the same beard and all the girls wore plaits and pantaloons. The food and coffee were superb, though, and simply the best toilets we had seen on our travels. Al said he didn't know whether to flush or take a photograph. We thought that the staff were a bit too chilled out, though, when we came to leave. The waiter who had been serving us our coffee and cakes asked us if we would like a table for two!

The campsite we were staying in was a dump, the weather was atrocious and further car trouble added to the damp and miserable atmosphere. As we left the Blue Mountains in a somewhat fed-up state, we headed towards Canberra and we knew we had to get the car sorted. Our trip would be taking us again back into the wilderness over the coming weeks and an unreliable car was not what we needed. Surely, we could find a mechanic to fix the problem.

TWENTY-THREE

THE EARLY YEARS CHANGING TIMES

1996

I WILL ALWAYS REMEMBER THE DAY. WE WERE IN A pub. We were spending a long-overdue weekend visiting my parents and catching up with our friends. One of my friends was drinking soft drinks; I should have seen what was coming. She was more a pint of lager kind of girl at the time. As we all loitered around the bar, she looked at her husband and the inevitable words came: 'We have some wonderful news. I'm pregnant.' The yelps of joy from all of us drowned out a strange, sinking sensation I felt inside. This feeling was, to be honest, not unexpected. Thoughts of having children over the last few years had been minimal, but I suppose it was inevitable that those thoughts would increase as time went by. Allister and I had been talking about it more and more of late, but even so I did not expect to stand in front of my friend and be thinking, 'I wish it was me.' Alas, this was what I was thinking. Allister and I were of course thrilled for our friends and at that moment I had no idea what Al was thinking; he looked as happy as I am sure I did. Was he feeling odd inside like me? When we talked about it later it seems he was but in a different way. He was just wondering how I was feeling about the news. It was the same kind of reaction from my parents when I told them about our night out. They, more than me, expected that the news of one of our closest friends being pregnant would have an impact.

What had been an occasional thought now became a much more frequent one. The realisation that I wanted children was foremost in my mind. I was twenty-seven and had been married for nearly five years, and it felt the right time to start a family. For me, I think, the innate desire we have as women to become a mum was kicking in and giving me sleepless nights. Our friend's news had no doubt helped, though, in bringing to the surface emotions that Al and I had done a good job of ignoring since we had found out that we could not have children.

To say we could not have children is perhaps a somewhat inaccurate sweeping statement. We could not conceive naturally is perhaps more accurate, but accuracy was not foremost in my mind at this time. My thoughts were about not just having a baby but having Allister's baby and it was this thought that would never leave me. It was this thought that put huge obstacles in our way as we started to talk about what the future might hold for us. Would we remain childless or could we explore other options that would fill our desire to raise a family?

And there was no denying it anymore: we did want children. In front of us were a few hard years, but even at this time I don't think we realised how hard. Our friends had not had their baby yet, our siblings were not even in the planning stage and we were still only in our twenties. Time and lives moving on was going to make things a lot harder.

We decided to put our house up for sale. Was this a reaction to the news that our friends were expecting their first child? If it was, it wasn't a conscious one. We were living in a small one-bedroom starter home and had been for nearly five years. I think that we did have thoughts that if we were to explore options for having a family then a one-bedroom house was not an ideal size, but I do think it was more about the need to move forward. We couldn't make a baby so let's move to a new house instead. It doesn't sound logical, I know, but emotions were a little confused at this time. It wasn't the right thing to do and only added to our feelings of uncertainty. The mid-nineties were a time of negative equity and we had been victims of this. We didn't realise by how much until we came to put our house up for sale. To be able to move we had a figure we couldn't sell below and unfortunately this figure was not low enough for us to find a buyer. After a couple of extremely frustrating months of minimal viewings and very little interest, we decided to take the house off the market. It was not an easy time.

The good news was that we were both doing well at work. I was still enjoying life working for the small electronics distributor and was pleased I had made the move from Sainsbury's. It was the right move for me, and I had a great job. Al had progressed well at Sainsbury's. He was promoted to deputy store manager in 1996 and his future career looked promising. Conversation in the Frost house, though, was not dominated by our successful working life. It was dominated by talking about having children, or more accurately not having them. We needed to investigate our options and the time had come to stop sticking our heads in the sand and do something proactive.

We had a lovely GP at the time, and we went to discuss our situation with her. Options were limited, of course – Al was not about to start producing the vital ingredient again – but options there were. Our GP referred us to a specialist, and it was one morning in 1996 that we did for the first time face our dilemma properly and explore what options we had available to us.

In summary we had two options. Number one was adoption. We would want to adopt a baby, which would be harder than adopting an older child, but achievable. Number two was using donor sperm. When the specialist said these words, I remember thinking of a scene in *All Creatures Great and Small* when one of the vets was artificially inseminating a cow. This image didn't make me warm to this idea instantly, I can tell you.

The specialist we were seeing was a fertility specialist; well, that is my memory anyway. If adoption was the route we wanted to take, he could give us information on whom to contact and how to proceed, but that was all. If donor sperm was the route we wanted to take, then it was him who would make that happen.

At this stage he needed to give us as much information as possible to help us decide. What followed was quite a mind-blowing appointment. The most alarming thing for me was the news that I would have to undergo some minor surgery to start with. It seemed that to qualify for donor sperm it had to be checked all was well with me. I therefore needed to go into theatre for an exploratory laparoscopy. I was not impressed by this news. I had never had surgery and was not expecting to start now. However, if we wanted to go ahead with donor sperm, then it was essential I was checked out to ensure everything was in good working order. This would only be the first stage; thereafter I would need to take pills to optimise my ability to conceive and there would be blood tests to ensure that the timing for the donation was correct. Allister's part in all of this was in no way physical. The only thing we would share would be our emotions. It was these that the doctor went on to discuss. The obvious question in our minds was that, if we decided to go ahead and I conceived, then would this baby feel equally mine and Allister's? Now, there was a question. The doctor spent a lot of time talking about the emotional side of this. He was very reassuring in explaining the support we would have during pregnancy and how during this time Allister would form a natural bond. By the time the baby was born we would feel equal as parents. He talked the good talk, but I am not sure I remember being convinced. I remember feeling quite detached from the conversation, a sense it was someone else in the room having to deal with this. I was a long way from being ready for this step, but was adoption a viable alternative for us?

We left the consultation armed with literature, armed with advice on taking some time to consider our options, and armed with the knowledge this was not going to be easy.

If people we care about are ever in difficult situations, we all try to be supportive and this often involves us telling those people that we understand how they feel. Do we, though? We may care a great deal about our friends and family and any difficult situation they are faced with, but we don't understand how they feel if we have not experienced the same situation ourselves. We think we do, and indeed we want to, but I truly believe that if I had tried to explain fully to my friends and family at the time what I was feeling they could not have understood. I didn't really know myself, so, how could they?

Allister and I did tell our parents we were looking into options and we did discuss what these were. I honestly don't recall what advice, if any, we got back. I don't think advice is something you can give in this situation. It had to be a decision Allister and I took all on our own. I think we just needed to know that our parents would support any decision we made. I am sure they would have done, but again until we told them what we were going to do it was an emotion they could not anticipate or understand. Would Allister's parents feel like grandparents if we decided to proceed with donor sperm? Would my parents feel sadness that their only daughter would never become pregnant if we decided to proceed with adoption? Would we be happy and fulfilled if we decided not to do anything and live our life without children? These were the kind of questions that started to become regular discussion points for Allister and me, and they were not easily answered.

When we found out just before we got married that we could not have children we told our parents the news. We never told any of our friends at that time, except for our dear friend Julie. I tell Julie everything, always have and always will, and so naturally she needed to know this news before our big day. She took it well; I suppose, like me at that age, babies seemed a long way off, so it was hard to get too emotional about it. We talked about it from time to time, but it never really became a big topic of conversation until after that night in the pub when our mutual friends broke their exciting baby news. The obvious question was how Allister and I felt about it, and so when we started to explore our options, she was a good listening ear. Like our parents, though, there was not much advice she could give, but at least she was more detached than Allister and she enabled me to explore my thoughts out loud.

Allister was wonderful at this time. He was thoughtful, loving and caring and above all told me he would support any decision I wanted to make. And there was the problem. This decision had to be a joint one. Did we adopt, have donor sperm or do nothing and live a life without becoming parents? Not a decision for one half of the marriage to make alone. The hardest thing for Allister was the thought that us not being able to have children was because of him. Now, of course this was just the way it was, and I looked at it as a joint problem, but sometimes how he talked clearly portrayed how he felt inside. To him, if I had married someone else, then I might already have been a mum. Consider as well that his first question to me after he broke the news about not being able to have children was whether I still wanted to marry him. These comments clearly demonstrated his feelings. Allister felt he was the problem. The solution to that, albeit not a conscious decision, was to want to do whatever made me happy. Adopt or have donor sperm or do nothing, all fine by Al as long it was what I wanted. I am sure you can see the problem here. I had a husband who adored me and wanted me to be happy. This does not sound like a problem, does it? It is, though, when you have to make the decision of your life. I could not do it alone, I needed to understand what he wanted too, and it was many months of talking before we started to get to the bottom of how we both really felt.

It was a hard time, a very hard time. Our thoughts and our conversations were dominated about what we wanted and what we should do. We didn't know and that was the problem. Did we want children? Yes. Knowing the answer to that question we thought would lead to deciding how, but it did not. At times I felt angry and cheated as my thoughts turned backwards to when Al received his chemotherapy treatment at fifteen. Why had steps not been taken to secure sperm samples before his treatment commenced? I did not and still do not know the answer to that. Maybe it was not known that the treatment could cause sterility and therefore it was not considered. Maybe it was simply overlooked. Maybe he was too young or maybe it just wasn't something that could be done at that time. I prefer to think it was the latter. Looking backwards is pointless. Allister and I needed to look forward. One thing did emerge more strongly than ever over this time and it was that I was having such a difficult time making a decision because I wanted the one thing I couldn't have. I wanted Allister's children, Allister's biological children. I wanted a baby with lots of curly hair that looked exactly like Al. Donor sperm, no matter how close a 'match', was not going to give me that and adoption certainly wasn't. Where did we go from here?

We didn't go anywhere. We didn't make a decision and somehow, we just kind of drifted into talking about it less and less. Of course, not making a decision was actually making a decision but time was on our side and we knew that there was time to do whatever we wanted. The years would move on and time would become a constraint and eventually lead to an end to our options. We were not at that stage yet, and I think 'putting it on the back burner' was our way of not having to come up with an answer. At the same time, we were not drawing a line under the problem, so we could still have children if we wanted to. Well, this is what we told ourselves. It was our way of dealing with something that we weren't dealing with at all.

Our friends had a little girl in the autumn of 1996. It was a lovely moment, the first of our friends to step properly into the grown-up world and a moment that signified a huge change, not only for them but for all of us who had yet to make this step. It was the first time I would go and buy a new baby card; the first time I would buy baby clothes and toys and the first time I can remember holding a baby in my arms. Allister and I were so thrilled for our friends, and it was great seeing their family and the rest of our friends happy and excited for them. It really was, but those thoughts about what Allister and I were going to do were there, niggling away and making us feel an overwhelming sadness that we couldn't shake off.

One Sunday afternoon after we had joined them for a very pleasant roast lunch, our friends asked Al to be godfather to their little girl. It was lovely of them to ask him, and he had no hesitation in saying yes.

It was to be the first of many christenings over the coming years, and news that other friends were now also expecting their first child really did signify the change of times.

We decided to put our house up for sale, again. It was the right time, we needed to move forward, the market had picked up a little and we were both keen to make that change. We wanted to move to Petersfield, a lovely market town in Hampshire. This time we were determined to find a way to make the move happen. In December 1996 we got an offer on our house. All we needed to do now was find a house in Petersfield. How hard could that be?

Twenty-Four

Countdown
The Task List

May 2010

Shredding seemed to be finished. Well, it's finished for the purposes of this book. I think we might still have been shredding the day before we flew, but I think enough said. I can only recommend that, if you ever pack your life into a storage container, buy a shredder!

May's task list involved a lot of carrying tasks forward to June. I was to be at home for the whole of June so the theory was I would have simply more than enough time to do everything we needed to do. My exhaustion during June did make me question this with hindsight, but it meant that most of May was quite relaxed. Now, this is not to say we didn't do anything – it's just that we should have done a lot more. At the end of May, as the outstanding list for June was compiled, the sense of calm that we had felt about our trip and its arrangements fell away and was replaced with a sense of panic. It was only mild panic but panic all the same. Al was happy in the knowledge he would be at work during June and I would be at home sorting everything out. His trust was flattering, I think!

When we look back now over the things we did and the planning we put in place, we realise that the biggest proportion of our time was spent in moving out, arranging to rent out our home and closing our life down here. We did little to plan our actual trip. We booked flights, got our jabs, sorted where we were staying the first couple of weeks, and let us not forget the financial planning that any accountant would have been proud of. Although this financial wizardry took some time, it was the moving out of home and country that took longer. Other than deciding which countries to visit, we had given little thought to where we would go and what we would do when we got there. You know what, though: I would recommend doing the exact same thing. When you arrive in a country, the 'not knowing' is part of the fun, and as you travel any plans you make will change anyway. It is all about discovery: the countries, the culture and above all yourself.

One of the interesting things about moving out of your home, be it into another one or into a storage container, as we did, is the things you find you have, covered in dust, which you have forgotten about. A case in point was a collection of old postcards that I had. I was given these as a young girl from a lady who worked with my dad. She was retiring and to me, as a girl of about ten, she was very old. She had owned the postcards for a long time too, so logic told me they must be very old. As a young girl with the same desire for tidiness and order that I have now, all the postcards were assembled into a folder and labelled. It was a job I was proud of and for a time it took pride of place on my extensive bookshelf and would be brought out and perused at bedtime. At some point I got older and gradually the postcards migrated from the bookshelf to a cupboard and then into a bottom drawer. As I moved around from the age of ten to the age of forty-two the postcards moved around with me, never looked at and gathering dust. I concluded they might be worth something, and, given that they would likely be in a bottom drawer for another thirty-two years, it seemed like a good idea to sell them.

I used the internet to search for postcard dealers or collectors (yes, they do exist) and found a few in the area. I emailed them and waited for the flood of offers. The flood did not arrive, but a chap did get in touch and said he would like to view said collection. We arranged to meet in a coffee shop. I insisted on meeting in a public place, and naturally I took my husband with me for protection. Anyway, the chap was very nice and offered to buy my collection on the spot. Did he seem too keen? I thought so and found myself questioning if there was a hidden gem in my collection that would make me a millionaire. The watch that Del Trotter in *Only Fools and Horses* found sprang to mind, if you can remember that far back!

Anyway, I took the chap's details and pondered the price. The trouble is when you are not a postcard expert you have no idea of their true value. There was nothing for it – they would have to go to auction. As this task stretched into June, I ventured, for the first time in my life, into an auction house. My collection was met with a positive response and I set a lowest value they could sell at. This would match what I had already been offered plus the commission the auction house would take. The day of the auction was very exciting, although I couldn't attend. I waited for my windfall. Alas, they didn't sell.

'We are very surprised,' said Mr Auctioneer, 'postcards usually sell so well.' Not this time, clearly. The decision to be made was: do I sell them to the nice man in the coffee shop or do

I keep them and let them gather dust for many years to come? I am not always the best at making a decision, so I spent some more time on the internet looking for copies of the cards I had and seeing if I could ascertain any value. After all, I had nothing else to do at this time, did I? To conclude, I rang Mr Coffee Shop, asked him if he would still like them, he said yes, came around with the cash and I handed over the merchandise. Handing the cash into the bank, I held my breath in case the nice lady said, 'I am very sorry, Mrs Frost, but these notes are forgeries.' I really must learn to trust more. She did not say this, and I enjoyed spending the cash in Australia.

Storage was the next big achievement in May. This task, left originally to Al, did not get off to the best of starts. To put it simply, I felt the arrangement he had a quote for did not protect all my worldly goods enough, and so I searched for an alternative. We settled on a company that provided steel containers hidden within a warehouse with great security. From the outside the place looked like a farm, indeed I think it had once been a pig farm, and you would have no idea it was full of storage units. Size does matter and thus affects the price. Allister and I agreed on the slightly smaller version to save money. Allister was convinced that we could fit everything we owned into this – what I thought to be too small – steel box. It would be July when he was proven right.

Another big moment was when we paid the final balance on our flights. It made leaving day feel very much closer! We also sold my car in May. It was sold to a friend of a friend and was to be picked up and paid for after 3rd June, as this was the day that I finished work. Thereafter we could survive with one car. This was good news. This money was to go into our Australian bank account and would be used to buy us a car to tour Australia. This was very exciting.

It was onwards to June, then.

Twenty-Five

Travelling Car Trouble and Heading South

November 2010

Our car had failed to start three times to date, and we were now the proud owners of a set of jump leads. In the Blue Mountains the RAC man said our battery was flat because 'something was draining it'. This was less precise than the previous two, who had declared that we had left the lights on and the stereo was taking the power. Number three obviously did not want to commit.

We were en route to Canberra and decided the best course of action was to take it to a garage to get it properly checked. We thought we needed a new battery despite all three RAC men telling us the battery was fine. We were certain we knew better.

We found a garage that looked acceptable and the mechanic there gave it the once-over. I must say he gave by far the best reason to date for our battery going flat so often. Apparently, this very common problem with the Holden Commodore was that the driver's seat would stick and drain the battery. Was he for real? The battery itself was of course as good as gold! The solution was to remove the fuse from the electric seat adjustment control. Well, ok then, we thought, why not?

We arrived in Canberra, pitched our lovely little home, lit the BBQ, had a beer and went to bed.

The next morning the car wouldn't start, as, believe it or not, we had a flat battery. Following a quick jump start (we were getting very efficient at these) we headed into the centre of Canberra and found ourselves another garage. Now, these chaps were very thorough, but like all those that had come before they told us that the battery was as good as gold. It was decided that the problem was loose corroded connections, so these were duly replaced. We felt a little more confident as we drove away as this was an entirely new kind of reason, but to be on the safe side we decided to stay another night and enjoy all the things that Canberra had to offer. In fairness, this is limited, but we treated ourselves to a meal at a Thai restaurant as we hadn't seen one of these in a long while. Having not eaten such a spicy meal for quite some time, the food did awaken our taste buds somewhat, but very enjoyable all the same.

The next morning the car wouldn't start, as, believe it or not, we had a flat battery. Following a quick jump start (we were even more efficient on this day) we headed into the centre of Canberra and popped into the garage we had visited the day before. We had paid for the repair and as it wasn't actually repaired it seemed only fair that they got another crack at fixing the problem. Despite the battery testing again as 'good as gold' they decided to remove it. A remarkable decision, we felt! As we looked at the corroded, bulging battery, we were struggling to see how this was 'as good as gold'. This battery was only four months old, as we had bought it when we purchased the car, so the very obliging man at the garage advised us it was under warranty and contacted the dealer in Western Australia where we had made the fine purchase. I think he felt a bit foolish over the 'good as gold' comments! Our luck ran out at this point, as the brand we had was only sold in Western Australia and thus did not have a countrywide warranty. I am sure you are not surprised by this, and neither were we. We paid for the new battery and kept the receipt with the view that we might seek recompense once we returned to Western Australia over Christmas.

We decided to stay another night, just in case the car failed to start the next morning. I do not think our lack of confidence was a surprise at this point. We amused ourselves with a trip to the Houses of Parliament and sat through the prime minister's question time. Very entertaining, although poor Al missed a fair amount as it seemed the spicy food from the night before had given him some unwanted repercussions. There is always a positive, though, and, as far as toilets go, the Houses of Parliament did not disappoint.

Our day ended well with a free feed as a large school trip had descended on our campsite. The school cook was a delight, and as Al worked the best of his charm on her I was able to enjoy lasagne and salad followed by jelly and ice cream. His charm was so successful we even got hot chocolate and biscuits before bedtime. I think she was one step away from tucking him in! We even got bedtime stories from our camping neighbours, who wanted to show us their guns! We declined a visit to their wilderness home for a shooting lesson and crawled into our sleeping bags, fully aware that the tent was not bulletproof. A traveller's life is always varied, you can be sure of that.

Our car started the next morning and filled with a new-found hope we packed up our tent, bid farewell to the cook and our new pro-gun friends and headed to the Snowy Mountains.

Australia does have mountains and it even has a ski season. This is not something we easily picture when we think of the vast red outback, but there is snow in Australia. We were not in the ski season, but as we camped in Mount Kosciusko mountain retreat, we were pleased to be able to light a campfire as the air was certainly cool. The camping was fantastic, beautiful location and we were surrounded by kangaroos and inquisitive possums.

The next day we hiked the Main Range Walk. It was a twenty-two-kilometre hike through alpine-like valleys and across snow-covered ridges. Our reward was a day without a cloud in the sky and a view at the top from the highest point in Australia. This was a truly wonderful feeling. Al enjoyed it that little bit more, as 100 nurses were doing a charity walk. It was strange how our pace seemed to match theirs throughout the day.

A celebratory night was called for and we lit the fire and cracked open a bottle of wine. Exercise, high altitude and wine are a great combination. As Al wandered off to the toilet it was unclear whether he would return as disorientation set in. Through the darkness I heard him walk into a post and then attempt to settle down in someone else's tent. I rescued him and we both certainly slept well that night.

The following morning, we ate breakfast whilst looking at the map. From our mountain retreat we were heading towards Melbourne but planned to camp at a place called Wilsons Promontory en route. We could have travelled the direct route on established roads, but where is the fun in that? Al felt it was much better to head off the beaten track a little, travelling over the mountains and down the other side, where we could camp overnight in a place called Bairnsdale. This would be a functional stop to catch up on emails, shopping and washing.

Al was correct that the route was certainly prettier, but the map was not quite accurate. It depicted sealed roads. These you may or may not recall from earlier chapters are roads covered in tarmac. There was about thirty kilometres of our route that had definitely not seen any tarmac, ever. As the car bounced its way across the mountains and shook us from top to toe, I worked hard at not blaming Al for his choice of route. This was a challenge.

To bring calm upon me again, on arrival in functional Bairnsdale, Al suggested we took a short ferry ride across to a place called Raymond Island. He had heard rumour of a large koala population, and if anything would make me smile again it was these cute, furry animals. We were not disappointed and as we toured the small island, we lost count of how many we saw. It was absolutely wonderful; we even came across a mother and baby in a tree at our eye level. This made for a fantastic photograph that is now a huge canvas hanging in our house. A constant reminder of our amazing trip and all that it had to offer.

Not all wildlife in Australia is great to be so close to, and we were soon to be reminded of this as we moved on to Wilsons Promontory and pitched our tent once more. Wilsons Promontory is very scenic and very popular. It is the southernmost point of mainland Australia. Our first day there was lovely, and we enjoyed the beautiful beaches. We planned our hike for the next day whilst enjoying a beer and hotdogs outside our tent that evening. I guess that was our mistake, as the rain soon started. We were not to be deterred the next day and set off on our hike in the pouring rain. Damp, wooded areas are a haven for leeches. We found this out to our cost and, despite our best efforts to avoid them, we soon found ourselves with new friends, firmly attached. We made our way out of the trees and onto a beach and stripped. The best and safest way to get these beasts off is to burn them off with a match. Obviously, our matches were back at camp, and there were no other idiots out and about in the area. As they gorged on our blood, we had no choice but to head back into the trees and make a dash for the car. Our pace was of an Olympic standard, but it did not stop another one getting stuck to Al's chin. On arrival back at the car park my little friends dropped off as they were so full of my blood that the weight simply pulled them down. To fully enjoy your blood, they inject something into you first to thin it so they can maximise their intake. The result of this is that as they detach you bleed quite a bit. As I emerged from trees into the car park, I looked like I had been attacked. The startled face of the woman I ran into said it all. I smiled in an attempt to assure her that all was well and then we headed back to camp for much-needed showers. My T-shirt ended up in the bin! We have a photo of the leeches stuck to my chest. Al seems to find this picture amusing, even today. I am less enthusiastic about the memories it brings back.

The rains followed us to Melbourne; fortunately, the leeches did not. I think we would have really enjoyed Melbourne had it not been for the continual lashing wind and rain. We did ride the tram to get a dry tour of the city, and from what we saw it looked great. Between downpours we explored on foot, but it was not as enjoyable as we had hoped. I was distracted by a small nagging worry, and as the weather was so bad, we decided to make use of our time in a city and visit a doctor.

I had already visited a doctor in Canberra to get a prescription and whilst there had asked the doctor to look at a mole that had appeared on my toe. I had not expected much response, but alas she decided to tell me it was worth checking out when I got home. At the time this event was seven months away, and so the seeds of doubt were sewn. I would later learn that doctors in Australia do take any mole questions very seriously and there is not always cause for alarm. Anyway, I decided to get a second opinion and my alarm increased dramatically in Melbourne, when the doctor advised it might need removing and would refer me to the hospital for a proper check. Sensing my panic, she decided to ask another doctor to take a look. It turned out I was seeing the newly qualified, not-so-confident doctor. The rather more senior doctor performed a thorough look through some fancy piece of equipment and announced it was trapped blood in a blister. I would have felt foolish had it not been for the fact that it took three doctors to correctly identify this!

Oddly, relief was replaced with a few weeks of mole paranoia on my part. I don't think the skin cancer posters and leaflets I was seeing everywhere helped, and when I spotted another new mole on another toe a few weeks later I knew I would have to get that one checked too before leaving Australia. If you do ever travel to Australia, get yourself a Medicare card on arrival. The reciprocal arrangement that is in place with the NHS entitles you to free doctors' appointments. I intended to maximise this once back in Perth for Christmas and get myself one of those readily available full skin checks!

Having visited the location of *Home and Away* in Sydney, I informed Allister that I could not leave Melbourne without visiting Ramsay Street and the home of *Neighbours*. It is unfortunately not central, and the drive took a little longer than planned. An empty, quiet cul-de-sac greeted us as we had yet again managed to pick a non-filming day. It was a bit of an anticlimax, I must say, but we took a few photos and bid Melbourne farewell.

As we reached the end of November, we left the city behind and headed towards the Great Ocean Road. This is a famous journey that snakes its way along a spectacular and scenic coastline from Melbourne to Adelaide. The weather was rubbish, of course, but we were getting used to that and not letting it spoil a single moment. Time seemed to be passing very quickly now and with Christmas on the horizon we were very aware that our time in Australia was going to end soon. Mind you, there were still a lot of miles to cover yet, and we knew it was going to get hotter. We couldn't wait for that!

Twenty-Six

Travelling Beyond the Great Ocean Road

December 2010

Leaving Melbourne marked the mid-point of our trip, and what better way to celebrate than a night out for a pizza? The weirdest pizza names we had ever seen were on the menu, but when the girl behind the counter shouted, 'Whose is the large winki?' Al happily collected.

We were staying in a place called Torquay, which our guidebook described as the gateway to the Great Ocean Road. This road extends approximately 175 miles east and is a truly beautiful drive. The highlight is the view of the Twelve Apostles. These are huge limestone pillars that rise as high as sixty-five metres out of the ocean and they make for an awe-inspiring sight. This drive had never been part of our original plan, despite its recommendation from several people before we travelled. Perhaps it was this that made it so enjoyable.

Before reaching the Twelve Apostles we stayed a couple of nights in a place called Apollo Bay. We took the opportunity to visit Cape Otway, a koala-populated headland that yet again kept me entranced for an afternoon. I did not fully understand my obsession with these animals. The obvious was that they were cute and cuddly looking, but I think it was more about seeing an animal I had never seen before and knowing that there was nowhere else in the world I would be able to see them. At the end of the headland was a lighthouse. Exceptionally high winds made for an interesting climb to the top. Al enjoyed some 'windsurfing' whilst I wondered if it would ever get hot down under. It was hard to believe we were in the middle of the Australian summer.

Apollo Bay will also be fondly remembered by me as the only place on our travels where I had a haircut. A cut and blow dry was a wonderful moment in time. When you have lived out of the back of a car for months, worn the same clothes over and over again, and more importantly coped admirably without a hairdryer, then, believe me, you would understand the joy I experienced. For a short while I actually felt quite feminine, and as I admired the magnificent views over the sunlit Twelve Apostles the next day, I was able to show off my new look to all the other tourists and travellers jostling for the same views. It certainly is a busy area, but that should not put anybody off making the trip.

Leaving the Great Ocean Road, we headed towards Adelaide. Thunderstorms were following us and so we stopped in a small cabin on a lake for a couple of nights to dry out and basically have a rest. It must sound odd that we needed a rest, but, believe me, endless travelling over many miles, living out

Sporting my new haircut. The Twelve Apostles, The Great Ocean Road, December 2010.

Early morning, talking to parrots!

Stunning Whitehaven Beach. The Whitsunday Islands, October 2010.

OPPOSITE: *The Big Day. Saturday 29th June 1991.*

I'm too hot! Nitmiluk National Park, Northern Territory, September 2010.

Feeding rock wallabies, Queensland, September 2010.

Feeding the ducks! Holiday with friends, Norfolk Broads, 1995.

Snowing in Hawaii! March 2011.

Uluru in the rain, September 2010.

What a view! Sydney, November 2010.

The land of Crocodile Dundee! *Kakadu National Park.*

King's Canyon, Northern Territory. Not a cloud in the sky.

Introducing me to motorbikes. Plymouth, summer 1989.

of the boot of your car and continually being on the move can get both monotonous and draining. The weather was having a massive influence on how we felt. I was often wet, often cold, and beautiful beaches were passing us by instead of us lounging on them for a few days in hot and sunny weather. The bad weather had its advantages, of course. We were seeing more of Australia than planned and Al was more agreeable to nights in a cabin. It was overstretching our budget, though, and we were tired and a little irritable.

The place where we stayed was called Meningie and it was a lovely and relaxing spot. It was just what we needed. We watched a movie in the evening, and I made the most of the private bathroom. Whenever these were available to me, I felt it was important to spend most of my time using them!

The rain had stopped the next morning and so we decided to explore the local area a little bit. It was Saturday 4th December and it turned out to be a pretty frustrating day. The expression that bad things come in threes held very true. The first issue of the day was the car. It would be, in the weeks ahead, taking us across the Nullabor Plain. This is a 725-mile trip across the Great Australian Bight, a flat, treeless, empty plain that lends itself only to the self-sufficient traveller for the most part. Having a reliable car, we therefore felt was important, and we thought we had sorted that when we got it fixed in Canberra. We hadn't it seemed. As we got in our car that morning it was clear we weren't going anywhere. We couldn't even get it started with our jump leads and so out came the RAC, again. At least we got our money's worth out of our subscription! We made a decision that on reaching Adelaide we would have to take the car to a proper Holden dealer, rather than a small independent, because the wilderness of Australia was not far away and we did not want to be stuck in the middle of nowhere, just us, the wildlife and our temperamental car.

Catching up on our emails later that day presented us with issues two and three. Our heating had broken down at home and given the cold and snowy conditions back in England this would no doubt be dealt with quickly by the agency. This led to a fear of the pending invoice settling over us. To add to our growing financial worries my dad had received a letter from our credit card company stating that they would cease trading from the end of January. The said credit card was our safety net. We had owned it for years, and it had a very large credit limit on it. We were not using it, but we had it there in case we ran out of money or had any emergencies that we needed to pay for. Our other credit card, with its very small credit limit, was working well for us for daily usage and was being paid off each month from our current account back home. It was not going to be much use, though, for any major or unforeseen expense or covering us if the travel pot ran out. Given that money seemed to be draining out of all areas, this was not good news at all. We had a beer and went to bed.

The car did not start again the next morning, but we decided to leave it until we left our lake cabin. We would call the RAC man on departure and drive straight to a Holden dealer in Adelaide, without stopping on the way. We would be keeping the engine running. The day improved with a visit from Father Christmas. He was selling cakes for charity and so we obliged by purchasing one of the smaller ones. Our charitable inclination quickly diminished when we realised that Santa had sold us an out-of-date cake. He was obviously clearing last year's stock. The sight of Allister chasing down Father Christmas on his sledge across the campsite was wrong on so many levels, but he did return with a correctly dated cake of a much larger size. I think Santa was mildly alarmed by the crazy English boy talking about the Sale of Goods Act, but a Sainsbury's man cannot cope with out-of-date and substandard food, whatever part of the world he is in. The irony was that Allister doesn't even like fruit cake!

We left our lake cabin the next morning, once the RAC had started the car, of course, and drove straight to Adelaide. Once our car was deposited at the main Holden dealer, we spent a very pleasant day strolling around Adelaide. We liked all the cities in Australia that we visited, but Adelaide had somehow a more understated style about it than elsewhere. It just felt nice. Not a terrific use of the English language, I know, but that does sum it up. After such a great day we did wonder whether our mood would be destroyed by the man at the Holden dealer, but Lady Luck was finally paying us a visit. When we collected the car, the bill was very modest as the only fault they found was that the connections on the new battery, which had been fitted by the garage in Canberra, had not been done up properly. We drove to find a campsite on the outskirts of Adelaide with mixed feelings. We were pleased that the problem was minor, but the niggling doubt was there that the car would break down again. After so many garages and mechanics, I am sure you can appreciate our doubts that this one would be any different.

Campsites around Adelaide were exceptionally busy, but we did manage to squeeze our tent into the corner of one eventually. Not being cricket followers, and in fairness not watching much television, we had failed to realise that the Ashes were in town. It turned out that the following day was the last day of play and it was concession day. Loving cricket as I do, not, I was thrilled to get two tickets. Actually, it was great. Neither of us had ever been to watch cricket and what better way to start than watch us Poms thrash the Aussies on their own turf? Unfortunately, we finished them off in under an hour and so our planned day of cricket, lunch and a few beers was not going to plan. We made full advantage of our time there, though, and enjoyed a singsong with the 'barmy army'.

Making the most of the extra time in Adelaide we drove to the aptly named Mount Lofty in the Adelaide Hills. We so love a good view and had a habit of heading to the highest points of wherever we stayed. The thunderstorm that hit us at the top took away any view we might have had, and, as my hair literally stood on end with the lightning that surrounded us, we did question the decision to be at the highest point for miles around. The good news was that our car had successfully started three times that day and it did not seem to be struggling with the torrential downpour. Had we reached a turning point in the life of our car?

Ever optimistic about improving weather, we left Adelaide for the Barossa Valley wine region. We had read about the pleasure of sunny days on bicycles touring the wineries, with the main aim being to fall off your bike at the end of the day when the last free sample tips you over the edge, so to speak.

I know that you know that we didn't hire bikes, and I know that you know that the sun did not shine. The cold and the floods simply did not lend themselves to such pursuits. We dropped in on Jacob's Creek, though, and stood by the aforementioned creek, but decided that we would instead attempt a winery tour on reaching the Margaret River over in Western Australia. Rumours of thirty-plus degrees were reaching us from Al's cousin in Perth, and we were hopeful that the Australian summer was imminent.

It had been a while since we had experienced some wilderness, so we drove to Wilpena Pound. We could have camped overnight but some apprehension about our car was still with us, so we decided to make it a day trip and pitched our tent in a nearby town, just in case we needed a mechanic in the morning.

Wilpena Pound is a huge crater rim coming out of the plain of the Flinders Ranges. Alas, our hike will be remembered not for the magnificent views but for the huge emu that we encountered on the track. It took a real liking to Al and we can laugh about it now, but a massive six-foot bird chasing you along a deserted track is very scary, I can tell you. It was scarier for Al, in fairness, as he was the object of the emu's affection. We like to think of it now as the pursuit of a lovesick girl emu, but we think these birds had learnt that rucksacks meant food, and it was the bright-red pack on Al's back that was the focus of its attention. We do not have any photos of the incident as I was cowering behind a tree, but the memory is strong. When Al finally picked up a large stick and waved it wildly at the creature it ran off. We were both very pleased to see it disappear into the trees. The good news was that the rush of adrenalin got us up to the top of the crater very quickly.

At the top we were soon distracted by the sound of two young children complaining to their dad they were thirsty. This rather irresponsible young father had hiked his children a long way up the volcano without enough supplies of water. Hearing him suggest they drink out of some puddles, we offered them some of our water. We always carried enough to last us about a week! His lack of responsible thinking reached new heights when his pride stepped in and he told us they were fine. It was warm by this time and they had a long hike back. As they were only about eight and ten years old, we decided to ignore him and offered some water again. When one of the children started to cry, he allowed his pride to take a back seat and took a water bottle from us. We added a couple of cereal bars for good measure. He still wanted to save face, though, so he handed the bottle back and didn't drink any himself. Allister and I managed to moan about him all the way back down to the car and that was quite a walk. Some people are just plain stupid.

Our travels continued and we were soon to be driving across the Nullabor Plain and back into Western Australia. We decided, though, to take a last-minute detour to the Eyre Peninsula. Time was on our side, and one of the things that is so important to do when you are travelling is not to fall into routines and timetables. Most of us live our lives that way and it is very easy to fall into that pattern once you have been travelling for a while. That is not to say that you don't need some kind of plan, but never be afraid to be spontaneous or wake up in the morning and go in the opposite direction to what you intended. I think that this philosophy should be applied to life in general, but this is harder to achieve. There was no excuse for not managing it on our travels, though. The freedom we were experiencing was like nothing we had ever felt before, and the more we travelled the better we became at making the most of it.

The Eyre Peninsula was not some breathtaking experience that made it all worthwhile, but it epitomised why we were doing what we were. We pitched our tent in a pretty woodland campsite surrounded by kangaroos, wombats and parrots. We were on the edge of a small town by the sea and it was fish and chips night at the yacht club. We chatted to the locals and later slept amongst the wildlife. The next day we travelled towards Ceduna and on a deserted stretch of road we came across a shack selling home-baked bread. There was not a person in sight, just a jar to leave your money in. The best bread we tasted on the whole trip concluded a couple of days that did indeed define why we were travelling.

Ceduna marks the eastern end, and for us the start, of the Nullabor Plain. We knew a desert wilderness was close as we pitched our tent that night. We were back on red rock and as the stones dug into my back I looked forward to our early start and the famous drive that lay ahead.

TWENTY-SEVEN

LIFE CHANGES
FINALLY HOME

AUGUST AND SEPTEMBER 2003

ON MONDAY 11TH AUGUST 2003 ALLISTER CAME home from hospital. My doubts that this day would never come dissolved and I felt a sense of relief. We both knew that there would be many more challenges ahead, and indeed we both knew, although we didn't say it, that Al might not beat the disease. We had much hope and belief though, and for Al to be at home, sitting on our sofa drinking a cup of tea, was truly an amazing moment.

One of Al's first comments was that the garden looked strange. The weather was lovely when he came home, and he wanted to sit in the garden. Months of being in hospital had made him lose touch with the sensations of being outside. He really did marvel at how green the grass was and that the trees looked so big and leafy. I think it was a special moment for him, although I had to make sure he sat in the shade and wore his sunglasses. Bright sunlight was something else he had lost touch with and he felt very sensitive to it.

At 6pm Allister asked me where his meal was. This was an odd moment and completely unexpected. During our life together we had always eaten our evening meal at sometime between 7.30pm and 8.30pm, depending on our work schedules. As far as I was concerned, 6pm was only late afternoon. I informed Al that his 'meal' would be later and then he got really agitated and upset. My husband was, it seemed, completely institutionalised. I did not see that one coming, but months in hospital had given Al an environment of routines and strict timetables. Hospital was a place where he was awoken at the same time every day, a place where doctors' rounds were at the same time every day, a place where he was given medication, had his blood pressure checked and was looked in on by a nurse at the same time every day and a place where his cups of tea and meals were served to him at the same time every day. I went and cooked Al a meal, and later tried to discuss with him the idea of having his 'meal' a little later the next day. He was not having any of it and was quite frankly very stroppy. Adjustment was going to take some time.

Allister was not the only one who needed to adjust. I had lived most of the year on my own. I had shopped for one, watched the television programmes I wanted to and kept the house clean, tidy and organised. This last part had helped me manage my stress; tidy house, tidy mind and all that. I never left my dirty underwear on the floor, close to but somehow not in the laundry basket, and I never, and I mean never, left the toilet seat up. All this was about to change, and it was not going to be a smooth ride.

We had an early night the first day Al was home. Lights out at the hospital was somewhat earlier than normal lights out in the Frost house, and the routine was set in stone. In fairness, I was tired – it had been a very emotional day – but that was not the point, obviously. I had eaten in what felt like the middle of the afternoon and was now going to bed at a time when in a previous life we would have been going out for the evening. As Al started to softly snore, I pondered my strategy. Allister Frost needed to be de-institutionalised and for both our sakes this needed to be swift and effective.

With Al being home, naturally people wanted to come and visit. That is not to say that he didn't have people wanting to visit him in hospital, but for a lot of the time that he was there he did not want visitors; he simply felt too unwell and just wanted to be left alone. I knew Al did not look great. He was painfully thin; his skin was translucent to look at and his hair was becoming a thing of the past. I had got used to how he looked, though, and in the hospital environment a lot of other people looked terrible too, so he blended in. Sitting in our garden or walking to the car, he was in the normal world, and he did look quite out of place. This was highlighted when friends came to visit. Those that hadn't seen him for months did a double take and then tried valiantly to look at Al as though he didn't look any different. Most didn't succeed but Al didn't notice or, if he did, he didn't care. The funny thing was that to me he was looking so much better. The most important thing, though, was that people called in and it started a process of returning to some normality in our life.

During this endeavour to return to normal Al decided he wanted to have a bath. This wasn't all that normal as Al never liked baths; a shower man through and through, but clearly, we were dealing with several personality quirks at this time, and Al wanting a bath was something I could cope with. I therefore set forth to make the bathing experience as enjoyable as possible, filling the bath with just the right temperature of hot water, infused of course with body-moisturising bath foam scented with a hint of jasmine. The lighting was soft, and a selection of his favourite magazines lay alongside the bath, waiting for him to peruse. As he lay in the bubbles looking calm and relaxed, I was delighted his wobbly legs had managed to climb in and pleased he seemed to be enjoying it. I left him to it, although I was never far away as thoughts of his delicate physique sliding under the water if he nodded off and the fear of him drowning kept me close by and alert.

I spent some time listening to him splashing around but it wasn't all that long before he got bored and I could hear the water draining away.

'I've got a problem and need your help,' I heard him shout. Mild panic followed as I went back to the bathroom. The problem, it transpired, was that Al could not get himself out of the bath. His arms and legs were twig-like at this time and muscle was hard to locate. Having a bath had made him tired and any strength he did have in getting in was not noticeable now. I had every confidence I could get him out but as I went to help him, I was surprised that to me he felt like a dead weight. He may not have weighed much but then neither did I. I was not initially alarmed but several attempts at trying to get him on his feet had achieved nothing. The moisturising bath foam with a hint of jasmine was all very lovely but now the water had drained away it had left a slippery surface behind. This was not helping, so I switched on the shower to wash it away. This would solve the problem. As I attempted to lift Al up again it was evident it had not. Al was getting cold and more tired and I was running out of ideas. The thought that I would have to call someone for help spurred me on. Allister, I felt, had been subjected to enough embarrassing moments over the last few months without adding to this list. I wrapped him in a big bath towel to keep him warm and this gave me the inspiration I needed. I climbed into the bath, put towels down in the bottom and wedged my feet into them. I then put my arms under his as I levered him into the standing position. Carefully I got him to climb over the edge of the bath, leaving him standing on the bathroom floor. This was good news. Al announced he would not be having another bath, dried off and went to bed for a bit of a sleep. I made a cup of tea and spent some time calming my nerves.

Al continued to make progress through August. He gained some weight and was increasingly more mobile. He still needed his crutches to help him walk any distance, such as the weekly visits to the hospital for chemotherapy, but around the house he was much more on his feet. The side effects of the chemotherapy increased, though. What little hair he had left was shaved off by his mum one day when I was out at work. I came home to find him totally bald, and weirdly with his head finally without a single strand it became much more obvious that he no longer had eyebrows. Water in his eyes was a constant problem in the shower and was made worse by the fact that his eyelashes had dropped out as well. He looked like one of those rare hairless cats. This we could laugh about but some of the other side effects were more difficult to handle. His mouth was full of ulcers and at a time when we were trying to get him to gain some weight this was not ideal as eating was very uncomfortable. The solution was to find foods that were soothing, and so a diet based around milk and ice cream ensued. Not the healthiest of options overall and I did think about getting my own cow at one point, but it helped Al deal with his painful ulcers and at least he was gaining some weight.

The next problem was a loss of sensation in his fingers and toes. Al said this was interspersed with a feeling of pins and needles and at times this was very uncomfortable for him. We were told this was common and that normal sensation should resume after treatment finished. Thankfully this was the case in his hands but even now I can sometimes stand on his toes and he doesn't know I have done it. Given my clumsy nature this does have its advantages.

My endeavours to de-institutionalise Al were working, and fortunately did not take as long as I thought they might. My tactics were at times a little sneaky. The first challenge was to break the mealtime clock. This was done by simply serving our evening meal five minutes later each day. Added to this was a regular sprinkling of late meals forced upon us by me coming in from work after 7pm. We were soon eating at about 7.30pm and he had barely noticed the change. Bedtime got later by me popping a good film on just before 'hospital bedtime' and this extra couple of hours soon meant he was sleeping later too. I cannot say that he didn't remain somewhat quirky for many months, and it took even longer for him to regain his self-confidence and function normally again in society. Every step was in the right direction, though, at this stage, and this was all good.

Not all that long after he came home, and I was well on the way to breaking up his days of strict routines, we decided some sea air would be good therapy, for both of us. My parents were in Lyme Regis, staying in their caravan. Spending a couple of nights with them seemed like a good idea. Their caravan is fully equipped with a nice shower room and two bedrooms, and so we were sure Al would be comfortable. We arrived at lunchtime and the first afternoon was lovely. We sat outside the caravan, enjoying the sea view, and Mum and Dad cooked us a nice meal in the evening. Al was naturally tired and went to bed quite early, but he seemed ok.

It was not easy for me to put aside the fact that as well as dealing with chemotherapy Al was also dealing with having a colostomy. When in hospital and so very sick this seemed like a minor problem, but as signs of normality were creeping back into our life this minor problem was becoming a huge inconvenience. Al coped by convincing himself that it was only temporary and that when he was better it would be reversed. We had been told that there was every chance this would be the case, but there were of course no guarantees. I am not sure if it was dealing with his colostomy in a small and not all that private place (there is not much in the way of soundproofing in a caravan), or if it was the feeling that he wanted to be out and about enjoying clifftop walks and a nice cold beer on the seafront like normal folks do, or if it was just that inevitable moment; whatever it was, Al decided he did not want to get out of bed the next morning and was really very low. My parents were naturally concerned, but they gave us some space by going out for a walk, leaving me to try to cajole my husband out of bed.

This was the only time I can recall that Al completely lost his positive, never-give-up approach. It is truly remarkable that this was the case. Al's strength of character, self-belief that he would recover, and never-failing sense of humour was unbelievable at times and without doubt a contributing factor to him recovering fully from everything that he went through. On this day, though, this had no relevance and it was important I got him up and about and feeling better about himself. He was a tearful, forlorn man that morning and I felt my heart breaking as I held him and tried to convince him that he would get better: we would have our life back again and do all the things we wanted to. Maybe it was at this moment that the dream of travelling the world started, I am not sure. I had already committed to climbing more mountains and learning to play golf with Al once he got better. One thing that I can say for certain is that, when you make promises based on the other person continuing to live, those promises won't be broken. I am so glad it was only golf, mountains and travel. I love the mountains and travel and I can tolerate golf, although I would not describe myself as talented in this area.

I got Al out of bed, through a combination of a soft and sensitive approach, followed by a tough-talk approach advising in simple terms that staying in bed all day and wallowing in self-pity would not make him feel better. This was followed by a lot of love and affection and tears from both of us. The good news was that, by the time my parents arrived back from their unscheduled walk, Al was up, showered and eating breakfast. We ventured out in the afternoon for a short while and got a bit of that sea air. Not moving far from the car, it was not quite what I had hoped for, but Al's mood was much improved from the morning and we later enjoyed another pleasant evening and nice meal at the caravan with Mum and Dad. Travelling home from Lyme Regis, I vowed we would go back when Al had a bit more strength so that he could really enjoy a break away.

August drifted into September, and our lives were a pattern of work for me and trips to the hospital for chemotherapy for Al. There was a sense, though, that things were getting better. Al was getting stronger and gaining weight, but still needed his crutches for walking any distance. As long as chemotherapy continued, he was always going to find it hard to get his fitness back, but he needed to exercise his mind as well as his body and he needed things to fill his day. As golf and hiking were not yet an option, an idea that had started whilst he was still in hospital came into fruition: we bought a tropical fish tank. I knew nothing about keeping tropical fish, but in the later stages of his hospital stay Al had read many books on the subject and quite frankly was an expert. With me at work, his parents helped him with the purchase and set-up of the tank. I swooped in during the latter stages of this project, as clearly, I wanted to be involved in choosing the fish. With a colourful selection of fish happily swimming around our new and very swish corner-unit fish tank, I had to conclude it had been a great idea. It was relaxing for us both in the evenings as we sat in our lounge and watched them swimming around, and most importantly it had given Al a project; he had used his brain again and could see the result of his efforts. Our fish kept us amused right up to when we went travelling. Nearing this time, the novelty had started to wear off; cleaning out the tank was a chore and we no longer had the same enthusiasm for buying fish. That aside, it had given us many years of pleasure, and 'Project Fish' will live long in the memory as the event that signified Al's life being more than just a routine of hospital visits and treatment.

TWENTY-EIGHT

TRAVELLING AT THE END WAS CHRISTMAS

DECEMBER 2010

CEDUNA IN SOUTH AUSTRALIA MUST BE DESCRIBED AS functional, and it is small enough to walk around in about twenty-five minutes. For such a small place it has an abundance of caravan and camping parks. Depending on your direction of travel, it is the last or the first bit of civilisation that you will see or have seen for a while before or after you cross the Nullabor Plain.

Nullabor comes from Latin and is translated as treeless. The description is very accurate. The plain is flat and infertile and, as we would soon discover, monotonous as it snakes away westwards, in our direction of travel, across the south of Australia from Ceduna to the town of Norseman in Western Australia.

It turned out that it wasn't all endless empty plain, as we discovered when we stopped for lunch on our first day of travel across this unique landscape. We hit the coast at a place called the 'Head of Bight' and the Bunda Cliffs. The Nullabor Plain ends at cliff edges that drop abruptly into the Southern Ocean. Sitting on these cliffs was a pretty amazing spot to have a sandwich.

After lunch we crossed the border from South Australia into Western Australia. All fruit and vegetables had to be left behind but given that our supplies of these things were rather light we were not delayed too much in the quarantine area.

As there was nothing to do or see we just kept driving and six hours later we arrived at the Balladonia Roadhouse. It was very cheap camping, which in Australia often set the alarm bells ringing, but it was getting dark and travelling at night on the Nullabor was not a good idea. The chances of hitting big and chunky wildlife were high and it was the type of accident we didn't want, especially on a road in a deserted wilderness.

We had driven about 700 miles that day. We had crossed two time zones, which had put our watches back two and half hours and we had driven along the longest section of straight road in Australia. We have a photo by the '90 Mile Straight' sign to prove it!

Putting up the tent had to be done with much speed. It was, at this point on our travels, the most fly-infested area we had been to. We felt pleased with ourselves as we put our fly nets over our heads and managed to cope, whilst other less well packed travellers flayed their arms around wildly and pointlessly, trying to get some relief.

Once dark the flies vanished, and an air of calm descended on the campsite. Al treated me to some beans on toast cooked beautifully on our little stove as I sat in the back of the car and watched this culinary masterpiece unfold. This meal failed to fill us up, as we had been on the road since daybreak, so we ventured inside the roadhouse and we were soon tempted to a beer and a plate of garlic bread. We ate, drank and watched *The Vicar of Dibley*. It was all a bit surreal; I must say.

Western Australia's time zone was all a bit strange and as dawn came at 4am the next morning we were up and gone from the campsite by 5.30am. At least we were ahead of the flies. We exited the Nullabor and arrived at Norseman and ate the kind of cooked breakfast that seems wonderful at the time, but you spend the rest of the day regretting.

It was great to be back in Western Australia, though. We were entering the final phase of our Australian journey and Christmas back in Perth was only a couple of weeks away. We had planned to visit this part of Australia at the start of our trip when we had stayed with Al's cousin the previous July. A lorry driving into our parked car on the first night had meant this plan had been abandoned as we sorted out repairs back in Perth. We had been disappointed at the time, so it was great to be given a second opportunity. We headed to Esperance, on the south coast, and as the sun started to shine there was a definite sign that the weather was set to improve from this point forward.

As a complete aside, we discovered an interesting fact whilst in Esperance, which I would like to share. Skylab, the USA's first space station, broke up over the Indian Ocean in 1979, and, as bits of it fell out of the sky and landed in Esperance, local residents at the time were none too pleased. The local authority decided to fine NASA $400 for littering, and remarkably NASA paid, and very promptly too.

Although this was interesting to hear at the time, it certainly was not the best part about this area. Without doubt we found the coastline and the beaches to the east and west of this town to be some of the best in Australia. Award-winning Twilight Beach took our breath away and was even more special as we were there on a warm and sunny day and had the beach all to ourselves. There was nothing to see but golden sand and an aqua-blue ocean. It really was stunning.

Camping in Esperance provided us with much entertainment as well. A group of middle-aged Australians on holiday were rather fascinated by us; me in particular. It turned out this was because of an undying love for *The Goodies*, and perhaps a touch of the lonely hearts within the group. One couple seemed keen to find a wife for their friend. As I sat in a very small and cramped caravan, sandwiched between the dog and the fluffy cushions, looking at photos of Bill Oddie and Tim Brooke-Taylor, I could only relish in the joy that travelling brings. It turned out that our new Australian friends had met Tim Brooke-Taylor at some sort of *Goodies* event somewhere in Europe, and it was without doubt their most favourite moment ever. Talking to me seemed to relive those memories. The funniest thing was that they could not remember my name, and just called me 'English Girl'. As the loud cries of 'Goodbye, English Girl' rang out across the campsite when we left, we concluded that perhaps it was a good thing we only stayed a couple of nights!

We wanted to camp on the beach: something we had always thought we would do a lot of in Australia but something that had just not happened. We headed into Cape Le Grande National Park and camped in the sand dunes. Cooking outside the tent in the evening, watching the sunset on the beach and drifting off to sleep after a few beers is what camping should be all about. Unfortunately for us, camping had been too many cold and wet nights with views over mud or rock. Our time in this area made up for it, though.

As always Al had to take me to the highest point in the area to get the best views, so we hiked up Frenchman's Peak, which was right in the middle of the National Park. I could not argue with Al as the hike was worth it; we did indeed get a magnificent view across the park and out to sea.

The beaches were not too shabby either and Thistle Cove proved to be as beautiful as Twilight Beach. Lucky Bay even had resident kangaroos and the sight of them sunning themselves in the sand was quite amazing.

We didn't want to move on from this area, but for the first time in a long time we had a timescale to adhere to and we were expected back in Perth at Al's cousins by 22nd December. I had a girls' night out planned, and, given these had been a little sparse in the preceding months, I was keen not to miss it.

We visited some interesting rock formations – well, the appropriately named 'Wave Rock' was a bit interesting – before arriving in the land of the tall trees.

The Tree Tops Walk in the Valley of the Giants was great fun. Walkways are suspended between the trees some forty metres from the ground and it makes for quite an experience when the wind starts to blow. We both enjoyed it, but Al was keener to visit the Gloucester Tree. This tree is over 200 feet high and has a lookout at the top. You pay your eleven dollars and then get the joy of climbing it via metal spikes that circle around the trunk. I must confess that after a few steps up the totally exposed exterior of this tree an overwhelming surge of panic ran through me and I decided to descend to ground level very quickly. Al of course surged to the top and spent the next few days ribbing me about my lack of courage. What I think was more concerning at this point was that we were planning skydiving and bungee jumping in New Zealand. Given that I couldn't even climb a tree, my confidence in my ability to fulfil these ambitions had taken something of a knock.

Our final camping spot before returning to Perth was Margaret River, a place of great scenery and great wine tasting. The Southern Ocean and Indian Ocean meet at a place called Cape Leeuwin and this is worth a visit. We had a lovely morning there, but the wineries were calling. I felt that Al owed me a tour after his breakfast at Wyndhams Winery in the Hunter valley, so

I set forth to make the most of my driver. The funny thing was that after a couple of tastings I got bored and fancied a coffee. At least I didn't part with as much cash as Al did!

On our way back to Perth the next day we called in at Busselton and were disappointed to find the jetty stretching out into the ocean was still closed. We had attempted to walk the 1.8-kilometre jetty on our first visit to Busselton the previous July. Unfortunately, the longest jetty in the Southern Hemisphere had been closed then and was still closed now. It was also the summer and flies were now in abundance in the area. There seemed no reason to stay, so we beat a hasty retreat and arrived back in Perth a couple of days ahead of schedule.

We had been away from Perth for 137 nights. In that time, we had spent ninety-two of them under canvas, thirty-one in cabins and fourteen in motels. The number of camping nights would have been higher had it not been for the deluge of rain on the east coast. We had visited every major city in mainland Australia, including all the state capitals. We had seen an incredible amount of wildlife we had never seen before. We had survived all of it despite being sucked on by leeches, bitten by spiders and being chased by a lovesick emu (which will always live long in our memories). We had driven 17,608 miles around Australia, completing a full circuit with a detour to the middle! Despite a little trouble along the way, the car had served us well and on Christmas Eve we sold it. After taking into account the repairs, new batteries, new tyres and a service to the air conditioning unit, we made a profit of 100 Australian dollars. Not bad at all, I think you will agree.

Our Australian tour had been truly amazing. There had been some incredible highs and one or two lows, but a life-changing experience it certainly had been. Life in Australia had a couple more weeks to run; there was Christmas to enjoy, and best of all it was forty degrees by the pool with not a raincloud in sight!

TWENTY-NINE

TRAVELLING
A BREAK FROM OUR BREAK

JANUARY 2011

IRONICALLY, AL'S COUSIN AND HER BOYS WERE heading to England immediately after Christmas. We had very happily agreed to stay in Perth, to house-sit and dog-sit, until our departure to New Zealand on 9th January.

Beforehand we enjoyed a truly fantastic Christmas. In the early part of our trip we thought we would be spending it on our own in our little tent, so to be with Al's family and their friends was extra special. They did a great job of ensuring we had a proper Australian Christmas and it kicked off with a night out to a local pub on Christmas Eve. Christmas Day started with breakfast on the beach. This was bright and early at 8.30am, as by 11am it was simply too hot to be there. After the weather we had endured on our trip I was not too fazed by the heat but Al, who was a little worse for wear after the celebrations the night before, took refuge under an umbrella for a fair amount of the morning. A day by the pool with a light BBQ lunch was followed by a traditional turkey dinner in the evening, once the weather cooled. The day was rounded off with singing and party games. A truly memorable Christmas and one that Al and I will always remember.

Al's family departed on Boxing Day, leaving us in charge of the house and Max the dog. The next couple of weeks drifted by with us doing very little. I think it was just so nice to be in a house again that we wanted to make the most of it. We sat by the pool, had BBQs and watched movies in the evening. We walked the dog every day and made the most of having easy access to a computer to plan our time in New Zealand and Hawaii. When I look back, I know that this time was worthwhile. Being on the road all the time can be tiring, both mentally and physically, and to have a break from it gave us both a real enthusiasm for the next part of our trip. It was like starting again and by the time we came to fly out of Australia we were ready to get on the road again.

The big advantage of spending some time planning the rest of our trip was definitely financial gain. With the cancellation of our backup credit card we had to think carefully about how our money would last. We were both keen to tour New Zealand in a campervan. The weather would be changeable, no doubt, and the thought of camping in the cold or having to spend money on accommodation was not appealing. A campervan was an obvious alternative and we were able to research for a good deal. We were able to use our credit card until the end of January, so we booked the campervan and accommodation for Hawaii on it. Being able to take the time to research properly where we were going was so useful and meant the next stage of our trip was well organised. We would worry about paying off the card when we got home, and in the meantime our cash flow was increased.

We enjoyed a quiet New Year that was made more special by some surprise phone calls from friends and family, particularly as they had remembered the time difference was seven hours and so phoned us at 4pm UK time!

The only other significant event in our lazy stay in Perth was my decision to have a mole on my toe checked out. You may recall from an earlier chapter that one mole on my toe was not a mole at all and after this discovery I then found another one. A mole or not a mole was the question, and as I did not want to spend the next four months worrying about it, I found a local doctors' surgery that advertised skin checks and went along. Just looking at the one mole was not an option, so a full skin check was booked. I thought this was a good thing anyway, not something we do much in the UK. I was happy to take advantage of what was on offer in Australia.

To be honest, I was only mildly concerned about my toe, but this mild concern turned to panic when the doctor decided the mole needed removing and sending away to be checked. I spent the next forty-eight hours with complete anxiety, and finally got the results the day before we flew to New Zealand. Everything was of course fine. In this country it probably would never have even been removed. A BBQ with Al's cousin's friends before we left revealed that lopping off moles was pretty common. They have a more cautious approach than perhaps we do in this country. Now, when I look at my feet, I laugh about my mole and my non-mole being removed. Some little pieces of me left in Australia!

We also had to put up with an unexpected expense when I sat on my glasses and broke them. At least I got a nice new pair that I felt were much more fashionable than the pair I had. Some would say I broke the old ones on purpose, but they would be so wrong!

You can probably tell from the lines I write in this short chapter that this couple of weeks was indeed a break from our break. Not much happening that would set the world on fire, but a very relaxing time, well, apart from the mole incident.

We boarded our flight from Perth to Sydney on the evening of Sunday 9th January. We would have quite a wait at Sydney Airport to get our connecting flight to Auckland, New Zealand, but we were so excited we didn't care.

Our fantastic Australia adventure really was finally over, and travelling was all about to change.

THIRTY

THE EARLY YEARS MOVING ON

1997

'I AM NOT LIVING HERE.' I LOOKED AT AL AND THIS time he agreed. The problem was that this must have been about the twelfth time I had said it in a week. It was January, it was cold, we had sold our house in Farnham and we needed to find something we liked in Petersfield as soon as possible. Actually, finding something we, or more accurately I, liked was not the problem. Finding something we, or more accurately I, liked within our budget was the problem.

There were up sides to house-hunting. I was able to have a good nose around people's houses, and I so loved that, and we fitted in plenty of pub lunches whilst we browsed house details, and Al so loved that.

The downside, of course, was that there was always something wrong. Nice house, no garden, great plot, house a disaster, lovely kitchen, bathroom a cupboard, not enough bedrooms, too small a lounge and so on and so on.

We looked at a lot of houses. The benefit was that it did help us understand what we wanted. Living in a small one-bedroom house for six years does limit your perspective somewhat on what a home can offer. The idea that we wanted to buy something older, in need of hours of devoted renovation work, so that we could create our dream home, soon disappeared. After we looked around aged buildings that we could never afford to spend money on, we realised more modern was the way to go, and suddenly our desire to be detached was quite overwhelming. I cannot tell you why.

We were about to give up for the day when a last walk around the estate agents of Petersfield provided us with a brochure for a house that had just come back onto the market. The owners had accepted an offer several weeks earlier and their buyers had pulled out at the eleventh hour. How mad does that make you, those of you who have experienced that? Anyway, we were able to go and have a look straight away, and we drove to the house without too much optimism. On arrival the outside gave us new hope. It was immaculate and ticked all those relevant boxes. It was detached, had a garage and driveway and was in a nice position. The inside added to our hope. The owners were packed and betrayed a sense that they needed to sell again as soon as possible. The house was slightly over our budget, so their urgency was encouraging, even if we did feel like a pair of vultures, circling over those whose day had not been the best, keen to take advantage of their situation. Hey, we were young and money, or lack of it, was an important factor! The real plus was that the house was just what we were looking for. We tried not to look too keen and thanked the owners for showing us around their lovely home.

Next stop was the estate agents. Now, I know that they can get some bad press from time to time, but in fairness it is not always deserved. We had met some very nice ones during our house-selling and house-buying quest, and on this day the lady in question was very pleasant. The problem was her reluctance to offer the owners the amount we requested. It was somewhat under the asking price, and just for good measure we wanted her to state that we wanted all carpets and curtains included. We had a very exact budget. We had accepted an offer on our house, but alas the negative equity problem had not disappeared for good. We were lucky, if you look at it from a certain perspective, that some mortgage companies were offering negative equity mortgages in the nineties. This meant folks like Allister and I could move to a new house and borrow more money than the price of the house we were buying. If you are still following me, then what this actually meant was that we could not go over a certain amount, and this is what we offered. Well, we were trying to offer it, if only we could convince the nice estate agent lady to make the phone call.

In her head I am sure she was trying to avoid seeing our disappointment, or was it that she was seeing her commission dwindle a bit? I am sure it was the former! She explained in her very knowing and professional way, that the owners had, some weeks ago, turned down offers quite a bit higher than ours. I know we were still quite young, but we were not as naïve as we had been when we bought our first house, and we sensed that the owners needed a quick sale. I am not sure the estate agent appreciated our more ruthless approach, but she of course had to make the call. She did so, still telling us as she dialled that they would not accept. The phone call lasted one minute, our offer was accepted, and the estate agent looked like she had eaten a lemon. She did squeeze out the words 'Well I am very surprised' and just about managed to smile and congratulate us. It may have been more of a grimace in all honesty, but we did not care.

Anyone who has sold or bought a house will know that several weeks can drift by in this process with seemingly nothing happening. We were lucky that this did not seem to be the case, but unlucky that our solicitor presented us with more and more worrying pieces of information and unlucky that some of this information was going to cost us financially far more than we bargained for.

The naivety we had when we bought our first home came back to haunt us at this time. I do prefer to think of it as misplaced trust; we did after all buy a one-bedroom starter home from a very well-known and reputable building company. We didn't have the money for a deposit at that time; actually, we didn't have it now we were buying our second home, but I digress. Our one-bedroom home was bought with a 95% mortgage and a 5% home loan. All offered and set up by the said well-known and reputable building company, which was of course keen to sell us a house at the time when the market had reached its peak and was teetering on a plummet that we did not see coming.

On this particular January day our solicitor was explaining to us that there was a very small paragraph in our home loan contract that had a not-so-small impact. It turned out that the term of the home loan was the same as the mortgage, which was twenty-five years. This in itself does not sound like an issue; we were of course paying off the old mortgage to take out our new negative equity mortgage for the purchase of our lovely new home. The issue was that paying off the home loan early had a rather large early redemption penalty. We had to find an amount of money we had not budgeted for, and we would end up paying back more than double the amount of money we had borrowed six years earlier. It was like we had dealt with an illegal backstreet loan company charging unachievable rates of interest and not with a reputable firm. It really was a complete disaster and it threatened to ruin our plans to move.

We sat down that evening and discussed our options. The solicitor we had was very good; she had done her homework and truly believed we had cause to take the building firm to court for a list of misdemeanours that I cannot fully recall. In summary they had sold a policy they shouldn't have done, and we had a case. The risk of doing this, though, was somewhat overwhelming. It would take time, meaning that if we went ahead immediately, we would not be able to move until it was sorted. Neither of us was sure we could cope with that, but more important was the risk that we could lose. That could cost us even more. We were really upset with ourselves. We felt stupid that we had not seen the clause in the contract for the home loan. It was a clause that the company would always win on. The loan was only a small percentage of a small mortgage and so who would take twenty-five years to pay it off? The answer to that was no one, so they were onto a big winner. We were not onto a winner. We had to find the money to pay it off so we could move, or not move and take them to court. The other problem with these things is that you don't have time on your side. We were in the middle of the whole moving-house process and we did not want to lose our buyer or the house we were buying. Our solicitor did give us some guidance. It helped us decide to pay off the home loan and then once we had moved give some consideration to employing the solicitor to take up the case afterwards. We needed to move and felt it was the best option. We did have the opportunity to pursue later if we wanted too.

Having made this decision, the next rather large problem presented itself. How were we going to the find the money? The mortgage we had taken out to buy our first home, which was at this point feeling like a curse, was an endowment mortgage. We had decided to keep the endowment going. Again, there would be a loss by cashing it in early and so we felt it was better to keep it. Cashing it in, though, would go some way to paying off the home loan, and so we didn't really have a choice. The only other cash we had was in a 'save as you earn' policy that Al had through work. This could be cashed in at any time, but the benefit of this policy was that it had a designated term. Paying into it until the end was going to give us share options, enabling us to buy shares at the price they were at the start of the policy. This was almost three years earlier. The benefit was that if the share price had gone up over the three years then we would make far more profit than earning interest alone. It was not sensible to cash this policy in as the share price was favourable, and we really didn't want to lose any more money. What to do? It was a cash flow problem really, because we knew that once we sold the endowment and the save-as-you-earn policy matured we would have enough money, just, to pay off the home loan as well as cover all our other moving costs. What we needed was a kind of bridging loan. We were so lucky because both our parents lent us the money, enabling us to proceed and giving us time to sort ourselves out before paying them back, something we would do once we were moved and, in a position, financially to do so.

It was all systems go again, not that they stopped; we were just panicking and juggling figures. Our solicitor didn't want us getting bored, though, and kindly phoned to tell us all about the consequences of another of our outstanding financial decisions.

When we had moved into our first home it was at the time deemed to be a private road. All this really meant was that at the time we moved in it was not yet under the care of the council services for road maintenance, lighting and whatever other kind of maintenance comes under that umbrella. I assume it was because it was a new development, we were one of the first to move in and it was pretty much still a building site. Writing this now I truly cannot believe we were so stupid. All residents of the development on moving in had to sign up to pay a management company for maintenance of the so-called private road we lived in. We were still paying them when we sold our house. The solicitor couldn't trace them or our money! The management fees were somehow supposed to carry on with the next owners. Given that they couldn't be found, this did not seem like a good plan. This was more cost to us to get this clause voided, and more misery as we counted the total amount that we had paid out in annual fees over the six years we had lived there. Allister and I consider that we are quite sensible, intelligent and not easily led. I think I can say with absolute certainty that we did not demonstrate these skills in the early years of our married life.

Our next issue was a relief. This issue felt very normal amidst the saga that was moving to a new house and discovering we were financial morons. There was a small delay as the solicitor had to sort out liability and ownership of the shared drive we were to have with our new neighbours. This seemed so minor that it hardly even registered as an issue.

Despite the stresses brought about by our own financial ineptitude, our moving process was speeding along quite nicely, and suddenly, we had a date for exchanging contracts. We were sensible enough not to dwell on what had happened, and it really was best not to think about how much out of pocket we were. We did therefore allow ourselves to start getting excited about our move. One good thing was that as we were living in a small house, we didn't have that much stuff, so hiring ourselves a van and moving ourselves was all we needed to do. There would be no big expense for a removal company for us. This almost sounded like a sensible financial decision. Could this be a turning point in the world of Frost finance?

The next couple of weeks drifted by, surprisingly, without any other hitches and suddenly moving day was upon us. Our van was loaded, and we closed the door on the first six years of our married life. We were very excited about our new house and arrived in Petersfield before the final stage of completion. I remember sitting in the pub (where else would we go?) and just waiting and waiting for the phone to ring from the estate agent. It seemed like forever, but I know it was only a very short wait until she phoned and told us we could come and pick up the keys. The estate agents were opposite the pub, so I dashed across. It was pointless rushing because Al and my father-in-law each had a full pint of beer, and there was no way that these could be left behind. Eventually they finished and we drove our van to our new home. I can remember opening the front door like it was yesterday. Allister and I walked in with his parents and I just burst into tears. It was relief. There were times when we had thought we would be stuck in our one-bedroom house forever, and so to be standing in our lovely new home was quite overwhelming.

I managed to pull myself together and after the obligatory moving-day cup of tea we unloaded the van. Some friends who lived nearby arrived with sandwiches and offered their help too. It wasn't long before the van was all unloaded and we were wondering how we were going to fill the empty rooms we had. All we had upstairs was our bed, a chest of drawers and a wooden shelf unit. Our house is a lot fuller these days!

There was at the time a pub at the end of the road. These days it is flats, but it served as a good venue to celebrate our new house that evening. A 'quick drink' turned into a long evening with our family and friends and we eventually staggered home in the early hours. I think I can be quite honest when I say my dear husband was a little worse for wear, and considerably more so than me. I only minded this fact when he would not get out of bed the next morning. I was up early, excited and very keen to finish unpacking all our stuff and to go out shopping for the things we needed. Allister was not in my good books that day!

We quickly settled into life in Petersfield, and soon it seemed our financial fortunes were going to take a turn for the better. House prices were increasing, and after about six months we had the house valued. It had increased in price enough for us to change our mortgage. We were able to swap from the negative equity mortgage to a standard repayment mortgage. This was great as the interest rate was less and we finally owed money on a mortgage that was less than the value of the property we were living in. This was indeed a turning point.

After receiving the cash from our endowment and Allister's 'save as you earn' policy maturing we were able to pay back our parents for their 'bridging' loans. We then both got a pay rise and suddenly we found we were a lot better off. We had learnt some valuable lessons, though, and it was the dawn of the age of financial shrewdness in our house. This is something that has remained with us ever since. We negotiate everything, check the small print very carefully and never pay more than we should for anything. I am sure the lessons we learnt from the mistakes we made buying our first house helped us manage our money successfully enough to travel around the world. Today I manage our finances with the deftness of a qualified accountant, and if figures are missing from my almost breathtaking spreadsheet then there is a quick house meeting to resolve the query.

We never did pursue the building company for selling, or should I say mis-selling, us the home loan. We couldn't face the prospect of losing; we felt it was too much of a risk for us. We did recoup our losses eventually, though in a rather surprising way. We had cashed in our endowment during our house move, as we needed the money it freed up. It seems that endowments had a lot of controversy during that time, and we received a letter some years later regarding the mis-selling of endowment policies. We got the letter at the time when Allister was ill and sitting by his bedside in hospital one afternoon, I filled in a lengthy form answering all the given questions fully and honestly. I had time to kill as Al slept a lot in those days. I pretty much forgot about it once I had posted it; I had more important things on my mind at that time.

Some months later the postman dropped a cheque through the letterbox for several thousand pounds. Weirdly, around the same time I got thousands of pounds in compensation paid into my private pension. It was another round of mis-selling in the nineties that form-filling rectified. When I left Sainsbury's, I transferred my company pension into a private pension and some years later private pension companies had to top up these pensions. They should never have advised people, like me, with company pensions to transfer them to private pension schemes. And so, Lady Luck finally came our way and we more than recovered the losses we endured during our house move. We may have ended up with some luck, but it didn't stop us from remembering what happened, and we have not made the same mistakes again.

THIRTY-ONE

COUNTDOWN THE TASK LIST

JUNE 2010

I LEFT MY JOB ON 3RD JUNE 2010 AFTER ELEVEN YEARS. This was a sad and a happy day. I had enjoyed my time as an IT trainer, but I knew it was time for a change and I felt excited as I drove out of the car park for the last time. The obligatory farewell drinks night was to be the following week so I would be back seeing my colleagues again soon, but I don't remember having ever felt quite so free before. Mind you, that feeling of freedom was surpassed the day our flight to Singapore took off. After the volume of tasks completed in June and July, the feeling on that flight of 'well there is nothing else we can do now' certainly was freedom!

June's task list resulted in a very busy month. Simple sentences in a task list do not necessarily reflect the time taken to complete. We filled every minute of every day. Boxes sealed with high-quality packing tape started to gather as Allister efficiently progressed with packing up our life. I am not very good at packing, as was pointed out to me one Sunday afternoon as we decided to work together on the whole packing up task. It was soon concluded that Al was in charge of this particular job, and I was only of any use when receiving careful and clear instructions.

At least my financial prowess did me proud on our trip, and I concluded this task with aplomb this month.

We bought our rucksacks in June. This was a fine balance for me between having a rucksack big enough to carry what I wanted to take and not being so big I couldn't carry it. We had a fun afternoon in the outdoor shop. Al tried one on filled with weights and decided it was perfect. I tried every single one that they had for women and finally settled on one. Naturally after getting it home, I decided it wasn't right and drove back the next day to change it for the one I did want. This was of course the very first one I had tried on the day before. I spent an afternoon on my own doing a trial run of deciding what I was taking and packing it. This I would recommend to anyone going away for a long period. Do not leave this to the last minute. I had to think carefully about what I would need and fight against packing that extra T-shirt and pair of flip-flops. You do only need one pair of those!

The goodbyes with friends started in June. This was both the fun bit and the emotional bit. The fun bit was all the time spent with friends that resulted in the consumption of too much wine and telling each other how much we loved each other. There were some great meals out, fun nights in and some really nice memories to see us around the world.

I even managed a trip to Wimbledon with my mum. I had been to Wimbledon once on a school trip. We had queued for the outside courts in the pouring rain, we had seen very little tennis all day and I had spent most of it in tears after rowing with my boyfriend, who, at the time, was obviously the centre of my whole world. As this wasn't the fondest of memories and given my mum had never been, it seemed like a great idea to apply online. I was lucky to land two tickets for No. 1 Court, and after dealing with my sulking husband, who suddenly decided he just loved tennis and wanted to come, I phoned my mum and told her we were having a day out. My mum loves Wimbledon to the extent that she avoids all social interaction for two weeks every year, and thus it is fair to say she was excited.

Andy Murray and Rafa Nadal were on No. 1 Court – alas, it was the day before we went – but even so we saw some great tennis and the weather was hot and sunny enough that we actually needed sun cream and 'rain did not stop play'. We had a lovely day, capped off by my best smile at a nice security guard who said it was fine for us to go and watch some end-of-day doubles on Centre Court. I think getting into Centre Court was a perfect end of the day for my mum, kind of like a mountaineer finally achieving their lifelong ambition and summiting Everest!

My biggest memory of June was the enjoyment I had in having a month at home, seeing family and friends, and working towards being ready to go. Allister was working, of course, and so the packing had to be done around him being at home. I wasn't allowed to do that unattended, but everything else I could do. I remember the task list continually growing. I will never forget how much we had to do to close our life down in the UK, whilst at the same time making sure we could access everything we needed when we were away. At the back of our minds we kept thinking: what happened to planning all the places we would visit and the routes we would take? Well, we did enough, and the trip proved it was more than enough. Book your flights, get some jabs, pack your rucksack, sort out accessing your money and get insurance. Do that and the rest works out fine!

We got ourselves some tenants in June. Well, the agent did but the result was a relief all round. The income from rent was part of our budget, and without it I would have been eating baked beans every day of our travels and not just for some of them! We would move out on 13th July and give our keys to the agent; the house would be cleaned on 14th July and the tenant would move in on 15th July – marvellous! The tenant was a very pleasant chap who had sold his house and needed to rent whilst he built his own home. He was a professional guy who had 'ideal tenant' written all over him. There was a slight hitch. He was to move in with his girlfriend – not an issue, of course – and his two big, fat, hairy house cats. Our no-pets stipulation had to be waived as we were leaving in a few weeks and were panicking about the lack of tenants. The two big, fat, hairy, house cats were moving in and I could almost feel my cat allergy tingling. A quick condition that all carpets and curtains were fumigated – sorry, I mean cleaned – upon the tenant vacating the property resulted in a six-month contract being signed. We needed ideally eleven months, but we were of the view that house building never goes to plan and he would not be leaving in six. We were so right on that one. It was lucky for us, although not lucky for him, that a snow-ridden UK delayed his project over the winter months. He remained in our house until we wanted to move back in. We then had to give him notice.

On Friday 25th June 2010 Allister finished work for a year. It was a fantastic feeling when he got home that night; we were leaving in two weeks and we were both very excited. I must confess to feeling a sense of relief as well, as there was a lot of packing to do. Al was going to be very busy!

Tuesday 29th June 2010 was our wedding anniversary. Nineteen years, which was celebrated with a day of packing!

It was onwards to July, then.

Thirty-Two

Travelling Falling in Love with Jucy

January 2011

On Wednesday 19th January 2011 Allister and I jumped out of a perfectly good aeroplane. New Zealand was set to be a truly fantastic and thrilling experience all round but allow me to come back to this.

It was Tuesday 11th January 2011, and after eighteen hours of travelling overnight from Perth, via Sydney and with a five-hour time difference, we arrived in Auckland, New Zealand, very shattered. With our rucksacks on our backs we boarded a bus and then walked the rest of the way to a hotel we had booked for a couple of nights. I remember thinking how different it felt from when we had arrived in Singapore the previous July. Landing in New Zealand, we felt like seasoned travellers, and with this came a new-found confidence and a certain amount of complacency. In Singapore the whole experience felt so alien; now it just felt normal. I guess we even looked like travellers now. The sun tans, odd bits of jewellery and dirty rucksacks gave it away, I am sure.

Seasoned travellers we might have been, but this did not prevent jet lag. The next day it was gone midday when Al finally got me out of the hotel room. I had been very surprised by the quality of the hotel. We were in a reasonably central city location, but it had been pretty cheap when we had found it online over our minibreak in Perth. We were soon to learn that the cost of travelling in New Zealand was to be a lot cheaper than Australia. We would eat better and enjoy the New Zealand wine and beer a lot!

We fell in love with New Zealand on day one. Some facts to digest are that it was only populated about 800 years ago. The arrival of the Polynesian people meant New Zealand was the last major landmass to be settled on by humans. The Maoris named their new discovery Aotearoa, meaning 'the land of the long white cloud'. The white Europeans, known as Pakeha, arrived on the island some years later and today biculturalism is the key word as Maoris seek to rediscover their heritage and Pakeha take notice of what has been around them for generations. One thing stands out across the differing cultures and that is that all 'Kiwi folk' are friendly and live well together in a beautiful country. New Zealand is a little larger than the UK but has a population of only 4.3 million and 1.3 of these live in Auckland. It has about forty million sheep, but the sheep population is well known about. Although agriculture has traditionally been the economy, two million visitors a year mean that tourism is now a very big earner. The country is simply packed full of magnificent scenery. There is something for everyone, from sweeping desolate beaches to snow-capped mountains, huge glaciers, stunning lakes and coastlines that take your breath away. If you add to this the wonderful wildlife, then it is no wonder that visitor numbers are growing. The variety in the landscape provides variety in the activities available. You can head off on multiday hikes, or tramps as they are called in New Zealand, enjoy gentle strolls along windswept shores or fill your day with adrenalin-charged activities like white water rafting and bungee jumping. The New Zealanders make great wine and great beer and the food is pretty good too. It is quite remarkable that Allister and I aren't still there!

Auckland itself had a modern, friendly feel to it and it is hard to put into words how we felt about the atmosphere of New Zealand, but it was just so different to that of Australia. We found in Australia we often had cautiousness about people when we spoke to them, and at times uneasiness about the places we were staying in or travelling through. Please do not think that Australia and its people weren't anything but fantastic, but New Zealand just seemed more laid back, I guess. People are more reserved – more 'English-like' is a good description – and perhaps this is why we always felt very safe in New Zealand. It is a place we could definitely live in. Our parents are pleased to say we haven't moved there, yet!

Auckland was the starting point of a wonderful two-month tour, and it started with a bit of shopping. Our clothes were getting a bit tired, so it was time to freshen up the wardrobe (well, rucksack) and spend some of the Christmas money we had received. I remember well the comments we got on our online travel blog when we posted photos that showed we were wearing new threads. It seemed our blog audience had got a little bored looking at the same T-shirts and fleeces for six months. I even bought a very smart T-shirt as I was hopeful, with the better prices in New Zealand, that we might be able to eat out on occasion.

We visited the city's Sky Tower for those all-important views that Allister strives for, and to round off a pretty perfect day for him we even splashed a few New Zealand dollars in the casino below.

It was a lovely couple of days, but we were itching to get on the open road, and we went to pick up our campervan with a lot of excitement. We had toured Australia in the shadow of campervans. We had so many nights huddled in our tiny tent in the rain, watching with envy those travellers who were sitting all warm and cosy in their campervans, glass of wine in hand, playing cards and looking so relaxed. We were about to join this complacent group, and we couldn't wait.

Our 'Jucy Condo' was lime green, and for me it was love at first sight. The seats and table in the back converted to a rather splendid-looking double bed. There was sleeping room in the roof, which would store our new clothes very nicely. It had a small sink and stove, plenty of cupboards and, best of all, a fridge. I was looking forward very much to filling that with New Zealand Sauvignon Blanc and chocolate!

As we headed off down the road in what was to be our home for the next couple of months, the first stop had to be a supermarket. Shopping in Australia at times had been difficult. When you only have a cool box for your perishable items you are reliant on finding freezers to refreeze your ice packs, or campsites that have fridges you can use for the duration of your stay. We did get a bit over-excited on our first shop, and somehow in our heads the small campervan fridge could hold the same amount of food as our large free-standing one back in England. We had to sacrifice some beers for the sake of milk, fruit juice and salad, but needs must and all that.

Armed with a deluge of yummy food, we headed for Rotorua. The North Island of New Zealand is all about the volcanoes. New Zealand lies on the Pacific Ocean's 'ring of fire' and earthquakes and volcanic activity are common. Visiting geysers, boiling mud pools and hot springs were all on our agenda. We knew we had arrived in Rotorua when the smell of sulphur wafted into the windows of our campervan. We parked up in a very nice campsite and enjoyed that first moment when all we had to do was plug the van in to get power and then we were done. Allister wasn't quite sure what to do as there was no tent to erect, and he didn't need to spend time nagging me to do some work. We decided to make the most of the extra time on our hands and headed into town. Allister's joy was very visible as we discovered a great pub, and best of all it was serving ale. Australia's pubs were a constant disappointment to Al. Not that we frequented them that often, as everything was so expensive in Australia, but when we did ale was not something that was often found, and Al had to put up with Australian lager. The ales of New Zealand were very lovely, and Al was set to be a very happy boy for the next couple of months.

We had a great time in Rotorua visiting all the geothermal sites. Wai-O-Tapu is probably the best of these, and we certainly did enjoy seeing the beautiful mineral coloured lakes. The bright blue, green and yellow waters were so eye-catching, and we were fascinated by the plopping mud pools and the geyser that erupts right on time every morning. As well as the geysers and colourful lakes, another real highlight was taking a dip in the Polynesian hot springs that overlooked Lake Rotorua. Meeting new people is a real highlight of travelling, and I spent a lovely half an hour in the pools chatting to a retired chap from Lancashire who had made New Zealand his home many years before. I don't know exactly what is in the water of these hot springs, but his daily visits were certainly keeping him looking very fit and well for his eighty-seven years.

The New Zealanders are truly very adept at maximising their tourist revenue. You can get drawn to visit some random rock formation by clever advertising that entices you to experience something unique. In many cases this is quite true, but if you do venture to the distant shores of this island nation be careful not to get sucked into following a much-defined route. New Zealand is so much smaller than Australia, so we found it was a lot harder to head off the beaten track, but there are always places you can go that are less commonly visited, and these often do provide the most memorable experiences. That said, it is great fun to partake in some of the more common tourist attractions, and a traditional Maori evening is one of these. We headed off to the 'Matai Village', where we enjoyed a traditional Maori welcome along with a Hangi. This is a feast cooked over hot rocks. Entertainment followed with dancing and the well-known haka, the eye-bulging and foot-stomping chant we see when watching the All Blacks play rugby. All in all, a very fun evening, but if you really want to get to the heart of the history and culture of New Zealand, then a visit to the Museum of New Zealand in Auckland should not be missed. We had done this, and as we travelled around the country, we were both really pleased we had. Something we loved about travelling was learning about the places we visited. As well as enjoying all that other countries have to offer, travelling is made more special by understanding the history and culture of where you are.

We left Rotorua behind, having had a great few days, and set forth for our next adventure.

Allister and I had quite different feelings at this point. We were heading to Taupo, and from the moment we had decided to take this trip Allister had said he wanted us to go skydiving when we got to Taupo. The town of Taupo sits on the northern shores of New Zealand's largest lake. Whilst this is truly stunning, it is viewing it from 15,000 feet whilst plummeting to the earth at 120 miles per hour that is the town's main attraction. Taupo has earned its name as the skydiving capital of New Zealand for good reason. Thousands flock to the many companies that offer you the ultimate adrenalin-fuelled experience. Of course, not all go through with it, and the question was: would I? Allister was very excited and in no doubt that he wanted to jump, and, whilst I also wanted to make sure I didn't miss out on this experience, I was, understandably, a little anxious.

We found a campsite to park our Jucy campervan on for a couple of nights and decided the best way to deal with the fear was to book the skydiving straight away. We were soon booked for the next day, but it did mean I now had twenty-four hours to get through. Al did his best to distract me, but my thoughts were consumed with the image of me jumping out of an aeroplane and the parachute failing. The next day dawned with perfect conditions and we headed off to the skydiving centre. The strangest thing then happened. Once we arrived and sat down for the introductory speech, my nerves disappeared. Even the signing of the 'it is not our fault if you die' disclaimer did not raise my pulse. I had read in the guidebooks that as you visit various places in New Zealand that offer a multitude of thrilling activities, you find yourself drawn into doing things you would never normally have considered doing. In fact, you feel like you are the one who is not normal if you don't throw yourself off a bridge on a piece of elastic or jump out of an aeroplane strapped to a young man who you hope remembers to pull the parachute cord.

It was a good thing that my nerves had vanished, as we had quite a wait, but eventually we were up at 15,000 feet and ready to take the plunge. Everyone else on the plane had jumped at 12,000 feet, but not us Frosts. If you are going to do these things, then do the maximum. This was Al's philosophy with this activity, not mine, but it did mean we would get a full minute of free fall before the parachute opened. We were so high we had to have oxygen before jumping, and I must admit I did feel pretty cool at this point.

I was strapped to a young lad from Liverpool and as we sat in the door waiting to jump, I actually felt like it was someone else sitting there. I had no concept in my head that I was about to fall out of a plane, but as he nudged me forward and we jumped, that concept quickly disappeared. I do not know what I expected, but the sensation of accelerating to 120 mph is without doubt the most exhilarating and terrifying experience I have ever encountered. I felt completely overwhelmed by the sensation and know that I screamed a lot. Quickly, though, terminal velocity is reached, and it is at this point that you feel like you are floating. It was amazing. Al jumped after me and we were able to wave to each other as we were free falling. We were being filmed so that we could get a DVD of our experience. The cameraman held my hands, making me feel like I was in some kind of action film.

I cannot deny a sense of relaxation once the parachute opened, but the free fall was truly unbelievable. My only regret is that I don't think I fully appreciated the views. Lake Taupo at 15,000 feet should have been stunning, but I have little recollection of what I was seeing. Would I do it again? I am not sure. Would I recommend it to someone else? I definitely would. It does feel like a bucket list item, and I am thrilled that I have ticked it off. Al and I had a great evening after the skydiving. The sense of euphoria it left us with was wonderful and the adrenalin seemed to take a while to disappear, so we were really buzzing. I felt very proud of myself. I have a history of hiding when rollercoasters loom into view and don't even like being in fast cars, so to jump out of a plane was some achievement for me. Our Jucy campervan came with a TV with a built-in DVD player and I am not sure how many times we played the DVD that night, but it was a lot. As the wine kicked in and the adrenalin surge faded, I fell asleep, and know for certain it was a better night's sleep than the one before the jump! Next up would be bungee jumping, but that was a few weeks away and I was confident that this would now be a cinch!

What attracted us to New Zealand the most was not actually adrenalin-fuelled sports but hiking, known as tramping in New Zealand. In our quest to make the most of the great outdoors we left Taupo to complete a one-day tramp in Tongariro National Park. The Tongariro Alpine Crossing is rated as one of the best one-day tramps in the country, which can make it very busy, but it is worth the rating. It is about a seven-hour walk across the lava flows and huge crater floor. There are some stunning lakes and active geothermal areas along the way. Part of the crossing takes you under the shadow of Mount Ngauruhoe. If you are a fan of the *Lord of the Rings* films, then you will know this as Mount Doom. This can be hiked up as part of the day and we had considered doing this. On our walk, though, there was a lot of mist, and from the base it did not look appealing. In fact, it looked like it did in the film and befitting of the name. We really did have a fantastic day, though, and did manage to ascend to the summit of Mount Tongariro to lengthen the experience.

We left Tongariro National Park for a more sedate leg to our journey. Some bad weather followed us, surprising as this may seem, and stopped us doing some more hiking in Egmont National Park. I was taking the bad weather in my stride, though. Our Jucy Condo provided adequate shelter and warmth, and the joy of not having to crawl inside a wet and cold tent meant that Al heard barely a grumble from me.

We spent our time experiencing some indoor activities, including underground caves with glow worms and a historic old lift buried in a hill at the end of a very long tunnel. Variety is important when you are travelling, after all.

We were heading south to get a ferry across to the South Island of New Zealand. This was probably the part of the trip we were most looking forward to as we were expecting wonderful scenery, fantastic hiking and amazing wildlife.

En route we called in at the home of the couple we had met in Australia. They had toured Australia on their motorbikes in the opposite direction to us and we had enjoyed their company when our paths had crossed. It was lovely to catch up again and experience some New Zealand life. Our new friends took us to a livestock market, and we helped them buy some sheep. Obviously, we bought the prettiest sheep, but knowing that they were only to be fattened up in their garden for future lamb dinners was a little upsetting! Our friends kept us updated sometime later with the sheep's weight gain, and finally the day that they made their way to the freezer. There is an expression about too much information. I just remember cute little sheep running around their garden, but we heard they were very tasty. We were made very welcome at the home of our new friends, enjoying a BBQ, some good wine and some great company. Travelling is a lot about the people you meet, and it was great to spend some time with like-minded people and reminisce about our Australian adventure. As our trip around New Zealand would see us head north again to Auckland in a few weeks' time, we agreed we would call in again on our way back. We had such a good time it would be great to see them again.

Wellington was our last stop on North Island, so we did the sights and rode in the cable car. The next day our alarm went off at 5.30am and we headed to the port to catch our ferry to South Island to start the next part of our trip, and the part we had been most looking forward to.

THIRTY-THREE

LIFE CHANGES
SUMMER ENDS

SEPTEMBER TO DECEMBER 2003

MY GRANDMA DIED IN THE AUTUMN OF 2003. SHE WAS my mum's mum and I loved her to bits. My childhood memories are full of days with Grandma, school holidays with Grandma and the classic memories of sweets in a jar and the smell of baking whenever we went to visit. My other grandparents had already passed away, and at ninety-one my Grandma was still as sharp as ever. She had been suffering all year with ill health, and this had certainly only added to the strain my parents were under with their constant worrying about Allister and me. She was taken into hospital with difficulties in breathing and eating and we were told that time was running short for my grandma.

The good news, if this could be called good news, was that we had the opportunity to say our goodbyes. Four children and ten grandchildren meant Grandma was surrounded by a lot of people who loved her in her last days. I visited with my cousin and we sat either side of Grandma's bed holding her hand and chatting to her about whatever she wanted to chat about. She wanted to know about Al, of course, and at least I was able to tell her he was improving and doing well. I didn't tell her he was in our car in the hospital car park unable to bring himself into the hospital to visit her and say goodbye. Al too was very fond of my grandma; he had known her a long time, but the prospect of walking into a hospital ward to see her in her final days was too hard for him, and I could not blame him for that. After all, his future was still so uncertain. Grandma must have known that her time was limited, but she seemed so at peace with that. She had a lot of faith, and no doubt believed she was simply moving on to the next place, where she would be reunited with Grandad. At the hardest times during Allister's illness I did wonder whether having that kind of faith would help me. If I had believed Al would be in another place and I would one day see him again, would that have comforted me if the worst had happened? Truthfully, I do not believe that, but for those that have that degree of faith it must bring a huge comfort.

Grandma died a few days later and I travelled to the funeral with my brother and his girlfriend. The service was in Coventry and heading up from Hampshire we had a break at Warwick Services for a coffee before the inevitable event. I remember sitting drinking that coffee thinking that a funeral was not the easiest of days out when your husband is struggling to overcome cancer. It was going to be a hard day. Al had stayed behind at home; a funeral was definitely not an option for him. I know he wanted to support me, but it was not a good place for Al to be and I didn't want him there any more than he wanted to be there. To this day I cannot fully explain my detachment once I arrived at Grandma's funeral. I barely shed a tear, and, although

I felt much sadness, my thoughts were constantly with Al. Was it wrong that I had a sense of feeling relieved that the funeral I was attending wasn't my husband's? Perhaps it was. I cannot feel guilty about how I was that day, though. I know I loved my grandma; I know I still miss her now and I also know she would understand. She was ninety-one and had lived a long, full and happy life. Her life was celebrated in a church full of friends and family who loved her dearly. She was the stereotypical grandma: little and round, kind and good, and, if her faith was to be believed, she was now happy with Grandad. We are all left with wonderful memories of Grandma and that is a great legacy to leave behind.

Towards the end of September, I took a week off from work. The caravan was empty, and Mum and Dad said Allister and I could have it for the week. Last time out had not been a huge success, but several weeks had passed since then and Al was in a better place. We would also be on our own and it would be a chance to have a week away. I know I needed it, and I was sure that this time Al would benefit from it too.

The car was packed, and we headed to Dorset. We did have a lovely week. The weather was pretty good, Lyme Regis was not too busy as school holidays were long over and the much-needed sea air was great therapy for us both. Al's face even had a little colour in it, although this wasn't much as his baseball cap was normally in place. He did of course have a bald head and very sensitive skin. I think this was the first time we were out and about for any prolonged period and, as Al made his way along Lyme Regis seafront on his crutches, we felt quite normal. I don't think others thought we looked normal, though, and we did gradually become aware of people staring. It is funny when people stare, because most people who want to stare don't want you to know that they are staring. This results in strange sideways glances with absolutely no one making eye contact with you. If you think about when you go out for a walk, normally, at some point, you will look at and smile at someone walking past you. This was not the case for us. We walked the whole of Lyme Regis promenade with not one single person acknowledging us. Al knew he was being stared at, albeit in a covert manner. Al did not care; well, why would he? He actually started to find it amusing.

On reflection, he did look odd. Although he had gained some weight, he was still painfully thin, and although his skin was no longer translucent, he was still extremely pale. It was a hot day, so he was wearing shorts and a T-shirt, the result being that he looked like one of those wire dolls with loose clothing hanging off stick-thin limbs. Added to this, he had no hair on his head, none on his legs or arms and no eyebrows or eyelashes. Who wouldn't want to take a look? By the time we reached Lyme Regis Cobb he was talking about his designs for a 'Yes, I Have Got Cancer' T-shirt. I appreciate wearing this might not have been appropriate and fortunately it never got past the 'design' stage but at least it made Al laugh. It was good to see him laugh, whatever the reason might have been.

Whilst I was enjoying our short and gentle strolls around Lyme Regis I did yearn for some real exercise, and Al agreed it was a good idea. We decided to head to a place called Golden Cap. Al could sit on the beach with something to read whilst I climbed up and over the hills so named that stretched up from the beach. I would be able to see him and him me and we both would have a nice afternoon. We took the obligatory picnic, blanket to sit on and books and magazines for Al. Getting Al across the shingle on his crutches to a nice spot near the sea was quite a challenge, but the newly determined Al was not giving up and somehow we landed where we wanted to. We had some lunch and then I left Al to read.

It was great to do a good walk and I headed up Golden Cap with much enthusiasm. It was clear but windy so walking into the wind gave me a good workout. I enjoyed the views and Al was in sight on the beach. I guess we were both having a good day. I didn't want to leave him for too long though, I never wanted him out of my sight much at this time, a feeling that stayed with me for many months. I headed back and found Al asleep. I gave him a nudge and we spent some more time enjoying a drink and watching the waves. A feeling of déjà vu descended on us when we came to leave. Al couldn't get up. He was tired and getting up off shingle was more challenging than anticipated. It was bath time all over again. Having experienced something so similar, though, a strategy was already in my head, and, as I buried my feet in the stones and put my arms under Al's, we were not surprised that he was soon vertical. Getting back across the beach was harder because he was so tired, but he made it and we headed back to the caravan having enjoyed a lovely afternoon.

Towards the end of the week we discussed the idea of going out for something to eat. This was something we had not done for a very, very long time. We had enjoyed a good break and we thought it would be a great way to finish it off. There is a place on the seafront in Lyme Regis and we had always enjoyed going there in the past, so I phoned and booked a table. My parents' caravan is on top of the hill leading out of Lyme Regis, and we would always walk there and back so we could enjoy a few drinks with our meal. Clearly this wasn't practical at the current time, so I would drive, and we would both drink Diet Coke all night. How times had changed. Al got his usual selection of looks as he manoeuvred his way with his crutches to our table, but people soon get bored and we had a lovely meal and a nice evening.

The strangest thing I recall about that evening was the reactions that Al evoked simply because of how he looked. We shouldn't really have been surprised as he had been getting sideways looks all day. The waiter and waitress who took our orders and served us directed their questions to me. Al's brain was fully intact, of that I was sure, and so we made sure that he ordered the meal to validate that point. It didn't matter how many times Al spoke, the next visit to the table would result in no eye contact with Al and a question to me. Finally, the bill came, and – yes, you have guessed it – it was handed to me. When the waiter came to collect payment, I sat looking vacant so that Al could get his wallet out and pay the bill. The waiter was no doubt astounded at Al's abilities in this area!

There can be no blame attached to anyone that day who failed to make any eye contact with Al. Human nature is strange, though, in that we assume if someone does not look the way we perceive is normal, then we behave towards them as if their brains are no longer working. Allister and I try to make sure we always smile and give eye contact to anyone who crosses our path. They are after all 'normal' inside – Allister certainly was.

Our break was over, and we returned home. The chemotherapy was tough on Allister during the weeks that followed. Looking like a hairless cat he could cope with, despite his constant moaning about soap and water in his eyes when he showered. He said I didn't appreciate the benefits of my eyebrows and eyelashes, and I should try showering without them sometime. I decided not to take him up on his offer to remove mine to try it and suggested baby shampoo to lessen the stinging. This reduced his complaining a small amount. I felt practical solutions were always better at this stage. The mouth ulcers were very hard for him to cope with. Our milk and ice cream bill was considerable, but he was making sure he ate healthy food as well, no matter how hard it was sometimes. He was very determined.

The problem that was not solvable by us, though, was the increasing tingling, and what was becoming total numbness, in his hands and toes. It was serious enough that it was decided to stop part of the chemotherapy treatment. It is a funny thing to be told that. Al said it was such a mixed feeling: good that something could be done but worrying that the treatment for the lymphoma was being reduced. As a patient and as a patient's partner, you can only trust that the doctors who are caring for you or your loved one are making the right decisions. It is such faith we put in others, and I know myself at times that it was hard not to question decisions. Ultimately, though, you have to trust, and this is what we did. I cannot recall if there were improvements following this change – I think there were some – but it was to be some time before Al could describe near normal sensations again in his hands and feet.

Allister walked, without the aid of crutches, to the post box at the end of our road at some point during October. I can say with certainty that this is not far; if I walk slowly it takes me about thirty seconds. Al was gone a long time and I stood at the door and watched as he inched his way to the post box and back. There wasn't even the reward of having something to post. The reward was, in reality, far greater. This was the first time Al had walked outside without crutches and it was a truly wonderful moment. It also signified the start of Al's endeavour to regain his fitness. From that day onwards until he returned to work, he went out for a walk every afternoon. To start with this was with me until both of us felt confident that he wasn't going to topple off the pavement into the path of an oncoming vehicle. He was ready for the solo trip before I was, and so he had to suffer me tagging along for longer than he would have liked. It was fantastic what he did, and as the weeks went by the distances increased. When things are done so gradually it is easy not to notice progress, but suddenly I was aware that my husband was off walking every day, at a normal pace, at good distances and getting fitter and fitter.

The desire he had to get fit again was increased when chemotherapy came to an end in mid-November. It is so hard to recall the exact timings for the hair reappearing, ulcers disappearing and fingers and toes not tingling, but these things did happen and did nothing but spur Allister on in his daily walking quest. I had, and still have, of course, so much admiration for the progress Al made during these months. His mental strength gave him the determination to make it to that post box, and from that point he only ever got stronger. His hair didn't grow back all thick and curly, though: alas, the curls were to be gone for forever. Al would be sticking to a grade-one clipper cut from now on. I don't think it was at the top of his concerns; at least he had eyebrows and eyelashes again, so the whole shower experience once again became an enjoyable event.

His improvement in fitness could not have been more clearly demonstrated than at the end of November. I took some holiday and we decided to do some decorating. As our life had some semblance of normality descending on it, there was a sense that a new look to our house would only serve to help the process of moving forward. We have an open plan-style house, which makes decorating any one room quite hard, and it was our lounge that was the priority. As this leads to the dining area and up the stairs and across the landing without any doors to break the flow, we had to do it all.

Al left me with the all the tricky bits, making some excuse about not being strong enough, and we roped his dad in to help with the high ceiling over the stairs. I cannot fault Al, though, for his efforts with the paint roller. As I painted around coving and skirting boards, he followed me with the roller. Unfortunately, we were changing colour schemes from very tired and outdated terracotta to a clean and calm ivory. This meant three coats. It took a while. The results were great, though. It was fantastic to be doing something together, and the bonus was that it was great for building up the muscles in Al's arms. As he complained about all the aches and pains, he was experiencing in the first couple of days, I kept pointing out it was good for him. As the aches subsided, he agreed, and as we surveyed our newly decorated pad a sense of achievement descended.

As November moved into December and Christmas loomed, we concluded that the latter end of the year had not been too bad, certainly much better than the earlier months. Al continued to get stronger; we went Christmas shopping and made plans to see friends and family over the festive season. I was working a four-day week at this time and so we benefited from having Friday as an extra day and enjoyed the occasional pub lunch. Al not working had its advantages: going Christmas shopping together was something we were not used to. Being married to a man in retail pretty much means that December is quite a solo month for me. This year not only did we shop together but we also wrote our cards together and even spent some lovely afternoons wrapping presents together. A sense of optimism surrounded us: the first time in a long time; 2004 would be a better year.

Things don't always go to plan, though, do they? On a day shortly before Christmas, when I felt quite relaxed, and the permanent sense of anxiety I felt over my gorgeous husband was safely stowed in a quiet corner of my brain, Al walked into the lounge and gave me a look. I knew instantly that my calm feelings were going.

'I've found a lump under my arm,' he said, looking at me with a mixture of sadness and worry. On examination I had to agree, and even though we didn't want to panic we both did, trying to make each other think that we weren't too worried and that it would be fine.

Al had an appointment immediately after Christmas, so there was nothing to do but try to enjoy the next few days and put it out of our minds. We discussed that we would keep this to ourselves for the time being until we knew what we were dealing with. We were not the only ones who had been through a traumatic year, and we knew our parents were looking forward to spending time with us over Christmas with that same optimism that we had been feeling only a day or so earlier.

We did enjoy our Christmas. We managed very well to put our thoughts and worries about the lump to one side and get into the Christmas spirit. We went out to the pub on Christmas Eve with both of our parents and Al entertained us well as he overindulged on rich food and a couple of beers. Diet is important when you have a colostomy, and with rich food comes gas and gas has nowhere to go. As Al inflated like a hot air balloon, he made a mental note to eat a lighter diet the next day! Al wanted to have a good time and feel like a normal bloke again. He certainly wasn't going to let a minor inconvenience like a colostomy get in his way, although all he really wanted for Christmas was to be without it. We hoped that day wasn't too far away, although a concern over the lump under his arm was again something else that pushed this thought to the back of our minds.

Christmas moved into New Year, and as we kissed at the stroke of midnight a lot was left unsaid. Would 2004 be a good year for us? As we looked into each other's eyes we were both certainly hoping it would be.

THIRTY-FOUR

TRAVELLING WHEN TIME FLIES

FEBRUARY 2011

I WOKE UP WITH A START, UNCERTAIN FOR A MOMENT where I was. Al was asleep next to me and I got a sense that we should be doing something.

As I looked at the people near me heading for an exit sign, I remembered we were on the ferry on our way to the South Island of New Zealand. Not so much on the way now as actually arriving in the Marlborough Sounds. Reports of a rough crossing between North and South Islands had convinced us to take anti-sickness pills with our breakfast. The good news was that we hadn't been sick, but we had fallen into a deep sleep and missed most of the crossing. More good news was that we were awake in time to join the throngs on deck for the cruise into Picton through the Marlborough Sounds. The sun was shining, and it was a fantastic trip in.

Our plan had been to head off in a southerly direction straight away, but as we felt like we had been injected with a mild sedative we decided to spend a couple of nights in Picton. It proved to be a wise decision as the following day set the tone for our journey around South Island over the following five weeks. We took a cruise out to a place called Ship Cove, where Captain Cook landed a number of times on his travels. We spent a wonderful day hiking, and Al particularly enjoyed the moment when I walked straight into a tree branch overhanging the path. As I landed on the ground, his laughter at the look of surprise on my face did not improve my somewhat dented ego. We got picked up at a designated point later in the day, and a scenic cruise back into Picton was made even better by being followed by a pod of dolphins. A great start to our time on South Island, and we moved on full of expectation.

New Zealand Sauvignon Blanc is one of my favourite drinks, so we visited some of the wineries in the Marlborough region and stocked up our fridge. The food did have to be squashed in at this point, but there was still space for chocolate. This fridge was certainly my new best friend!

We had enjoyed some amazing wildlife in Australia, and New Zealand did not disappoint either. We were travelling towards a place called Kaikoura along the coastal road when we spotted the seal colony. We were lucky enough to see lots of pups, and once again on our trip Allister's camera was put to good use.

Our wildlife experience continued in Kaikoura as we headed out whale-watching. We had never done this in Australia as our budget was tight and it was very expensive. As the trip was in its later stages now, budgeting was easier, but more significantly it was a lot cheaper in New Zealand. Warnings of rough seas and high risk of seasickness greeted us as we bought our tickets, but we were used to this and had pre-armed ourselves with the

'Kaikoura Cracker'. The pharmacist in the town had assured us it would prevent us seeing our breakfast again and promised we would stay awake. We did not see much point going whale-watching and sleeping through the entire experience. We were not disappointed and watching the giant sperm whales launch out of the water was truly breathtaking. Those on board who had taken no notice of the rough sea warnings did not enjoy the experience quite so much.

Allister yet again put his camera to good use and it was to be a rare thing for me to see his face whilst we were on South Island. It was behind the camera for a lot of the time. When we look back at our photo collection from the whole of our trip it is amazing what proportion of them are from South Island, given that this part was only five weeks. It is safe to say, though, that it was our favourite time. The whole trip was amazing but something about the lifestyle of those five weeks just stands out in our memories.

For me it was everything I had imagined travelling to be. It was the freedom of the open road, waking up in the morning wondering what the day would bring, being immersed in beautiful and unique landscapes, seeing wildlife never seen before, spending days hiking in truly stunning places and ending our days with food and wine under the stars. Being with Allister was wonderful: we loved doing the same things and spending all our time together was fantastic. Travelling is more fun when you have someone to share the experience with, and who better than your best friend? Having the campervan made travelling easier, as we could park it anywhere, and with the experience that we had gained over the preceding months of travelling we knew how to make the most of every minute. For me it was one of the happiest times of my life, and as I look back at photographs of Allister's smiling face, I can conclude it was for him as well.

Given our desire for remoteness and getting back to nature we left Kaikoura and headed west across to Arthur's Pass. Linking Greymouth in the west to Christchurch in the east, this route across the Southern Alps is stunning. Allister and I cannot pass through the mountains without climbing one, so we parked up overnight at one of New Zealand's Department of Conservation, or DOC, campsites. This spot was populated by us and one other camper and to say it was idyllic would not do it justice at all.

On this site DOC did provide a toilet, but any call of nature was spent at one with nature as the open air was a better option. That night a clear sky and no artificial light gave me the most enjoyable call of nature I have ever had. The sky was simply packed full of stars: I had never seen anything like it. I was so astounded I knew I had to wake Allister and share the experience with him. Waking him in the middle of the night would not normally have gone down very well, but he forgave me. It was the best middle-of-the-night experience we have ever had!

The following morning, we were up early, despite our disrupted night's sleep. We were going to climb Avalanche Peak. Allister had developed a habit of looking in the guidebook and finding hikes under the category of 'most challenging'. As I struggled to scramble up exceptionally steep cliff faces and cover only six miles in three hours, I felt certain Allister had achieved his goal. Reaching the summit at 6,100 feet we were rewarded with spectacular views, and at that point I knew it had been worth the climb. We had even had some company for the duration. A kea, a parrot-like bird known as the mountain clown, had followed us most of the way. We assumed rucksacks meant food to this comical bird, but I was pleased its rather large and hooked beak did nothing more that fly alongside us.

The end of the day left us filthy and shattered but an overnight stay further along Arthur's Pass at a campsite with rather splendid hot showers refreshed us, and a nearby pub provided us with a location to celebrate a pretty fabulous twenty-four hours.

I find myself wanting to use the words stunning, amazing, beautiful and fantastic too often when writing about our time on South Island, but our next stop was the glaciers and yet again these words say it all. To get onto the glaciers themselves you need to book a tour but our arrival the first afternoon was a little late in the day, so we took a stroll to the base of the Franz Josef Glacier and admired the spectacular view. I think travelling had made us a little naughty as we found the view even better when we crossed over the barrier marked 'Guided Tours Only Past This Point'. Whether it was remorse at our actions or simply getting a taste for being on the glacier itself, we did, the next day, go on a tour of the Fox Glacier. Wearing crampons on our boots it was fantastic to explore the huge expanse of ice. We opted for the Fox Glacier tour because after all we had already explored the Franz Josef Glacier. We were lucky enough on the tour that caverns and tunnels had formed so we were able to get right inside the ice. The colours were amazing: a blue expanse changing to indigo and aqua in the bright sunlight. Despite my best attempt to use a different adjective here, amazing is the best word for the colours we saw, although incredible and breathtaking also work well.

Moving on from the glaciers, time started to pass us by very quickly. We were filling every minute of the day, there was always something to do, and the days really were flying past. We had headed south from the glaciers through the Haast Pass and had enjoyed another night in the wilderness. The next day we arrived in the town of Wanaka and this was a good base for a few nights. It is a beautiful town right on a lake and gave us a good mix of shops, bars and restaurants whilst at the same time allowing us to explore further afield into the great outdoors. A twenty-mile drive along a gravel road through fords took us to a place called the Matukituki Valley. From here a great hike took us across a suspension bridge up another valley to a rather marvellous lunch spot with views over the Rob Roy Glacier.

Our trip around South Island was not always about great hikes, and a morning spent at Puzzling World in Wanaka was a good change of pace. You would think my love of hiking would give me a great sense of direction, but alas this is not the case. As we entered the giant elevated maze I should not have been surprised when Allister finished the course and exited successfully in thirty minutes. The exit took him into a courtyard where coffee was served and where he was able to watch me wandering aimlessly across the walkways above him. The heckling coming my way from him only increased my determination to find the way out. I never did, and after two hours Allister came and rescued me. I am not sure I will ever enter a maze again.

The non-hiking period continued as we arrived in Queenstown. If you travel to the South Island of New Zealand and do not experience at least one night in this crazy place, then you will have missed out. It is a traveller's dream, with entertainment at every turn. It turns calm, mellow people into adrenalin junkies. People with no intention of doing anything other than enjoying the town's eating and drinking establishments will look down over the edge of a bridge into a gorge below and suddenly find themselves dangling from what looks like an elastic band. I am of course referring to bungee jumping, and, with the confidence I had gained skydiving a few weeks earlier, there was no way that I would miss out on this experience.

Queenstown is a slick marketing machine and it is hard to escape the draw of bungee jumping. Even if you keep your sanity and are not brainwashed into jumping, fantastic viewing platforms allow you to watch those that have succumbed, and their screams do a great job of convincing you that you made the right decision. Partaking in the watching first resulted in me having some second thoughts. We were planning on taking the plunge the next day and I was more nervous than I was about skydiving. There was no logic to this but to me jumping from a plane strapped to a lad from Liverpool seemed a lot less dangerous than jumping off a bridge over a steep-sided gorge that ended in a swirling, rocky river, with only a giant rubber band keeping me safe.

The next day I put on my 'happy to be doing this' face and arrived at AJ Hackett's Kawarau Bridge Bungee Centre. It looked just as scary as it had the day before, but pride was now kicking in. Alongside this was a sense that, if Al did this and I did not, then I would not hear the last of it in the weeks, if not months, to come. On the plus side it was the first day of the Valentine Special. This was an excellent discount for couples to do a tandem jump and live the romantic dream that is bungee jumping. I obviously had a mentality that being strapped to someone made these ridiculous pursuits safer, and as Al jumped, taking me with him, I was confident we would survive. Al would argue that my screams did not reflect this, but the experience was soon over and yet again I felt a sense of superiority as I basked in the stares of those who did not have the courage.

I felt one jump was enough to prove my bravery and show the watching world that I was overall a very awesome and cool chick. I was happy to watch Allister jump again, as he took advantage of the 'buy one jump and get a second very cheap' offer. I was mildly concerned about his blurred vision afterwards, but he was so happy that not being able to see was a minor inconvenience. Naturally we bought the DVD. On boring nights back home in the UK now we can often be found watching ourselves on our big flat-screen TV jumping out of a plane or off a bridge from the safety of our sofa.

With the lure of adrenalin still overcoming all logic, we decided to partake in the next crazy activity that Queenstown had to offer. A four-wheel drive, close to the edge of a perilous drop along the breathtaking Skippers Road, saw us arrive at the Shotover River. A jet boat ride at over 50 mph skimming the edge of the canyon walls combined with 360-degree turns and a few of those 'stopping just before you hit the cliff' moments was exhilarating. The screams of two American girls behind us added to the atmosphere of fear.

The fun had to end as we had to move on from Queenstown. It was time to hike again, and for us another new experience was just around the corner. We were to undertake a three-day hike in the mountains, and a different kind of excitement was building. New Zealand was quite exhausting!

Thirty-Five

Travelling
A Long Way South

February and March 2011

I HAD NO IDEA WHAT TIME IT WAS, BUT I HAD TO
assume it was early, as the thirty or so other people I was sharing
a room with were not stirring. I could hear Allister softly snoring
in the bunk bed above me, so I got out of my sleeping bag and
crept out of the room.

We had spent the night in the Luxmore Hut, having
completed day one of our three-day hike along the Kepler
Track. Classed as one of New Zealand's great walks, it had so
far not disappointed. Hiking up to the mountain hut the day
before with our rucksacks full of food, water, sleeping bags,
waterproofs and spare clothes had been hard work. It was even
harder for me than it was for Al, as I was not as strong and not
used to carrying such a weight when hiking. I had slept very

well as a result, despite being close to complete strangers and worrying about whether I would talk in my sleep.

I stepped out of the hut that morning and was simply astounded. I had one of those moments where I could feel a lump in my throat. I was standing just above the cloud and a white sea surrounded me with the sun and blue sky gleaming above. It was spectacular, and I knew Al had to be with me. Yet again in New Zealand I found myself waking him up to share an experience, and yet again he thanked me for it. We made a coffee and simply stared across the landscape. There were mountain peaks poking through the cloud, adding to the incredible view and emphasising how high we were. It was so peaceful and the sense we were floating above the earth was truly remarkable. Even now I can look back at the photos we took and feel a tingle down my spine. Allister and I do not know if we will ever see something like that again, and this no doubt makes the memory more vivid.

The second day of our hike was to take us to the summit of Mount Luxmore. It took us longer than was expected as we kept stopping to look at the view. As the morning progressed the cloud below us started to break, and gradually the landscape changed as the mountains emerged and the lakes below came into view. Neither of us believed at this stage that we would have a better day of hiking in New Zealand. Some days later we matched it, but in that moment, we were quite simply blown away. We had heard tales of these New Zealand great walks being overcrowded and disappointing, as bad weather was frequent, and wet, grey and misty conditions do not make for magnificent views. We found time alone, as people do naturally spread out during the day, and the weather was perfect. The whole day was spent walking along the ridge, before descending into the forest to stay at the Iris Hut on our second night. We could hear the repetitive piercing sound of the kiwi bird in the night and given its rarity this was another memorable moment.

Our third and final day of the hike was at lower altitudes and we enjoyed lunch at Lake Manapouri. As we ate the last of our food it was good to know that the hike was nearly over, and our rucksacks were now a lot lighter. For us the end of the hike was Rainbow Reach and a shuttle bus back to our campervan, which was parked waiting for us at a campsite in a town called Te Anau. Hot showers were quickly followed by hot food, which was quickly followed by falling asleep. What a truly memorable three days.

A more leisurely few days followed as we made our way to Milford Sound. We were in Fiordland, and of the fifteen fiords the area boasts, Milford Sound is the most easily accessible. It is spectacular even on a rainy day, and it sees plenty of those. Its accessibility by road paves the way for the endless stream of coaches, but that should not put anyone off visiting. To appreciate the grandeur of this drowned glacial valley we joined a boat cruise that took us along the sound to the edge of the Tasman Sea. Taking a cruise on the sound allowed us to really appreciate the 1,200-metre towering cliffs and the waterfalls plunging down them. It was a wet and misty day, but this only added to the atmosphere, and we both enjoyed the boat cruising right up to the falls to get us nice and wet.

On the water the breeze kept away the dreaded sand flies, but back on land in damp conditions they were swarming. It did limit our outside activities that day as they drove us potty, but to be honest it was nice to have a rest. The weather was wet, so an afternoon of drinking coffee, playing cards and reading a book followed. For once we were quite happy to be out of our hiking boots and warm and dry. The campsite had great facilities and we were able to sit on a proper sofa for the afternoon in a lovely lounge area. What a rare treat – I had forgotten all about the joys of furniture.

Recharged and ready to go the next day it was all about heading south to enjoy some wild and less travelled landscapes and to seek out wildlife a little rarer. We drove along the south coast and we certainly felt remote. We stopped at a place called Slope Point for the obligatory photo. A yellow sign marked the southernmost tip of New Zealand, and as the icy wind whipped around us, we certainly felt cold enough to know that Antarctica was the next stop. I really did love the feeling of being the furthest south I had ever been. The bleak atmosphere and no sign of anyone else really added to the sensation of being absolutely miles from anywhere. We spotted rare Hector's dolphins as we ate some lunch and parking up on the beach that night, we shared our space with sea lions. What else is there to say?

We had a primary mission, though, and this was to see if we could spot yellow-eyed penguins. This endangered species is found only in southern New Zealand, with numbers of around 4,000. As it is also considered to be the most ancient penguin species, we were keen to find it. We had done our research, but as our alarm clock went off at 4am I did for a moment question my sanity. It was dark and freezing cold and I was about to go and stand on a cliff in the hope that the information we had was accurate. At sunrise the penguins were supposed to make their way down the cliffs from their overnight resting places and head out to sea.

We drove out to the deserted spot and waited. We were frozen, but as the light appeared so did the penguins. First one appeared, and then another, and soon we could see many more making their way, at quite a pace, down the cliffs. We spent a magical hour watching them descend to the beach and into the open sea. Watching the adult penguins coax the youngsters into the water was a bonus. They were quite a way off, and the low light made it harder to see them, but worth every minute all the same. We left, hoping we would get another chance to see them.

We didn't know it then, but we were to experience them again in a way we would never forget.

Our day continued with a wildlife theme as we made our way to the Otago Peninsula to visit an albatross colony. Apparently, this is the only one on the mainland in the world, and it certainly was interesting. We were lucky enough to see chicks and watching them and the adult birds take off was a fascinating sight. As they ran and flapped in their quest to get airborne, their size did make us wonder if they would get off the ground. Once in flight a gliding elegance takes over and they look magnificent.

Near the colony were more penguins. These were the more common blue penguins, which look as their name suggests due to their slate-blue plumage. They are the smallest breed of penguin and they are often also referred to as fairy or little penguins. Seeing them as well did not disappoint.

Penguin day will always be remembered by us as a bad day too. Our route was taking us towards Christchurch and the difference of only a few days meant we were not there when an earthquake hit. When we heard the news that there had been fatalities, we were deeply saddened. We had met other travellers en route to Christchurch and we could only wonder if they had been there. It was important that we let our family and friends know that we were safe. Those with reasonable geographic knowledge would know we were in the area. The benefits of social media were clear when we posted on Facebook that we were fine. Some texts to those less online meant that on waking up in England to hear the news about the earthquake they would know we were ok. My mum did get a phone call from a worried relative before she had even heard about the earthquake, but fortunately her panic was short-lived when her mobile bleeped with my text.

A quick break from our wildlife tour landed us in Dunedin, and by total contrast a tour of the Cadbury chocolate factory.

Crossing the Nullabor Plain, Western Australia, December 2010.

Back from our honeymoon opening all the presents.

The love of travelling is starting. Niagara Falls, 1998.

The stunning glaciers of Mount Sefton, South Island, New Zealand, February 2011.

Skydiving over Lake Taupo.

The furthest south we have ever been. Slope Point, South Island, New Zealand, February 2011.

Loving my 'Jucy' campervan!

Bungee jumping off Kawarau Bridge.
Queenstown, New Zealand, February 2011.

A view over the Na Pali coast, island of Kauai, March 2011.

Mount Kosciusko, New South Wales, Australia, November 2010.

The Kepler Track, South Island, New Zealand, February 2011.

TOP LEFT: *Emotional moment. Angel's Landing, Zion National Park, USA, 2005.*

ABOVE: *Returning to happier times, Polperro, 2005.*

LEFT AND BELOW: *Hawaiian life, March 2011.*

Time to stop travelling! Monday 13th June 2011.

There is always 'one more mountain'. The Cuillin Ridge, Isle of Skye, September 2009.

Willy Wonka had a day off, but there were lots of treats to enjoy. I did get a little upset in the quiz when I answered a question correctly and someone took my chocolate prize. It was the end of the tour, so Al decided to escort me out of the factory before my 'chocolate rage' got out of control. We also walked up the steepest street in the world whilst we were in Dunedin. Whilst it felt like the title had to be true, we had some reservations. New Zealand loves to advertise the longest, highest, oldest whatever to entice you to visit, and invariably you do. Whether you have been duped or not does not really matter if you enjoy the experience. That is what we thought, anyway, and the 'steepest' street did not disappoint, particularly as we had to race to the top to see who was fittest and fastest.

Whilst at times the ramblings of other travellers can get on your nerves, and I must be honest when I say we had those moments, it is still a very important part of travelling. Not only do you get to meet many different characters and enjoy their company, you do also at times gain valuable information about the area you are in or are heading too. One such occasion for us was staying in a small out of the way village called Moeraki. A fellow traveller had recommended a small campsite overlooking the sea and advised us to chat to the owner about a fantastic nearby spot to see yellow-eyed penguins. We did just that and what an evening we had.

This time it was the other end of the day as we walked along the cliff top in the hope of seeing at least one penguin waddle out of the sea and head up the cliffs. As we walked along moaning that there was nothing to see and what a waste of time it was, we pretty much stood on one. As the penguins make their way up the cliffs, they overheat and stop. They put their wings out to cool down before moving on. As our eyes became more aware of how they were blending into the grass, we realised we were surrounded. Nobody else was around, and what a fantastic moment it was. We kept our distance, kept quiet and took a lot of photos. I do not recall how long we were there, but it was a long time. It is hard to tear yourself away from such an experience, because you know the likelihood is that you will never experience it again. I remember feeling something similar in Australia when I knew I had seen my last koala. This moment was probably a little more special, due to the remote environment and knowing we were seeing a rare and endangered species.

The end of our time in New Zealand was drawing near, and the final days did not disappoint. We spent some time in the Aoraki Mount Cook National Park. We camped again in one of the DOC sites not far from the village. The village itself is a small collection of buildings, but it sits at 760 metres with the mountains circling all around. It is a breathtaking area, and its mountains are famous for being the location for much of the climbing that Sir Edmund Hillary did in his early years. The Alpine Centre opened in his name is worth a visit, and I certainly learnt a lot about the man who conquered Everest in 1953.

Following in his footsteps (sort of) we set off from our campsite early on our first morning to ascend to the Mueller Hut. A cloudy and cold start in the mountains did not exactly inspire me, but after some time a sudden change in weather gave Allister and me a truly heart stopping experience. We climbed to a ridge, and as we got to the top the cloud vanished. In front of us were the huge glaciers of Mount Sefton. Having not seen anything much all morning, the view was quite overwhelming. The sun hit the ice and a wall of white filled the sky. As we stood and stared, we could hear the creaking of the ice and the distant rumblings of avalanches. We were both lost for words, and the sudden impact of the glaciers was quite an emotional moment.

Mueller Hut itself, sitting at 6,000 feet, was a good resting point. The hut provides shelter and overnight accommodation, but we preferred the long day option on this occasion and made our way back down the mountain. As we descended to the lower levels that had been shrouded in cloud all morning, we were able to see what we had missed out on. The sun was shining and illuminating the lakes. Areas that were deserted that morning were now full of walkers making the most of the weather and scenery.

There is plenty of other walking in the area and we made the most of our time there. The campervan was a bit chilly at night and washing facilities were ice-cold water taps. There were flushing toilets, though, and, with a location like that, what else is really needed?

Time was passing us by, and we needed to head north. We were heading to Hanmer Springs and the route we would have taken was through Christchurch. We had no option but to follow the diversions to go around the earthquake zone. Poor signs and little information led us close to the city centre and we came face to face with the reality of the damage an earthquake can do. Demolished buildings and debris everywhere made for a very long and difficult journey. The rapid contrasts we saw were quite astounding. When we finally got on the right road, we passed collapsed houses with owners sitting on their roofs, getting water from hoses or waiting to use the portable toilets that had popped up everywhere. Houses next door to each other were completely different. One would be standing with no damage and one would be destroyed. Five minutes down the road and all the houses were fine; people were playing golf and drinking lattes. The earthquake was very destructive and yet confined to a relatively small area. It was a strange and sad experience, and once through the area we stopped and donated to the fund to help those people sitting on their roofs.

Hanmer Springs is all about the thermal mineral pools. It is a natural environment of thermal waters containing a wide variety of minerals such as sulphur, magnesium and calcium carbonates. They are reported to be very good for you, so we made sure we enjoyed them before heading off. It was a very relaxing experience and my skin certainly did feel rather lovely afterwards.

We were going north to get the ferry back to North Island, but we decided to head east first across the Lewis Pass. We wanted to visit a place called Pancake Rocks on the west coast and this was the route to take. One of the challenges with driving on the South Island of New Zealand is that to get from one place to another there is normally only one road, two if you are lucky. This is fine if the road is open. Lewis Pass was not on this day, but alas we only knew this once we had been driving along it for a few hours. There had been a huge landslide and there is no detour for such events, so we had to retrace our drive and then travel along the only other road that goes across the island. This was Arthur's Pass, and at least we had been along it before, so were optimistic it was open. Travelling is a different world. A whole day lost driving the campervan and we never reached our destination. In the world of life back home this would cause high stress levels for any individual. We just shrugged our shoulders, played some music and enjoyed the views.

We did finally arrive back on the west coast, visiting Pancake Rocks. For the scientists out there, a process called stylobedding has created layers of weathered limestone that resemble stacks of pancakes. It is a photographer's dream and given that the whole area sits on huge caverns that send the surging sea up through blowholes, it is understandable why it is on the 'must see' list. We therefore had no regrets about our slightly longer than planned journey to get there.

We then made our way back to North Island on the ferry. Somewhat inclement weather meant that the only place we didn't feel sick was on deck in the wind and rain. Our seasickness pills were not so effective on this crossing.

We called in again on the friends we had met in Australia. Yet again they made us very welcome and we thoroughly enjoyed their company. It is such a shame to meet such great people and yet live on opposite sides of the world. At least social media maintains a link, and one day we will knock on their front door again, even if they are not expecting it.

Our final day in New Zealand was overshadowed by the news of a massive earthquake and tsunami in Japan. This was followed by tsunami warnings for Hawaii and news of evacuations. As we were flying there the following day, we were unsure what would unfold. As it turned out there was no problem with our flights, but it was a strange day of watching the news and wondering if we would be staying in New Zealand a little while longer.

Saturday 12th March 2011 was our last night in our campervan home in New Zealand. As we handed the keys back the following morning and boarded our flight to Hawaii, we did feel sad. I know that it sounds wrong to be sad about flying to Hawaii; the next part of our trip was of course about to start, but we truly had experienced an amazing adventure in New Zealand. Everything we both wanted travelling to be was contained within the two months we spent touring this wonderful country. It made all the planning, the time and distance away from home, the difficult days that happened along the way, and let us not forget the cost, all so very worthwhile. I have no doubt that one day we will go back there. I think the only difference there will be is that I might – just might – hire a slightly bigger campervan.

THIRTY-SIX

LIFE CHANGES
CHANGING FORTUNES

JANUARY TO APRIL 2004

ALLISTER HAD A ROUTINE CHECK-UP APPOINTMENT immediately after Christmas. This was with the surgeon who had done the operation to remove part of his colon and put in the colostomy. All Al wanted to talk about was having the colostomy reversed, and when this could happen. This conversation never progressed as we expressed first our concern over the lump that Al had found under his arm just before Christmas. On looking, the surgeon said getting this looked at by the oncology team was the priority, and he would get Al an appointment straight away. It seemed the subject of reversal would have to wait.

We got a date for this oncology appointment through very quickly. I will never be able to explain why I did not go with Al to this appointment. The surgeon was obviously concerned enough to organise it very quickly. I now have theories when I look back, of course, but none of them really get to the real reason because the real reason is unknown. I can speculate that I thought Al was in good health and getting better, and the lump under his arm was nothing at all. By attending the appointment, I was showing I was worried, and the lump seemed more real. Al also discouraged me from going with him. I needed to go to work and he was fine on his own was what he said to me. He too was in denial. By us both treating the appointment as a routine check-up, our concerns over the lump diminished, and indeed the festive season had helped us shove this inconvenience into the background. It was and still is the only appointment that Al went to alone. After this time Al was always escorted by me or one or both of his parents, despite at times his huge protestations. These days I am always by Allister's side when he has any hospital appointment and I always will be. He really can't be trusted on his own: who knows what can happen.

The reason for my lifelong declaration is that during this appointment the doctor told Allister that he should prepare for the worst. I do not know of course the exact words that were used during this consultation, but when I arrived home from work, I saw Al on the sofa with a look of total despair in his eyes. A look I will never forget. As I sat down next to him and held his hand, I will never forget the words that followed, either. Al looked at me and started to talk. He told me that the doctor (not his usual oncology consultant, incidentally) had said that a lump appearing so soon after the end of chemotherapy was a likely indicator that the cancer was very aggressive. When I asked Al exactly what she meant by that, he told me that we had to prepare for him not surviving this. I remember a sense of disbelief at this point. Al was fitter and stronger than he had been in a long time; we were getting our life back. How could this be true?

A biopsy was going to be arranged straight away, followed probably by radiotherapy, and I think it was at this point that I decided I would not start 'preparing for the worst' until we had the results from this and a more conclusive assessment. I know this was my way of dealing with such terrible news but what followed was even stranger. We just had our dinner and watched television. This was complete denial, I know. We did talk about the more practical aspects of the coming days. I was due at work the next day to run a training course. Of course, I wanted to be with Al, and initial thoughts were that we should have the day together. Was I really in the right state of mind to run a training course anyway?

As the evening progressed though, we somehow concluded that doing this was giving in. We would carry on with life as normal, and this meant me going to work. I do not think for one minute that we were thinking or behaving in a normal way, but I did go to work the next day. I ran a training course and thoughts of my husband not surviving were just not real. Allister spent the day with his parents and had a pleasant day. I am sure a psychologist would have much fun analysing our behaviour during this twenty-four-hour period, but when I look back at this, I truly believe that I just knew Allister wasn't going to die.

The day for Allister's biopsy followed swiftly. This was a strange day. The doctor inserted a needle to take a biopsy from what was assumed to be a cancerous growth. The lump burst, shooting white pus all over the rather surprised doctor. This was not a normal event. There was not much of the lump left after this explosion. The doctor cleaned himself up and secured some of the debris for sending away for analysis. The very nice doctor told Al that it was very unlikely to be cancerous; some sort of infection seemed far more likely. We should perhaps have felt angry that only the week before a doctor was telling Al that he should prepare for the worst. Maybe, just maybe, more facts should have been gathered before telling this to a lone young man. Anger was not the emotion we felt though, it was more a cautious relief. Cautious, as we needed the results to come back to know for certain, and we needed to find out what would happen next.

What happened next was that the results of the biopsy showed that it was some sort of bird virus. There was not much surprise to this news from either of us. Having a bird virus is not something you are likely to be told on a regular basis, but during his illness we had experienced numerous occasions of being told Al was an unusual case and odd things were happening. Somehow having a bird virus seemed quite normal.

Allister's consultant decided that continuing with the plan for a course of radiotherapy was a good idea. Caution had become a common trait amongst the medical profession where Al was concerned, and the unusual circumstances that had led to him developing the lump meant 'a better safe than sorry' approach was adopted.

Radiotherapy followed for several weeks. Compared to the chemotherapy this seemed like only a minor inconvenience to Al. Apart from a little bit of redness he had no side effects and his keep fit routine was not disrupted. The only lasting memory we have of this experience is that Al has a couple of small tattoos. It was important that the radiotherapy was given in exactly the same spot every week, so permanent ink marked the location. It is the only tattoos my husband has and ever will have, but he does like to joke from time to time that he does have some. They are the size of pinheads and look like specks of dust, but this is of course irrelevant to him: the point is that he has tattoos!

It would be a long time before Al was discharged as an outpatient: he would be under the care of the oncologist for many months ahead, but we found ourselves realising that

Allister was doing pretty well. It is an odd transition because we didn't wake up one morning and think, 'Al is better, let's get on with our life.' We were just getting on with our life.

There were some practical problems to deal with along the way. One of these was that Al, having been off work for so long, was no longer getting paid. We cannot fault his employers for their generosity with his pay in what was a long absence from work. He continued on full company sick pay for many months, but eventually this ended, and we were left with only a small amount of statutory sick pay and this was to stop also. I was only working four days a week at this time and had been from the time that Al became seriously ill. At the start of the year we didn't know when Al would return to work and when he did it was likely to be some months before he would be full time again.

The good news was that we had some reasonable savings. We didn't spend much money in 2003. Al was in hospital for the most part, but on full pay, and I just spent my time working and visiting him. This meant we had no holidays, had no social life, spent little on food and never visited a shopping centre. The result of this sparse living was that I had squirrelled away a fair few pounds, knowing that the full company sick pay would end and not knowing when my husband would return to work. We were therefore now spending some of these savings on living costs, treating ourselves to a few things like some new clothes and things for the house. We were also enjoying a gradual return to a social life with family and friends.

These savings would not last forever, and although my salary could cover all our bills and living expenses, and the odd night out, it didn't leave much for anything else and so I took the decision to go back to work five days a week. I didn't want to, partly because I had got used to not being full time and rather liked it, but mainly because it was one less day a week, I would be spending with Al. When looking back I know now that these feelings of not wanting to be apart from Al were the start of a difficult time for me. Surprising, perhaps, that the hardest time for me personally was as Al got better, but I guess it was because I didn't need to be so strong anymore. My strength and willpower to deal with every crisis vanished and was replaced with tears, worry and irrational fear. I will come back to this later.

With me working five days a week and Al feeling almost like a normal human being again, our thoughts turned to Al returning to work. He was actually getting a bit bored. The problem was that, although his fitness was greatly improved, his confidence was not. A lot of his low confidence came from being so long out of society. He had not made any decisions unaided for a long time, and in many ways was still very much looking to me for assurance that he was doing the right things and making the correct decisions about the simplest things. His company's personnel team visited us and there was no pressure on him to go back, but after such a long absence a return to work would need to be structured and gradual. Again, the benefits of working for a large company were evident, as this understanding approach I think helped Al go back to work sooner than he might have done.

Another big hurdle for Al was dealing with his colostomy. At home this was manageable, for the most part, but at work he wasn't sure how he would cope. We still had no reason not to believe that this would be reversed, and with Al doing so well we hoped it was a conversation that we could have with his doctors soon. We were not at this point yet, and a return to work was going to happen sooner.

Al went back to work in April 2004. This was an emotional day. More so for me than for Al, as I think he was dealing more with his nerves rather than understanding that his wife was in pieces because it was a moment that she thought might never happen again. He hadn't worked for over a year, a year spent mainly in hospital, at times unaware of who he was or what was happening to him. His return to work was therefore a truly wonderful event, but he still had more operations to face and he was a long way from the person he was before he became ill. Serious illness not only affects your body but also changes the person you are. A once witty, confident, life and soul of the party type was nervous, quiet and needing a lot of support and reassurance. That is not to say that Allister's inner strength was gone; this was very much intact. It was his amazing willpower and commitment to rebuild his strength and life that ultimately gave us both the desire to make sure we valued and enjoyed every minute in the future. As his recovery continued, we started to talk a lot about renting out our house and seeing the world.

Small steps though, and work was the first of these. He went back to work at the store he was at before he became ill. He started back at work for nine hours a week. It doesn't sound much, does it? For the first few weeks it was more than enough as it made him mentally very tired. His brain was getting a workout for the first time in well over a year. Al had to regain his confidence in the workplace. In his role as a deputy store manager, not only did he need to know what he should be doing; he also needed to be motivating others to do what they should be doing. These skills were a long way from returning, but Sainsbury's approach of the gradual return allowed Al the time to do this. Retail is a fast-paced and ever-changing environment. As well as needing to redevelop his management skills, Al had to catch up with all the changes to procedures, technology, product ranges and policy. It was going to be a long way back.

THIRTY-SEVEN

THE EARLY YEARS
ALL ABOUT THE CHILDREN

1997 TO 2000

MOVING TO A NEW HOUSE HAD DISTRACTED US WELL
from thinking about having children, but it was only a
distraction. We had been married for some time and obvious
questions were being raised. When asked about having children
we always gave a vague answer. I don't really know why, and one
day we decided there really was no reason not to be more open
with people when they asked. After this time, anyone who asked
got an honest answer, and this has been our way ever since.

Sometime earlier, on one of our visits to the Midlands to see
friends and family, we had taken the plunge and told just our
closest friends about our situation. I remember the silence and
the looks of total surprise. It was probably only brief as quickly
our friends asked us questions and asked us how we felt. I know

it must have been awkward for them, far more so than it was for us. We had known for quite some time and talking about it had become normal, but for our friends it was all very new. We never wanted to make it awkward for them, but the endless questions about when we were going take the next step and have a baby needed to be answered, and it was easier for us that they knew. It was hard being vague with our closest friends when they asked us about having children, and we were starting to feel dishonest. I don't know why we kept it to ourselves for as long as we did; we had nothing to be ashamed of and nothing to hide. I think we weren't ready to tell them until we had come to terms with it ourselves. Had we come to terms with it at this stage? Well, we knew what our options were, and we had got used to the fact that it wasn't going to be easy, but we certainly weren't any closer to making a decision.

We carried on not making a decision and just kind of got on with our life without children, and this didn't change for the following few years. I know it was denial and it was not the best thing to do, but time was not making the decision any easier. I still wanted Allister's biological children, we couldn't have that, and the alternatives were not any more appealing. Sadness hung over us, and yet we still couldn't make a decision or find any closure. We were talking about it less and less, and I suppose some kind of acceptance of our situation was starting to form. Other changes started to happen in our life too. Notably, one of these was our relationships with our friends. Their lives were so very different, with ever-growing families, but we were all still great friends. This meant being involved every step of the way. There were endless christenings, birthday parties and other gatherings for reasons that I cannot recall. Weekends spent together meant activities involving the children, and conversations were typically about the children. Instead of spending time down the pub with our friends, we would spend afternoons at the park, and the evenings would involve bath time and then waiting until the children had gone to sleep to have dinner, whilst listening to the baby monitor gurgle away in the background.

Even our annual girls' weekend away had changed beyond recognition. Instead of ridiculously late nights spent discussing all our darkest and deepest secrets and days spent recovering in the spa, we entertained new small members of the group with cuddly toys and peek-a-boo. When the girls came to stay with me one year with a little one in tow, I recall cleaning up a small accident on my carpet that occurred between the nappy changes. I knew then for certain that the annual bash would not be the same again.

There is another evening that I will always recall as one that perhaps really did drive home the reality that our life was, and might well remain forever, without children. We were spending the weekend with my parents and had plans to meet up with our friends on the Saturday night. Our friends had got babysitters, and so it was a rare opportunity to have a night out at the pub. Usually a Saturday night meant everyone gathering at one house for a few drinks and a Chinese takeaway. Nights out at the pub had been replaced with nights in and baby monitors. On this occasion, though, we were going out, and, with it being the first time in a long time that there were no children present, I expected conversation to be a little more varied. It wasn't. The whole evening was spent talking about first steps, potty training, suitable nurseries, wonderful grandparents, solid foods and of course the next birthday party.

Please do not think that I am indicating I was bored by the conversation; far from it, the problem was the overwhelming sadness I felt at not being able to contribute. I wanted to be talking about my own children and I couldn't. Our lives had been very much like our friends' lives had been and in some ways we all had conformed to the 'get an education, get a job, get married, and buy a house' expectation. Not having children broke the pattern, and suddenly Allister and I were no longer conforming, and we felt like misfits. I felt like an outsider, far removed from my friends' lives, and as we drove home, I was left with a sense that it really wasn't going to happen for us. After all, how could it if we couldn't bring ourselves to take any action? Perhaps it really was time to move on.

Moving on is not easy, though, when you are invited to attend another christening or another birthday party or spend another weekend entertaining your friends' children. Allister and I did not want to lose touch with our friends and enjoyed seeing them and being part of their lives, but as time passed, we did find our desire to do these things was lessening. I do not think it was all about avoiding reminders of our own childless life, although of course a significant part of it was, but also about our life changing to one that didn't involve children. I think the best example of this came about one New Year's Eve. We always got together with our friends at New Year, and for many years, before children came along, we used to stay in hotels, and we had some fantastic party nights. Staying in hotels changed to gatherings at someone's house, as babysitters are not easy to come by at this time of the year, and to start with we did of course join in. One year, the annual conversation started about New Year. We looked at our friends and simply said, 'We will be doing something different this year.' It was a tricky one and met with varied reaction: breaking a tradition is not always easy. We spent that New Year, and many more since, with my cousin and his wife. Very dear friends of ours who, albeit for different reasons, also had no children. This signified the start of Allister and me acknowledging that actually we didn't have children. We realised that it was ok if sometimes we didn't want to watch *Coco the Clown's Magic Afternoon* or spend our Saturdays at a third birthday party with our friends' parents and grandparents playing pass the parcel and blowing out candles on a cake.

We were beginning to want to live our life differently. We were living our life as if we had children, taking on the responsibilities of careers, a home and providing. We were of course only providing for ourselves, and although this is necessary it doesn't come with the same degree of responsibility that having children does.

It is hard to define when exactly things changed, but I do know our love for travel started in 1998. With no little mouths to feed, jobs going well and our finances back under control, we had for the first time enough money to go abroad. To date, other than our honeymoon, holidays had been cheap and cheerful UK-based affairs. During 1998 we spent two weeks touring Canada and the USA. We loved it. The freedom of not knowing where we would spend the night, the whole open-road feel and the excitement of seeing new places and meeting new people was something that clearly suited us. We did not know at the time how much travel would come to dominate our life but looking back it was a turning point. Finally, we were able to see some advantages to not having children. This is not to say we had made a final decision about our future regarding children, but I think we were starting to see that life without them really could be enjoyable.

THIRTY-EIGHT

COUNTDOWN THE TASK LIST

JULY 2010

THIS WAS IT: THE FINAL SURGE, COMPLETION OF JULY'S task list and then we would be leaving. There would be no 'Countdown, The Task List, August 2010'. August 2010 would be exploring the outback of Australia. Now that sounded good – scary, but good.

July was so much fun and so much hard work, but we were doing it together, now that work was well and truly behind us, and that really was great.

The only thing that ended up being a waste of time really was setting up a site on which to store photos. I knew we would take a lot of pictures but hadn't considered that this would mean a lot of hours in internet cafes trying to upload them off the camera onto the site. It is fair to say that the speed of the internet in some of the more remote parts of Australia was slow at best, if it existed at all, and as costs mounted as we tried to upload them we soon realised that it would be better just to buy a high-capacity memory stick and back them up to that whenever we could. This proved to be a good solution. We did use Facebook to stay in touch, and when the internet was cheap and speedy, we would upload some photos for our friends and family to enjoy. If I were to travel again for a long period of time (well actually for any period of time) I would now have my iPad with me. With the availability of free Wi-Fi this would now be a much better option.

In the context of keeping in touch, the best thing we did was set up a blog. Again, this was used when the internet was cheap and speedy, and it allowed us to tell tales of our trip and add photos. We made sure our friends and family all had access before we left, and they were able to leave us comments on the blog entries as well. It has also given us a lasting diary of our trip and is great to read back over now. It is worth the time in doing if you are going to take that travelling plunge.

July had to be primarily about leaving, because, well, because we were leaving! We set forth very quickly in completing our list of the kit we needed to take and packing our rucksacks. Our third bedroom was a small box room, which we emptied completely and then used it as the room for putting in what we were taking with us. This room allocation was a vital process. Al was packing the house up like a man possessed, and it was important not to pack what we were taking. The third bedroom was the only place it was safe to leave anything.

The kit list that we had been compiling for six months ended up with not that much on it. It was such a useful thing to do, though, as over the six months it got added to as we thought of things and I would recommend doing it, rather than just opening your cupboards and seeing what you can fit in your rucksack.

Kit highlights, or better described as those items you must not forget to take when travelling around the world for a year are, in addition to main rucksacks: day packs, money wallets, good-quality sunglasses, cameras, mobile phones, chargers and travel adapter, hiking boots, waterproof jacket and trousers, first aid kit, insect repellent, sunscreen, mosquito nets for the head (a must in some of the fly-infested outback landscapes of Australia), a tent and sleeping bags (if camping, of course), torch, Swiss army knife, some sort of security seal for rucksacks, and of course clothes, comprising something for the hot and the cold climates, swimwear, footwear, for me some cheap jewellery, some toiletries to start the trip with, a book for the long flight, a pen, pack of cards, for me glasses and contact lenses, medication and all relevant travel documents in some sort of document wallet that will endure the test of time, and of course passports! We would need more kit for camping, but the plan for that was to buy the car in Australia and then buy what we needed to camp with, like cooking stuff, sleep mats, groundsheet and camping chairs!

Did I get everything in my rucksack? Yes. Could I carry it? Yes. Did I take anything I didn't wear? Yes. Not that bad, though, as it was only one skirt! Did Allister achieve the same? Yes. And he had spare space. How is that even possible? I did want to add some more of my stuff to it, but of course that was not allowed. I have a final tip for the world traveller. If you are travelling with someone else, split some of your clothes and key items over both your rucksacks. A missing bag will mean at least you will have a change of clothes and some contact lenses to hand in the other bag whilst your lost luggage is retrieved from storage in an airport in a far-flung country you never even visited!

We spent a lot of time during our last two weeks with family and friends. Goodbyes were hard and got harder as the time for departure got closer. We said goodbye to Allister's parents on 7th July. They were heading to France on the 8th. One set of parents down and one to go. We just knew emotions were very mixed between being happy for us and yet knowing it would be many months until they saw us again. I think they hid it well. Better than some of our friends, who I am sure would have cried less if not so full of wine! I have to say, though, it is better to know that people care and will miss you than to head off around the world without anyone noticing you have gone.

Allister kept a written diary of our whole trip. He started to write this on 1st July whilst we were still at home, packing. It is an interesting read that tells me that from 1st July until 6th July we did nothing but meet family and friends, have BBQs, eat out and have a lot of fun! I am sure we should have been packing! It seems we hit the packing hard on 7th and 8th July as we were picking up the keys to our storage unit on the 9th. The van wasn't booked until the Monday, which was the 12th, so we spent the weekend moving over smaller items in the car, and by Sunday night we had shifted a lot of stuff. Was I panicking? I was a bit. This was because the storage unit was looking quite full and there was a lot of stuff to be shifted into the van on Monday. Allister was very calm and kept telling me it would all fit. We watched the World Cup final on the Sunday night and the TV was packed on the final whistle. All the time Allister continued to reassure me it would all go in!

Sunday night was our last night in our bed. Monday morning dawned, we picked up our van, our big, strong mate arrived to assist with heavy lifting, and by lunchtime all our worldly goods, apart from a few last-minute items to be dropped off on Tuesday morning, were packed tightly and securely in a metal container, in what was once a pig farm, in the middle of the Meon Valley.

We sat in our almost empty house on Monday afternoon with a computer, a couple of camping chairs, a kettle, four mugs and a couple of bowls and plates and a strangely large amount of dirty washing. Let us not forget the blow-up bed we would be sleeping on that night and of course our perfectly packed rucksacks, waiting for sealing after the final additions of toothbrushes and deodorant and other ad hoc toiletries on Tuesday morning.

My mum and dad arrived on Monday afternoon. The house also contained a little pile of things that my mum and dad would be taking home with them to store at their house. Valuables such as jewellery, photos and all our documents. Storage units are great, and we were insured. This is fine if it burns to the ground or you are robbed, because you can go and buy a new sofa, a bed, and new clothes, but we felt some things were better placed in my parents' loft. Now, in my eyes these items were only a small pile, but to my dad's it was a pile that was most certainly not going to fit in his car. Al would get it all in my dad's car. After his storage unit success, I had no doubts.

As we were unable to offer my parents anywhere to sit it was decided to head to the pub. Mum and Dad were staying in the local Premier Inn overnight, as we clearly couldn't offer them a bed. We had a meal out because we had nothing to cook with either! This was great, although my dad was not very well. He coughed his way through dinner whilst telling me he was fine, and it was not a problem to drive us to the airport the next day and then drive the 300 miles home. I was not convinced, but circumstances were such that the alternatives were none.

We decided on an early night and Mum and Dad headed to the Premier Inn. Once we got home there was little for us to do other than go to sleep, and so we lay on our airbed for our last night in England for a while.

I don't think either of us can be sure of our thoughts that night. I can't describe our feelings as excitement, as somehow the reality still hadn't sunk in. Lists of tasks had dominated our life for several months. In that time somehow it seemed we found little time to actually think about the trip. I think relief that we were finally going was a better description of our feelings. Whatever it was, I don't think either of us slept particularly well: maybe – just maybe – the nerves were also kicking in.

Thirty-Nine

Countdown
Departure Day

Tuesday 13th July 2010

'WAKE UP, WE ARE LEAVING TONIGHT, YOU HAVE STUFF to do and I want a cup of tea.' The sound of Allister's voice was making its way through the fog that was my brain. In fairness, it was not that early, but having finally got to sleep I was not in the mood for waking up. The reality of the day hit quite quickly, though, and my stomach did a flip. Al was grinning at me, looking like an excited child at Christmas, and this was infectious. We were going travelling and flying to Singapore that night, wow!

Despite this it was still unthinkable to start the day without a cup of tea, so I followed my instructions and headed to the kitchen. Tea was drunk and showers were taken. My mum and dad arrived, and whilst sitting on camping chairs and drinking coffee they surveyed the remaining items in our lounge. One end contained our rucksacks and remaining few items to be packed inside, and the other end contained the items destined for my dad's car for the onward journey to their loft. I should mention my parents' caravan in Lyme Regis at this point. This is relevant, because my parents had driven to our house from their caravan, but they would be heading home to Shropshire after the airport run. This route meant that my dad's car already contained a large amount of luggage. I could sense the growing alarm in Dad's voice as he asked, 'Will all this stuff fit in my car with you two as well?' He clearly hadn't seen Allister's superhuman skill at packing lots of stuff into small spaces, but to be on the safe side we all did a run over to the storage unit to squeeze in a few more bits. This left the jewellery, photos, documents, some dirty washing (can't put that in storage, obviously) and outfits for my auntie's wedding! To this day I can't work out why my poor mum ended up with so much dirty washing. I was convinced I had cleared it a couple of days before; I guess that wasn't the case.

There wasn't much left to do, and we weren't flying until 10pm, but somehow the day just sort of slipped past us. Allister and my dad delivered our car to our brother-in-law, as he was borrowing it in our absence, and then it was pretty much lunchtime. As catering facilities were very restricted in our house, we headed to the pub for a very leisurely lunch. I think we felt a sense of limbo and feelings that we should be somehow more frantic, but it was after all a good thing that we weren't.

After lunch we could not delay the inevitable any longer, and it was time to seal our rucksacks. Our last few toiletries got safely stowed, and as Al embarked on the sealing process, he looked at me and said, 'Now, are you sure everything is packed and there is nothing you need to have out of here?' Many years of holidaying with me had taught Al that I always wanted to add, or take out, a little something after the cases were locked.

Al would often hear me frantically reopening them as I tried to justify my actions. This was of course a slightly different situation as all my other belongings were a few miles down the road in a metal container, but Al still felt he'd better check. Our rucksacks were sealed around the zips with cable ties and then placed inside a wonderful piece of kit called Pacsafe. Money well spent on these, we thought. Pacsafe is a sort of mesh casing for your rucksack and something I would recommend for the rucksack traveller. It protects the exterior of your pack from damage and more importantly makes it very hard for anyone to get inside. All we had to do was remember where the keys were once we got to Singapore.

The process took a little longer than planned as Al ensured every zip was secure and the Pacsafes were properly in place. I hoped it wouldn't take quite so long to open them at the other end!

The time came to load the car and leave. My dad's stress level was increasing a tad as we moved our stuff in the direction of the car. Al was very impressive as always in the packing into small spaces, but even he had misjudged slightly. All I can say is that during the trip to Heathrow I had a limited view out of the window, my lap was crushed, and my dad was hyperventilating.

Locking our front door on our empty house was a very memorable moment. We have lots of memorable moments, it is true to say, but that moment of shutting and locking the door felt like our life in England was closing; it was very final and a real sense of 'no turning back now'. I expected to feel emotional at this point, especially as I had to deal with the thought that other people would be moving into my home, but I didn't. There is much to be said for how we adapted. Six months of planning to move out meant the emotion of moving out was gone. We were left with a sense of moving forward and the excitement of what lay ahead. We did have to drop the keys off with the agent, and the only challenge here was getting one of us out of the car to do this without the entire contents of the car spilling out onto the street after us. We managed it and then headed to Heathrow, not the most comfortable of journeys but fortunately the traffic was kind and we arrived in good time.

The several weeks of goodbyes to friends and family spilled over into a deluge of tears as I said goodbye at the departure gate to my mum and dad. I had been so controlled with everyone else, but alas the dam broke and all the pent-up emotion spilled out into a small flood. There is nothing like an emotional farewell with hundreds of people milling around. My dad successfully lightened the moment as we passed through the departure gate. Taking photos of this area is not allowed. Obviously, the need to take that final snap of his number one daughter turned my dad into a belligerent law-breaking individual and he was not to be deterred by the cries of the security guard. I am sure not everyone heads through departures wondering if their dad has been arrested. A text to my mum from the bar a few moments later reassured me that Dad was once again a pillar of society. I think Mum was still crying, but at least they were together! Al did what Al does best and bought me a drink and gave me a hug. We sat in the bar awaiting our flight, just looking at each other and knowing there was nothing left to do. Weirdly, we didn't have much to say to each other. I put it down to exhaustion, and as we boarded our flight to Singapore it turned out that sleep was not far away.

FORTY

TRAVELLING
A MAI TAI IN HAWAII

MARCH AND APRIL 2011

WE HAD LEFT OUR CAMPSITE IN NEW ZEALAND AT
11am on Sunday 13th March 2011. We arrived at our hotel in
Hawaii, at 11am on Sunday 13th March 2011. We had been
travelling for twenty-four hours and crossing the date line
meant we got to do the same day again in a different country.
Now, that is a strange thing to do. It was even stranger given the
simply huge contrast between the two countries.

I don't think twenty-four hours of travelling prepared me
well for arriving in Honolulu. We took a bus from the airport
to Waikiki Beach. My vision of Hawaii was one of golden sands,
palm trees and waves lapping peacefully on the shore with gentle
music playing in the background. This vision disintegrated
into a roar of honking horns, heavy congestion, endless rows

of hideous souvenir shops, people everywhere and of course a McDonald's on every corner. There was not a mountain, glacier, deserted wilderness or penguin in sight. We were not quite sure how we were going to adjust!

Arrival at our hotel did help ease the pain. We had booked all our accommodation for Hawaii in advance, and first up was the beachfront hotel. The lobby was made to look like a surf shack, colours were a blend of lime green and orange, and as hula girls greeted me, I did wonder if I would ever feel normal again.

Funny thing with moods, though. If you ever find yourself sleeping in a small campervan for two months, I promise that, when you open the door to a hotel room and see a double bed, clean bed linen and a private shower, whatever mood you are in will be instantly replaced with a feeling of euphoria. Mine was only enhanced by a small balcony twenty-three floors up overlooking the ocean. It was quite a view. Both Allister and I suddenly relished the challenge of Waikiki Beach, and it didn't take us long to unpack – emptying a rucksack doesn't take long – and head off for some lunch.

It was apparent that mai tais were the cocktail of choice, and keen to get into the spirit, quite literally, we ordered two. Once we had found our way through the fruit, foliage and 'fun glass accessories' they were actually rather yummy. Allister wasn't quite sure what to do with his miniature hula dancer on a straw, but he had conquered bigger challenges in his life.

Let me digress for a moment with a little geography and our Hawaiian plan. Hawaii is a group of islands. We were at this point on the island of Oahu. Waikiki Beach, where our hotel was, is a surfer's paradise and the beach area of Honolulu, the place where most Hawaiians live. We planned to stay only a few days on this island, to enjoy some beach time, but mainly to visit Pearl Harbor. Our next island was to be Big Island, the land of the volcanoes, and then onwards to Kauai where hopefully the golden beaches and stunning scenery would reappear. The total trip would be about three weeks, all accommodation and inter-island flights were pre-booked, and with the mai tais slipping down rather nicely I was starting to look forward to the change.

I cannot talk about our stay in Waikiki Beach without first mentioning breakfast at the hotel. We did go for the bed and breakfast option, but to say it wasn't quite what I expected would be a significant understatement.

On arrival every guest is given a luminous orange cool bag. It is called BOB and the hotel informed us this acronym was for 'breakfast on the beach'. 'Bun fight on the balcony' we soon affectionately called it as we joined the hordes on the patio each morning to fill our BOB. The theory was that you gave your room number and then headed to the buffet to fill your BOB with an assortment of breads and pastries. You could then take your BOB and sit around the pool or head to the beach. There were strict rules about one BOB visit to the buffet per room. The hotel was woefully poor at checking room numbers, and we soon took full advantage of refills, giving us enough food for breakfast and lunch. We still have BOB today and it can be occasionally spotted when we head off for a long journey.

We did have a good few days on the island of Oahu and the highlight was our visit to Pearl Harbor; it was so incredibly interesting. I am not known for my historical knowledge or interest, but I left feeling educated and moved. Al felt much the same, although he certainly didn't learn as much as me given that his prior knowledge was far greater than mine.

Our trip to Hawaii, though, was mainly to satisfy our desire to see two wonders of nature. The first was to visit active volcanoes and see for the first time lava flows. The second was to take a trip to the summit of Mauna Kea. Standing tall at 13,740 feet this mountain enjoys 340 cloudless days a year and provides spectacular views from its summit. On one of these clear days you can see the curvature of the earth, and as darkness descends a spectacular night sky develops. We headed to Big Island, on the inter-island 'rattle and shake' airways, with much excitement.

Nature cannot always be relied on to give us what we wish for. Ten days before we arrived on Big Island there had been a spectacular volcanic eruption. All lava flows had subsequently stopped. We were told this was the first time in twenty-eight years. We did see some craters glowing in the distance, but as each day drifted by so did our hope of watching hot molten lava pour into the bubbling sea. Still we maintained our optimism and saved our four-wheel drive trip up to the summit of Mauna Kea until the end of our stay on Big Island. I look back now at the photos of me standing in a blizzard and can only give a wry smile that we did not manage to stand on the summit on one of the 340 clear days. We saw absolutely nothing at all. At least we experienced the rare event of snow in Hawaii. Every cloud, quite literally, has a silver lining. Nature can be very disappointing.

Our accommodation on Big Island was rather unique and splendid, though. We stayed in the aptly named village of Volcano in the grounds of an artist's gallery. Our little cabin was surrounded by statues, next to a garden of tranquillity and under the watchful eye of the resident goat. I am not sure Allister coped well with the whole feng shui vibe, but I loved it.

Big Island boasts the most southerly point of the USA, so we stood on the cliffs and watched the crazy jumpers as they hurtled down into the waves. Despite my new-found love of everything adrenalin fuelled, I decided against jumping off huge cliffs into the rough and wild sea below. A girl has her limits, after all.

We did stay in two places on Big Island, and our move to a hotel in the resort area of Kona was somewhat different to our artist's retreat. Some damage from the recent tsunami was visible and we were not surprised to find that only a ground-floor room on the seafront was available. There was not a room above the fifth floor free anywhere, but ground-floor availability was plentiful. We enjoyed the location, though, and the sea remained calm. A few more mai tais helped relax us each evening as we went to bed to the sound of the waves breaking on the shore.

Another trip on the inter-island 'rattle and shake' airways landed us on our next island. Kauai proved to be a good example of saving the best to last. Ten days of island life, living in a local community and being a beach bum was truly enjoyable. As well as the beaches there were tropical forests, mountains, breathtaking coastal scenery and a return to great hiking. We stayed in a condo, which was one of many that were laid out in squares with a pool in the middle. It was a mixture of short-terms renters like us and permanent residents. It was a far cry from the big resort hotels that did exist on the island, but such a great way to feel absorbed into Hawaiian life. The local cockerel with its regular built-in alarm clock at 3am, 4am and 5am was perhaps not ideal, but at least we didn't have to get up for work.

Kauai's beauty has meant that it has been the location of many films: *Jurassic Park, King Kong, South Pacific* and *Raiders of the Lost Ark*, to name only a few. We had just missed the filming of *The Descendants*, but a trip to the Tahiti Nui bar, where George Clooney had filmed a few scenes, made me feel close to the action. It was particularly enjoyable when the film was finally released in the UK and we got to see George sitting in my seat at the bar.

Our hiking allowed us to take in some truly beautiful surroundings. We had a fantastic day on the Kalalau Trail. We started along the coast with fantastic views before walking into Hanakapi'ai Valley. The walk became trickier, and it was lucky Al was on hand with his first aid kit to help a damsel in distress who slipped whilst crossing the river over slippery rocks. My hero, the damsel and I made it as far as a stunning 300-foot waterfall that was well worth the hike. The whole trail needs a full day and overnight camp before the return journey, so for us the waterfall was as far as we went before turning around. Al managed a good swim under the waterfall first, whilst I just took advantage of the opportunity to have a rest. It was a great day.

More stunning hiking followed as we explored the cliff tops of the Na Pali coast. I really could ramble on for pages about Kauai, but I think it is best summarised by saying that I would love to go back, and if ever you get to Hawaii then don't bypass this island. The Na Pali coast is particularly spectacular and should not be missed if you ever do make it and having seen it from the land, we could not resist ending our Hawaiian experience from the air. A 'doors off' helicopter flight around the island was awesome. What a dramatic way to end our island adventure.

A 4am alarm call the next morning, courtesy of a clock and a cockerel, was to ensure we caught our final inter-island 'rattle and shake' airways flight back to Honolulu in time for the connecting flight to San Francisco. There was no denying it. We would soon be heading back to the UK.

FORTY-ONE

LIFE CHANGES
SURGERY AND TEARS

MAY TO DECEMBER 2004

APRIL BECAME MAY AND MAY BECAME JUNE AND
Allister was getting on well at work. He exceeded all expectations:
his own, mine and his employer. His hours were increasing
gradually and there was more than a glimmer showing of the
man I had married. His confidence was improving, and he was
getting better at making decisions. I knew this because I was not
able to be quite so bossy. Rather annoyingly, I was not getting
everything my own way anymore. Every silver lining has a cloud!

Sainsbury's continued to be very supportive and in June he
was offered a move to a store closer to home. It was a smaller
store, but with only a fifteen-minute drive it was thought it would
help him get back to full-time work quicker. This proved to be
true and over the summer he started working full time again.

I was so very proud of him, and even today I still sometimes look at him and wonder how he did it. He had his difficult times during this period of course: dealing with his colostomy at work was not always easy, but he never kept anything secret from his colleagues. He was very open about the problems it presented and could even tell a few good jokes on the subject. I asked Allister how he would feel if I was successful in publishing this book and the details of his life were then out in the world for all to read. He told me he had nothing to be ashamed of or embarrassed about and would tell anybody anything about himself if they asked. This was the approach he took at work. He always said it stopped the gossip by talking about it himself. I am not convinced it did – he was good material – but as it helped him, I wasn't going to argue otherwise.

A long absence from work meant a bit of work for the personnel department in getting him reinstated correctly on various computer systems, the most important one being payroll, of course. All of this went smoothly, and the transfer to a new store also went without a hitch. Allister also took the opportunity to remind himself of his terms and conditions, and it was with very sheepish body language that he arrived home one day and said, 'It seems I have private medical insurance cover through work. You get this when you become a deputy store manager.' Al had been a deputy store manager for many years. I wasn't too sure whether to laugh at this point or not. I did, as it stopped me crying with frustration. Al had been having the most fantastic care over the previous eighteen months, but when faced with the choice of staying in a private room in a private hospital or sleeping on a ward with seven other men in an NHS hospital then I would have put Al in the private room every night. Ironically, Sainsbury's private health cover was for everything, including all pre-existing medical conditions. There would have been no reason not to use it. Once I calmed down and we thought about it rationally, though, there were lots of reasons that we could not have used the private hospital. He was too ill for a lot of the time and needed twenty-four-hour care in specialist units but moving forward we needed to find out our options.

In the summer of 2004 Allister was still seeing his oncologist for regular check-ups. It transpired that she didn't see patients privately. To change his oncologist made no sense. We were so grateful for the wonderful care that she and her team had given Allister. His illness had been long and complicated, and it was important that he was monitored closely. We felt at this time that continuity of care was vital, and so no change was made. When the time came for more surgery, we had a very different attitude.

With Al feeling so much better and the semblance of a normal life resuming, his thoughts about having his colostomy reversed were getting more frequent. Several consultations at the hospital and discussion between the doctors in charge of his oncology and gastroenterology care concluded that this could be attempted.

Allister wanted only the surgeon who had done the original operation to do the surgery. We both had a lot of confidence in this man. It was he who had performed the original operation for what was thought to be only Crohn's disease. It was his thorough investigation and care that got Al correctly diagnosed with lymphoma and this no doubt ultimately saved his life. He had also arranged for Al to see the oncology team so quickly when he examined the lump under Allister's arm at the beginning of 2004. There really was no other man for the job, and the good news was that he saw private patients. Private room and good food would be such a bonus, not to mention speed. Switching to seeing him privately meant the operation could take place as soon as we wanted. There was a little administration to undertake. The surgeon had to agree to the switch from NHS to private: this was no problem. The insurance company had to agree to the switch: this was no problem. Al needed to let work know he would be going back into hospital for surgery and would be off work for a while again: this was no problem.

Allister went back into hospital in September 2004. It was a hospital he hadn't visited before and it was into a lovely private room in a very calm atmosphere. The environment did help. My levels of stress had rapidly risen since we knew the date Al was to be admitted. I was thrilled, of course, that Al was having the surgery. Al had coped with living with a colostomy because he had convinced himself it was only temporary. If he had been told the surgery could not be done and it was permanent, I am not sure how he would have reacted. However, with surgery comes risks, and there was no guarantee.

The surgeon sat down with us on arrival and explained what might happen during the surgery. There were three scenarios. The first was that it would be a complete success, the bowel would be rejoined and the colostomy would be gone. The second would be that the surgeon would choose to do the operation in two parts. This part would mean the bowel would be rejoined, but then a temporary ileostomy would be put in for a few weeks to rest the new join. An ileostomy is basically higher up the bowel than a colostomy and for Al this would mean putting up with a bag for a few more weeks, but in a different place. He would then have another operation to take that out, be fully rejoined and good to go, literally. The final scenario would be that the surgeon would be unable to remove the colostomy successfully and Al would be stuck with it for life. We didn't want to think about scenario three too much and were hoping very much for scenario one.

It was nice to see the surgeon again and I could not help but lighten the mood by reminding him of something that happened the first time he operated on Al in April 2003. I joked with him that he needed to be careful not to 'snip' anything he shouldn't be when operating on Al that afternoon.

In 2003 the surgeon visited Allister on the ward after the operation. I was at home having some needed rest and missed the moment. It appeared that, despite having just undergone major surgery and being in pretty poor health, my husband still had a sense of humour. Al told me later that the surgeon, having examined him, explained that the surgery had gone well and talked to him about his colostomy. He then seemed a little awkward. He asked Al if he had children or plans to have any in the future. It turned out that Al was a bit of a mess inside (well, we knew that anyway) but in cutting away what needed to be cut, the surgeon inadvertently cut what he shouldn't have done, and Al had also undergone an unplanned vasectomy. Al said he really felt the urge to say children were in our plans – naughty, I know – but he didn't have the heart and reassured the surgeon that he need not panic as Al was sterile and had been since he was fifteen. The relief from the surgeon was apparently very evident.

Seeing the surgeon again now that Al was about to have another operation, I couldn't help my quip. The surgeon remembered the situation well, laughed, and promised to be careful!

Al went into theatre and I went shopping. I needed to distract myself, and shopping seemed a good idea. I didn't buy a single thing and spent a lot of time staring into space. I was surprised at the time at how high my anxiety was over this operation. Looking back, the reasons are clear. Our life had an air of normality to it once again, and, after such a long period of this not being the case, being back in hospital disrupted that normal feeling and brought back a lot of stressful memories. I was finding that hard to cope with. A greater feeling, though, was that of worry that the operation would not be a success. I knew without any doubt that Allister had coped with the colostomy so well because he believed it to be temporary. If this operation was not a success and Allister had to face having a colostomy for the rest of his life, then I was uncertain of the impact this would have on him.

My nerves and I headed back to the hospital. My nerves increased even further when there was no sign yet of Allister coming out of surgery. It was some time before his surgeon appeared to give me an update, and by this stage I was a wreck. Allister had been in surgery far longer than was estimated and so of course I assumed bad news. It wasn't all bad and the length of the operation was explained by the fact that the decision had been taken to put in a temporary ileostomy to rest the rejoined section of the bowel. It was felt that it was safer to allow time for it to fully heal before it was used again. This was scenario two, and whilst I would have been more thrilled with scenario one, I was delighted that it was not scenario three. Al would need further surgery in about a month's time to remove the temporary ileostomy, but he would be fully repaired at the end of it. I had a huge sense of relief and I knew that when Al came out of recovery, he too would be so very pleased. He was indeed very pleased, but the news was initially overshadowed by the enthusiastic attempts of a nurse to get him out of bed. As she tried to move him the pain was so severe for poor Al that I watched him go completely green and then he started making a strange groaning sound. It was decided it was a little soon to have him up and about, but he soon recovered well. It was not long before he was discharged with nothing more to do than wait a month for the second operation.

This return to hospital had definitely had a negative impact on me. Al was of course delighted that he would be fully reassembled in a few weeks' time and, while I of course felt the same way, I seemed to be having trouble relaxing.

I know now that everything that had happened had caught up with me and somehow Al returning to hospital had caused my protective wall to crumble away. I was bad tempered, tearful and not sleeping well. I had no desire to see anyone other than Al, and all I really wanted to do was sit and watch television and hold his hand. Wanting to hold his hand developed into never wanting to let him out of my sight and a constant feeling that something bad was about to happen. Looking back, I can see that these feelings lasted well beyond this period of time, and I believe now that it was another good eighteen months until I fully put behind me what had happened. The immediate problem was how I was going to stop crying at the smallest thing, get some rest and start to feel less on edge.

Al and I talked about it and, given that he was going to be off work for a good few weeks again, we thought about the option of me taking some leave of absence from my job. Ironically, Al was back on full sick pay. A return to work meant that when having to take time off again for his surgery his company sick pay started again. This gave us the option for me to take some unpaid leave along with some paid holiday that I had left for the year. This was of course all dependent on my company agreeing. I arranged a meeting with my boss, and, after what was only a short conversation, it was agreed that I would have six weeks off work: two weeks' holiday and four weeks' unpaid leave. It was easy in part because the company was going through a quiet period work wise and giving me unpaid leave suited them as well as me. That is not to say that they weren't both thoughtful and considerate of how I was feeling, but I guess it was an arrangement that worked well for us both at that time.

I started my leave almost straight away and Al and I spent a lovely couple of weeks relaxing at home. I did some odd jobs around the house, enjoyed going swimming and to the gym and just valuing some relaxed time. We cooked some nice meals, watched movies and avoided seeing people as much as we could. In truth, it was me who was having the social problem and I cannot to this day give any reason for it. If I was to guess, I would say that I was still having trouble with letting Al out of my sight. The reality of how close I had come to losing him was foremost in my mind. It was a feeling that I had suppressed continually at the times when he was most sick, and at the time we were given the news that a lump under his arm meant that the cancer was very aggressive. Somehow, I felt now the need to hold on to him and I did not want to share him. When it was just him and me, I felt safe, and somehow it made me feel less worried that he could get really sick again. I was obviously having some issues at this time, but I knew I would be ok eventually. Well, as long as Al didn't throw me another curve ball!

Al, unlike his wife, was doing rather well. He was relaxed about his upcoming operation and of course so thrilled that he would be all put back together. The ileostomy was proving a little more challenging than anticipated and it was good news it was only for a month. I will spare you all the detail, but managing it was not always easy for Al and one particular evening he was in the bathroom for a very long time. On opening the door, he told me not to go in and that he needed cleaning materials. He was in our bathroom for what seemed like most of the evening. He didn't want to talk about it that night, but the next day when I was looking at my gleaming bathroom and wondering what all the fuss was about, he revealed that there had been a little problem with control. He described the effect a fireman's hose has when it is pumping out water at maximum pressure and a fireman lets go. This is what happened to Al, only it wasn't water that was pumping out. How we laugh now!

Small bathroom incidents aside, it was a quiet and relaxing couple of weeks and in a blink of an eye we were back in the hospital awaiting the final operation.

I went shopping again whilst Al was in theatre. Again, I bought nothing and spent a lot of time staring into space. The difference this time was that when I returned to the hospital he was already out of theatre and on the ward. I saw his surgeon as I walked in and he smiled at me. I knew in that moment it had been a success and in an instant all my anxiety vanished. It was clear that I had been so fearful of the operation not working and Al having to face up to that. This was not the case. The surgeon confirmed that it had been a complete success, but we had to wait for a key moment before he could be discharged. It is unusual to get excited when your husband sits on the loo, but when it happened for Al, I was very excited. He hadn't been in that position for a long time and it was a big moment, so to speak. I got to share the joyous moment with my parents as they were visiting Al at the time, and as cries of 'the eagle has landed' came from the bathroom we all felt that we needed to applaud.

Al was discharged and the first few days at home were not easy. It took some time for his system to get working normally again, but Al got through it ok and we were both thrilled.

It was a couple of weeks until I had to return to work and about the same for Al, so we made a brave decision and decided to go away for a few days. A change of scenery was needed, and Al was fine to go away. Going abroad would not have been sensible at this early stage so we decided to go to St Andrews in Scotland. I had never been, but Al had once before to play golf and with a lovely coastline, plenty of accommodation to choose from and a nice selection of restaurants it sounded ideal. We decided to have a couple of nights in Edinburgh en route and we really did have a lovely time. To be doing what I can only describe as normal things was so fantastic. We enjoyed the nice restaurants (maybe a little too much for Al on one evening and he did pay the price for that) but apart from that he was well. As for me, well I still had a feeling of impending doom hanging over me, but it was lessening, and I was sleeping well and enjoying the break.

We returned home and went back to work, and before we knew it Christmas arrived. Al had been discharged by his surgeon some weeks before and on the day the surgeon shook our hands and wished us well I knew he was delighted to see the man who was standing in front of him. Al was a very different person to the weak, thin and malnourished individual that he had first operated on in April 2003. He would have known then that the odds were not stacked overly well in Allister's favour, so to be able to wish us good health and future happiness must have been a good moment for him. It certainly was for us, and I will be forever grateful for the part that this man played in keeping my husband alive for me.

There was a realisation from us both that as we looked ahead to 2005, we were planning a year like the rest of our friends and families were. We were talking about our jobs, holidays we may book, a family wedding and for Al there was a lot of talk about playing golf. How fantastic was that? It was very fantastic, so why did I feel that I was waiting for something bad to happen? I knew this was a negative state of mind, but the fear of losing my husband was hard to shake. I looked at him on New Year's Eve as 2005 dawned and I could not quite believe he was standing there with me. He was, and still is, a truly remarkable man.

FORTY-TWO

TRAVELLING NOT QUITE HOME

APRIL AND MAY 2011

ARRIVING IN SAN FRANCISCO GAVE US MIXED FEELINGS. It is a city we had visited some years earlier and we were looking forward to spending a few days there again, but it did signify the final stage of our trip. Our next flight would be taking us back to Heathrow. We were determined to enjoy ourselves and make the most of the ten days we had left.

Checking into our hotel, though, made me realise we needed a change of attire. Catching myself in the lobby mirror, I realised I looked like I had never done anything but travel, and the receptionist called Al 'Crocodile Dundee'. The kangaroo leather hat had to come off his head with some urgency, I felt. We showered, dressed more conservatively and headed to a late-night diner for some food.

Given that we had visited San Francisco before, we were keen to do something different, so we hired some push bikes and cycled over the Golden Gate Bridge. This was a mode of transport we had not used over our time travelling so we were very pleased with ourselves. It is a lovely way to explore the waterfront, see the bridge and an opportunity to see the town of Sausalito. Many people who hire the bikes catch the ferry back across the water but based on the principle of 'we have paid for the bikes, so we will use them as much as possible' we cycled back.

San Francisco is a great place to mooch, so we did much of that over the next couple of days. We felt compelled to ride the tram, even though we had done it before, and it was as much fun as we remembered. We frequented a few diners, drank plenty of coffee and just wandered.

It was then time to see a new part of the USA and we picked up a hire car and headed north into the land of the giant redwood trees. We spent our first night in a motel that was offering an early evening cheese and wine reception to its guests. This seemed like a very good idea. As very seasoned travellers, we never missed an opportunity to get something at no extra cost. We planned to go and find a place to have a pizza afterwards, but the crackers, cheese and wine kept coming so we were soon full and a little worse for wear. We headed back to our room, decided to watch a film and then fell asleep.

With a slightly woolly head the next morning we travelled into Humboldt Redwoods State Park. The trees are sequoia and seeing some at over 400 feet high was quite spectacular. We continued our travels to Redwood National Park and then drove through snow-cleared roads in Lassen Volcanic National Park. It was all very beautiful and relaxing. This cannot be said of our overnight stay in Reno. We did not fall in love with this place and venturing out was only a short five-minute excursion that saw us quickly retreat into the safety of our hotel, once we realised that we were not in the nicest part of town.

Things improved greatly when we arrived in Lake Tahoe. I have no doubts that in the peak ski season or during the peak summer season Lake Tahoe is packed and perhaps not quite so appealing, but luckily, we were visiting between seasons. There was enough snow around to make it very pretty and few enough people around to make accommodation cheap. We booked ourselves into a lovely little cabin on the lake, with breakfast thrown in, of course, for our last three nights away from English soil.

The Nevada/California state line runs through the town. On one side of the road are the casinos of Nevada, built as close to the state line as is physically possible, so as you step out of them and over the road you are in California and not a single casino can be seen. Allister was keen to enjoy the Nevada side of the road and entered a poker tournament. There were decent cash prizes for finishing in the top three. Obviously, he came fourth! He had a good time, though, and it is after all the taking part that counts. What am I saying? I don't mean that. We had been travelling for months and funds were a little light. It was, for me, all about the money!

With our accommodation came some cut-price activities, so a boat trip on the beautiful lake was on the agenda. We heard stories of spectacular colours and idyllic spots. We will never know if they are true as the fog closed in on us and we pretty much only saw each other.

Going out on snowmobiles in the mountains was far better. I was a little overwhelmed when I first climbed aboard mine, as I had never driven one before. These machines are large, heavy and powerful and everyone set off at a great speed around narrow bends with the mountain slipping away to the side. Not to be beaten, though, I soon caught up and got the general hang of the machine, at least enough to avoid falling off the mountain or hitting a tree. It was fantastic, I must say. The weather was perfect and the views when we stopped for hot chocolate at 9,000 feet were awesome.

At 8.30am on Thursday 14th April our alarm sounded, signifying the last day of what had been a truly incredible nine months. Although our trip would continue, with visits to Scotland and France planned over the coming weeks, we were flying back to Heathrow, and this meant we awoke with a whole mix of emotions. We were looking forward to seeing friends and family and of course continuing our travels on the other side of the Atlantic, but it was impossible not to feel a little sad that it was coming to an end.

It was a lovely trip back to San Francisco, though. We were flying later in the day and had time to enjoy a leisurely drive through snow-covered mountains en route and then a final drive into San Francisco across the harbour.

At 5.30pm our flight to Heathrow took off. Nine months earlier we had flown out of Heathrow heading for Singapore. It was inevitable, I suppose, that as darkness descended on our flight Allister and I were still talking about the most amazing nine months of our life.

It was a good job we had plenty to talk about, as a sleepless night on our ten-hour flight ensued. The lack of sleep, the awful food, the sound of a vomiting passenger and our bodies complaining that we had been awake for about twenty-four hours made arriving in Heathrow a little surreal.

It was about midday, I think, on Friday 15th April and a set of emotional parents greeted us as we walked through into departures. We headed to the pub for lunch. As I tucked into a burger and chips, I knew my digestive system was asking me if this meal should be breakfast, and perhaps some cereal or yoghurt would be better.

Arriving back in the UK was without doubt an extremely odd experience, and not being able to return to our own home only made it even more emotional than it was already destined to be.

The expression that hindsight is a wonderful thing is very apt about our arrival home. Our return was, for want of a better word, staggered. It turned out that this really didn't suit us. It was staggered because we arrived back in the UK but did not actually go home. We couldn't go home as our house was still rented out to our tenants. This was intentional, of course, as our travels were going to continue for two more months, during which time we planned to tour Scotland and then head to France. It was to be two weeks before we left for Scotland, though, and this was to be two weeks of visiting and staying with friends and family. That is not to say that it wasn't fantastic to see all our friends and family – it most certainly was – but we felt completely in limbo and in our heads, we weren't home at all. We were still travelling.

Our emotions were all over the place. Jet lag did not help, but the most overwhelming sensation was one of detachment. Living with friends and family after spending nine months on your own is very strange indeed. If you have ever experienced returning to your loved ones after a long absence, then you will understand the sense you have that they are just the same and their lives seem exactly as you left them. You, on the other hand, feel as though you have changed a great deal and that your life has somehow moved significantly forward.

We had undergone a unique experience. Travelling is not just about visiting places; it is about living away from the constraints of everyday life; it is about waking up in the morning and just doing what takes your fancy; it is about learning things about yourself because you have time to try things you have never tried before; it is about meeting people whose lives are nothing like your own; it is about immersing yourself in new cultures; and it is about freedom. To go from that to being surrounded by the life we left behind, and feeling that it had been frozen in time, was just plain weird. Suddenly we were sitting having dinner with our parents, we were visiting our niece and nephews, chatting to friends, getting together for dinner and even attending a wedding. Allister and I believed travelling had made us very sociable, which it probably had, but I don't think we really appreciated that, while we would chat away to anyone we met, for the most part it was just us. Not being just us anymore was quite difficult to get used to, and it was hard to feel part of life back home because we were actually still travelling. Hindsight tells me that, if there is to be another trip for us, it will end when we land at Heathrow and we will definitely make sure our house is vacant.

Emotions aside, we did have a lovely two weeks, and everyone made us welcome in their homes, fed us, watered us and gave us a bed. We are lucky to have so many people in our life who love us, and who were thrilled to have us back in the country and very keen to spend time with us. Two weeks passed quickly, though, and with our own car firmly back in our possession we headed north for our Scottish tour.

Most people will know that the weather in Scotland can be somewhat unpredictable. Our camping gear was packed, and I was working very hard at being enthusiastic as it was raining heavily. One of the big problems for me was that I had spent two weeks in the comfort of our parents' homes, enjoying home-cooked food, frequent and peaceful long hot showers and the plenty of other home comforts that were at my disposal. I may have struggled with some adjustment on arriving back in the UK, but we humans are quick to adapt, and I was quite happy sleeping in warm, clean and comfortable beds. I now had to adapt all over again and return to the world of living out of the boot of a car, sleeping under canvas and middle-of-the-night treks to the toilets in the freezing rain.

I was able to delay the inevitable as we started our Scottish tour in St Andrews because plentiful bed and breakfast options lured us in and convinced us to leave the camping gear in the car.

After a very pleasant couple of days we headed off to Aviemore and with very good weather I had run out of excuses. We pitched the tent in a lovely wooded campsite, and despite my misgivings it was great to be camping again. Weather changes quickly in Scotland, though, and heavy rain delayed our hiking. Eventually, though, not to be deterred, we headed up the mountain of Cairngorm. Allister and I love mountain hiking and 'bagging a few Munros' was our plan for Scotland. For those not in the know, a Munro is a Scottish mountain of 3,000 feet or more. There are 282 of these and we have so far bagged about twenty. We do have a fair way to go. Cairngorm falls into the Munro category and so it was a must for this part of our trip.

At the heart of a busy ski centre it does in fact have a cable car that takes you to a restaurant, not too far from the summit. This is so not the way you reach the top of a Munro, and as the weather was verging on the reasonable, we set off on our hike with much optimism. The mist rolled in and visibility became poor, but it was a straightforward route, so this did not deter us.

As is always the case, a call of nature was needed just as the rains came, and as I ducked down with the lashing rain and swirling mist engulfing me, I did question my sanity. I questioned it even more five minutes later as the mist cleared, and the mountaintop restaurant loomed before us. It seemed that my comfort break had been right under the windows where visitors enjoy the spectacular views. As I sat enjoying a coffee a few minutes later in the warm and dry, I was able to look down and reflect on the spot I had so recently visited.

We moved on from the restaurant and made it to the summit. We hiked all day, it rained on and off and I was certainly pleased to get back to the hot showers of the campsite. A cold and wet tent was less appealing, and I was feeling a little uncertain about how much enthusiasm I could muster for the coming weeks.

It turned out that I could muster very little. Our journey around Scotland was to take us up the east coast, across the top and down the west coast, finishing with a few days in Glencoe in the heart of the Highlands. We had never been to the north coast before and travelling down the west coast from there would allow us to visit other places we had never seen, and of course hike up some mountains along the way. I should have been looking forward to it, but I was fed up. Al was doing his best to get me in the mood for travelling again, but I think the moment had simply passed. I had tasted the comforts of warm and dry homes, enjoyed seeing friends and family again, and now I was driving in the wilds of the northernmost shores of the UK, wet and cold and in search of a campsite.

I don't remember exactly where we were or what day it was, but we pulled into a campsite in what was a gorgeous location. We were in the north and the campsite was above a deserted, golden, windswept beach. It was truly lovely, but as I got out of the car it started to rain and the wind was fierce. I just looked at Al and he knew that this was the end. I simply was not putting the tent up. At this point I felt truly miserable. It is such an awful thing to admit to. I was still lucky enough to be in the midst of a trip of a lifetime. I was in a beautiful location with my wonderful husband, and yet all I could do was complain. I had no more interest in travelling and I simply wanted to go home.

As we sat in the car, with me in tears and Al trying to reason with me, we weren't sure what to do next. We couldn't go home. Al reminded me that we did still have tenants in our house, and to do that would have been ridiculous. He had a point and I knew

I was being unreasonable. Al drove us to a bed and breakfast; I had a hot shower and a mug of tea and then we discussed more rationally what we were going to do. The long-range forecast was awful, so we agreed to abandon the camping. A few weeks of youth hostels, bed and breakfasts and even a few days in a cottage followed. The cottage was somewhat run down and in need of much care and attention, but it was warm and dry and had the benefit of a log fire, so this was all fine by me.

After a stern talking to, from Al and to myself, I had a great few weeks in Scotland. I got back into the swing and in-between the rain and storms we both enjoyed fantastic hiking in some breathtaking scenery.

Scotland is a beautiful country; there is no question of that. We walked along deserted golden beaches, hiked along rugged coastlines and stood on the top of the most spectacular mountain ranges. Hanging over a perilous cliff face so we could watch the puffins was memorable too. We had been on a world trip but were finishing close to home in one of the most amazing countries in the world. It proved that you don't have to travel thousands of miles to have a fantastic experience; sometimes the opportunity is right in front of you.

Our trip around Scotland ended with a few days in Glencoe. We stayed in a pub right in the heart of the mountains and it was a great way to finish. The weather didn't disappoint, culminating in a spectacular storm that gave us views of waterfalls being blown up the mountains and trees disappearing in front of our bedroom window.

We left Scotland in the rain, naturally, and headed back to Shropshire for a few days with my parents. Next up was France and then home. Home was something we were both looking forward to.

FORTY-THREE

THE EARLY YEARS
JUST THE TWO OF US

2000 AND BEYOND

OUR NIECE WAS BORN IN THE YEAR 2000. OUR FEELINGS were a little different from those we had when our friends had children. The shared happiness and joy for the new parents was the same, but somehow when the new child is your family there is just that extra closeness that comes instantly. She was beautiful, and as we have watched her grow into a charming, funny and articulate young teenager we can only be happy that she is part of our life. The addition of her brother a couple of years later gave us a bright, sporty, kind and thoughtful young nephew, and we enjoy greatly being their aunty and uncle.

More nephews came along on the other side of our family a few years later. My parents were thrilled with the arrival of their first grandchild in 2005 and the addition of his brother in 2007 completed the set. One looks like his mum and has the personality of his dad and one looks like his dad and has the personality of his mum. Well, kind of, but they are very different. The excitement they show when we come to visit is wonderful and we love spending time with them. One chats to us for hours on end about his day and every detail of what he has done, while the other looks on more thoughtfully, taking everything in and happy if we want to play a game or two. We are lucky to have our niece and nephews, and being an aunty and uncle means we get to enjoy the fun parts!

It is the not the same as having our own; we know that, and our parents know that too. When first hearing the news that they were to become grandparents they were of course elated. We remember feeling, though, that at times their faces also showed other emotions. Maybe they didn't and it was only a projection of our own inner feelings. I am not sure, but we did feel that they looked at us with eyes that reflected some sadness, or maybe a better word is wistfulness. Whatever it was, it was definitely emotions that reflected their compassion. It was only natural that they would consider that they would never hear the same news from us. It was sadness for them as well, I am sure, to know that not both of their children would be giving them grandchildren.

I remember my mum asking me, not long after my nephew, her first grandson, was born, how it made me feel. She was so happy to be a nana and I know I was not going to say anything to take away from that. The interesting thing was that it did make me stop and think properly about how it made me feel. It was indeed a mixture of emotions. It was 2005 and a time when Allister and I were moving on from his fight against cancer and rediscovering our life together. Thoughts about children had disappeared when Allister became ill and it was the arrival of our second nephew in 2005 that did stir some old feelings.

Some new ones too as I thought about how I would never hand my mum my baby and make her a nana. Time had meant a great deal of change for Allister and me, but after a surge of old feelings subsided, I was able to answer my mum with complete honesty. I was thrilled that she and my dad were grandparents. I did have some relief that my brother had taken the plunge – I mean, imagine my poor parents if he had decided not to have children. That would have meant no grandchildren at all! I told my mum I had accepted that Allister and I would not have children. Dominating my thoughts daily were feelings of relief and gratitude. I was not walking alongside her as a widow and the happiness I felt that I still had my Al was so overwhelming that not having children seemed so much less important now. I think she gave me a hug at this point, and I am not sure we have talked about it much since. Not much left to say really.

For Allister and me life did indeed change beyond recognition amidst the arrival of our niece and nephews. Our passion for travelling was growing and our enjoyment of our trip to the USA in 1998 prompted a return in 2001, when we spent three weeks touring the west coast. We returned to the USA again in 2002 and this time toured the east coast, including a trip along the Florida Keys. I know at this time we had still not fully given up on having children, but we were no closer to making a decision and the scales were most definitely tipping towards a life without them. We were very content and enjoying our life together. With our newly discovered love of the open road we had even started to tentatively talk about whether we could take a year off work and 'see the world'. Not a very serious discussion at this stage, but a sign that we were moving past having children.

Life has a way of taking decisions away from you though, and the onset of Allister's cancer in 2003 and the difficulties he faced over the next couple of years most certainly did put closure on whether we would have children or not. I often wonder how I would have coped with a young family during the time that Allister was ill. Would I have been able to support him as much as I did, and could we have fought together the way we did? Well, these questions cannot be answered, but I believe now it was meant to be. It was right that we didn't have children. Allister is still here, that is the main thing, and our life does feel fulfilled. I will not dwell on what might have been. I am only grateful that I met and married such a wonderful man. Some people, like us, can't have children, some have the children, but the marriage fails, and some find themselves widows at an early age. Few people get it all, so it is important to feel grateful for what you do have, and I know I am that.

I know that Allister and I never sat down and made a decision. Our denial, lack of decision and ultimately Allister's illness made it for us. I truly believe if the desire had been overwhelming, we would have made a step towards adoption or donor sperm. For us, not having Allister's biological children was not solvable. Our relationship was strong enough that we found happiness with each other, and this is more than enough. We will have to deal with not being grandparents one day as we watch our friends' children and our niece and nephews have children of their own. It is the next step in the pattern of life, and being grandparents looks kind of fun, but you know what? I think we will handle it just fine.

Not being able to have children gives rise to so many emotions. It is how you handle these emotions that dictates whether you can be accepting of the situation you find yourself in, or whether you allow those emotions to dominate and potentially destroy your happiness. I know we became accepting and have no doubts that we never let our happiness be lost. Sad times – yes – and hard times – yes – but we were never prepared to let not having children stop us from being happy. I know we have succeeded in that, and, while our future will be without children and indeed grandchildren, we will still enjoy every minute and be grateful for what we do have and not dwell on what we don't. Life is too short to do that. A cliché, I know, but how true.

We do have friends who still have young families. We enjoy spending time with them, and for me there is no longer a tugging sensation in my heart or feelings of sadness. We both have acceptance and closure and, most importantly, no regrets. That is not to say I don't have any emotions. I still ponder what might have been. I sometimes look on at family life and wish it could have been me, but there are other times when children are having tantrums or a mum is being run ragged by the endless demands of our modern-day schools and children's activities that I think, thank goodness it isn't me. Mind you, if you want to moan about your kids and your hectic family life then I am perhaps not the person to come to. One left-over legacy for me is that I do not deal very well with parents who moan about their life. To me they should be happy and grateful to have children. I know it is not as simple as that, but what I know and what I sometimes feel are a little different.

Allister and I could have had children in our life: we had options and many people in our position would have taken one of those options. Life gifted me with a wonderful husband: sadly, he couldn't give me his children. The alternatives were not for us and so we live our life just the two of us. As I sit here today waiting for Allister to walk through our front door, I know now that I wouldn't have had it any other way.

FORTY-FOUR

TRAVELLING
THE ADVENTURE ENDS

JUNE 2011

ONE OF THE BEST THINGS ABOUT OUR FRIENDS AND family when we returned to the UK in April 2011 was their unquestioning generosity. We had a bed where we needed it, and there were no locks on the food cupboards. The final few weeks of our trip were extremely enjoyable, and this was down to some wonderful hospitality from those closest to us.

We arrived in Shropshire at my parents' home, after enjoying, and in part enduring, our trip around Scotland. Suitably pampered, we headed south and arrived on the doorstep of our dear friends in Fareham. There is nothing better than a night out with friends, and I am sure after several drinks we were telling them that. Absence can make you a little sentimental when you return.

We were off to France next and an early-morning alarm call reminded us that we had a ferry to catch. We bid farewell to our friends, although only for a couple of weeks as we would take up residence at their house again on our return.

Allister's parents have a house in the Dordogne area of France, and it was to be our home for the next couple of weeks. They were there to welcome us and a very relaxing end to our trip began.

We swam in the pool, drank plenty of wine, enjoyed quite a few BBQs, played a bit of golf and slept quite a lot. It seemed we had run out of steam. To be in one place for a whole two weeks, to have clothes in a wardrobe and not in a rucksack, and to not have to think about where we might be sleeping the next night was rather great.

It did give us the opportunity to reflect on our trip before going home and back to the world of work. It was a chance to really think about what we had achieved and to really appreciate every minute of what we had done, the places we had been to and the things we had experienced. In some ways it was a strange couple of weeks as we were waiting to move back home and it did feel like a lull before normal life, if there is such a thing, started again. We had a great time, though, and in a blink of an eye we were back on the ferry returning to the southern shores of England.

On Saturday 11th June we arrived back with our friends; we went to the pub again and had a few drinks again. As a result of this, Sunday was a very lazy day. The weather was rubbish, such a fitting end to our trip, so we stayed in. Our friends were lucky, though: we had plenty of photos to entertain them with! We did squeeze in some movies, some more drinks and plenty of snacks.

Monday 13th June 2011 was a day that we always remember. We said goodbye to our friends and drove back to Petersfield.

We were going home, and we did feel quite excited. On Tuesday 13th July 2010 we had locked the front door to our home and boarded a flight to Singapore. Eleven months later we were pulling onto our drive about to open our front door once more.

Al put the key in the lock, gave me a grin and then there we were, standing in our empty house. It was a truly wonderful moment and an incredibly sad one all at the same time. We were home, but our travels were over. It was the end of what had been an incredible trip. We were so happy we had done it, so sad it was over, feeling like it happened in a flash, wanting to do it all over again and yet happy to be home. Confusing emotions, for sure, but as I looked at Al, I knew that it was an experience that we would both value for the rest of our life.

After such a rush of emotions the rest of the day turned out to be a bit of an anticlimax. We didn't really have much to do. We were picking up a hire van the next day so we could empty our storage container and get all our stuff home. We had not been totally sure what time we would be able to get into our house on that Monday, so it made sense to hire the van the next day. It turned out that we were sitting on our lounge floor wondering what to do at around 9.30am, so in hindsight the van would have been useful.

Some decisions were soon made about the best use of our time, and we headed to the storage container in our car to pick up a few essentials. It was then time for a much-needed trip to Sainsbury's. The expression 'not much food in the house' did not apply to us. There was simply nothing in the house and a hefty shop of food and drink, toiletries and those all-important household items such as toilet roll was much needed. Our trolley was soon overflowing, and it was best not to think about the bill.

The day passed very quickly, and we made plans to get up early the next day to collect the van and get all our stuff home. Most of it would just be moved from the storage container into our garage. Al would be going back to work in two weeks' time, and I would be job-hunting. Whilst this exploration of the job market was going on, I planned to redecorate the house from top to bottom. The house was in good order, but an empty house was easy to decorate, and it was long overdue. We were going to rip up all the carpet, decorate room by room and then buy new carpet. There was therefore no point moving everything back into the house. It would be essentials only and it was to be a fair few weeks before all our worldly belongings were finally unpacked. After living out of a rucksack for the best part of the last year we were not concerned about this transitional period.

As we lay on our airbed in our bedroom that night, we did decide that one essential was our bed. That would be moved back in the next day; we saw no point in sleeping on an airbed for any longer than necessary.

I don't think we slept much that night. I think it felt like a last night of freedom. The next day and over the days that were to follow we would have a great deal to do. Waking up to the choice of simply spending the day drifting around a local town, walking in the mountains or simply lounging on a deserted beach would not be an option. We had to return to our life, and finally drifting off to sleep that night without doubt signified the end of our travelling adventure.

FORTY-FIVE

LIFE CHANGES
MORE SURGERY AND TEARS

2005

THE FUNNY THING ABOUT RECOVERING FROM CANCER is that it is such a gradual process. It is so gradual that you almost don't notice a change and then suddenly it hits you: life has returned to normal. I think that does sum up 2005 for us. We were living our life again and enjoying it.

It was a year of holidays for us and we kicked off with a week in Polperro, Cornwall. When Al was young, he used to stay there with his parents. They rented a cottage from someone his mum knew. It was a lovely place at the end of what is called 'The Warren', with wonderful views over the harbour, the rocks and out to sea. As students in Plymouth, Allister and I were not far from Polperro, so he introduced me to this lovely Cornish fishing village and his favourite pub, the Blue Peter. After we finished our time at Plymouth, we started booking odd weeks in the same cottage Al stayed in with his parents and so began a routine that saw us visit most years for at least a week. We were booked for a week in 2003 when Al became ill and so we had no choice at the time: we had to cancel the holiday. It seemed therefore somehow quite fitting that our first proper holiday destination since his recovery was to be Polperro, a place so special in our hearts.

Alas, things do not always go to plan, and when we phoned to book a week in our favourite cottage, we found out it had been sold. The new owners were currently renovating it and it was unclear whether it would be a holiday rental property in the future. There were of course plenty of other places to stay in the village, so we picked one and headed down there in February.

It had been three or four years since our last visit, and it was great to see that it looked and felt just the same. We slipped into our old habits very easily, out walking during the day followed by cosy evenings in the Blue Peter. Familiar faces smiled and said hello, and of course our absence wasn't questioned. Why would it be? We were after all just visitors who arrived at irregular intervals. This was great. We sat in the pub chatting to people who had no idea what Allister had been through. It is of course wonderful to have family and friends who care, but it does mean that they want to know how you are and in some cases are wondering if you are really ok. Chatting with relative strangers meant we did not think about what had happened and we felt like ourselves again. Nobody was looking at Al with that sympathetic look in his or her eyes, and no one had any thoughts about what had happened during our last two years. There is a lot to be said for anonymity. What a wonderful week we had, and it really made us appreciate that it was always doing the simplest things that we enjoyed the most. It was walking in the sea air, enjoying fantastic scenery, a few beers in the pub and the odd game of cards that made us happy. Twenty-something years on from the first time Al took me for a drink in the Blue Peter and we are still visiting every year and it is still the simplest pastimes that make us the happiest. All you need is a pair of hiking boots and a good pub to relax in at the end of a long walk. Whether the walk is the coastal paths of Cornwall or the mountains of Scotland, the result is the same: a sense of freedom, satisfaction and, in the case of the mountains, the odd adrenalin surge!

I certainly did feel better after our week in Polperro, but underneath I knew I wasn't myself. Put simply, I expected something to disrupt our happiness; I just couldn't shake the feeling that something bad was going to happen. It didn't of course stop us planning the rest of the year and we booked two holidays. We decided to go to Rhodes at the end of June for a week of relaxing in the sun and we booked two weeks in America in September. We planned to do a road trip and the main attraction was to be a visit to Yellowstone National Park. Al's love of all things geological meant that a trip to one of the remotest and largest volcanic areas on the planet was without doubt a great idea.

Rhodes was a very enjoyable week overall but will always be remembered for two significant events. The first of these was when all my pent-up emotions came to a head and I released all of them in the space of about three exhausting hours. It was our wedding anniversary and Al had booked us a table in the nicest restaurant in the resort. We arrived at a rose petal covered table and a bottle of champagne on ice. And so, it began. Champagne, it seems, was the emotional release I needed, but unfortunately what started as a romantic and loving conversation soon drifted into a dark place where I started stressing over the food Al was eating and how much he was drinking. I was blissfully happy one minute and overwhelmed with the emotion that I was going to lose him the next.

Have you ever walked into a room when the lights are off and felt that prickly feeling on the back of your neck because you think someone, or something, is lurking in the shadows? It is fear, albeit brief and irrational, that makes you feel on edge. This kind of feeling had been with me on and off for about eighteen months, although I did not fully realise it at the time. It was a sense of apprehension and the feeling that something was in those shadows waiting to upset me again. On 29th June 2005, on our wedding anniversary night, those feelings that had been simmering away tumbled out over our romantic dinner table and turned me into a wailing banshee. Al really did not know what to do with me, and successfully managed to say all the wrong things. To be fair anything he said was likely to be wrong, and it was evident the best place for me was not in public, so we retreated to the privacy of our room.

I cannot recall what we talked about, what started me off or how it ended: I only know that the next morning I felt better. I don't think Al fully understood at the time. He was better; this was a good thing, so why was I so upset? He had a point. He says now that he understands fully and like so many things, we do laugh about it, but at the time it was so hard to think logically and deal with the emotions I had. This rather eventful night did signify a turning point, though. The feeling of apprehension gradually melted away, leaving in its place a feeling of relief and optimism, more like the feeling you get when you open the curtains in the morning to a bright and sunny day. I experienced more tears on our trip to the USA some weeks later, but those were tears of joy. Those were good tears.

The end of our week in Rhodes landed us with significant event number two. After a pleasant evening we headed to bed and Al announced that something wasn't right with his stomach.

This did not help me get rid of the feelings I had that something bad was about to happen. Anyway, after a late-night examination by both of us, we concluded he had a hernia of some sorts. It looked like something was sticking out that shouldn't be. The good news was we were heading home the next day.

A trip to his GP confirmed that Allister did indeed have a hernia and needed to be referred to the hospital to see a consultant. The benefits of the recently discovered private health insurance proved advantageous as he got an appointment relatively quickly. The consultant confirmed the hernia and advised he needed surgery to repair the weakened area. Apparently, it was not uncommon after having had a colostomy for the area to be weak and a hernia to occur. A typical good news and bad news conversation followed. The good news was that it was a simple operation; the bad news was that the timing for when the surgery could be done was four weeks before we were due to fly to America. This was a tight timescale should anything unexpected occur in the surgery and for recovery from the operation. There was no choice, though, and the surgery was booked.

And so, it was that I found myself wandering around the shops again a couple of weeks later as Al underwent surgery, again. I was surprisingly relaxed, a sure sign that I was feeling much better. My relaxed state was proven to be the right way to be as the surgery went without a hitch and we headed home for Al to recover. Of course, this needed to be a quick recovery, as we did have to catch a flight to America in less than four weeks. We both found ourselves pleasantly surprised at how quick the recovery was. It was it seemed normal for it to be quick; it was a routine and uncomplicated operation. We had got used to Al undergoing complicated surgery when he was unwell and therefore weak. He was of course fit and well for this operation and thus recovery was at a normal speed. How things had changed for us.

We flew into Las Vegas in early September, picked up our hire car and drove straight to a place called Zion National Park. We had planned a two-week road trip, which was to include staying for a few days in Yellowstone, and we would end the trip with a couple of nights in the crazy playground of Las Vegas. Our jet lag meant on the first morning we were up, dressed and looking for breakfast very early. We were staying just outside the park and fortunately for us there was a lovely little coffee shop that was open and awake as early as we were.

After a lovely breakfast we headed into the park with hiking boots on and rucksacks packed. Our plan was to hike the Angels Landing Trail. This would, to start with, take us for about two miles up well-maintained paths in very picturesque surroundings. To the end of this path and back is, for many people, the total walk. However, the walk extends across a narrow sandstone ridge with sheer drop-offs on both sides. There are even anchored support chains to help you pull yourself up the steep cliffs, and to hold on to in case you suddenly slip. The elevation is quite high by this point, but you don't really want to stop in this part to enjoy the views; the sheer drops do take the edge off a bit! Allister was determined to tackle the hardest walk in the park on our first day, and of course why wouldn't he want to do this when he was just four weeks out of surgery? I probably would have settled for an easier walk, but who was I to stand in the way of the man who needed to prove to himself that he could achieve anything he wanted to now?

And so, we made the climb, I fought the urge to shut my eyes at certain points and we reached the top. It was certainly worth the terrifying climb. The views were truly magnificent, and it felt very rewarding to look down on the people whose walk concluded at the end of the maintained path. It was so rewarding, in fact, that, as I looked at Al with his arms raised above his head in victory, the tears came again. The good news was that these were tears of joy. I think there had also been a fair amount of adrenalin flowing around whilst we completed the climb as I worried about the sheer drop-offs and whether Al should be doing this. Al looked momentarily alarmed as I started to snivel, no doubt panicking that it was a Rhodes moment all over again. He soon realised that I was just happy. I was so proud of what he had achieved in overcoming his illness, getting fit again and loving life all over again. I felt quite overwhelmed that we were there, doing things that at times I thought we would never do again. Allister was fully recovered. There was no doubt about it. What a moment: tears were inevitable.

The rest of our holiday was amazing, and I kept the tears to a minimum. The varied experiences of the trip were fantastic. We left Zion in shorts and T-shirts, headed north and kept driving north all day. By the time we stopped for the night in a place just outside Yellowstone National Park it was snowing. We were much underdressed! I would recommend a visit to Yellowstone National Park to anyone. It is remote, wild and stunning, and walking around this simmering volcano is a truly spectacular experience.

Arriving back in Las Vegas at the end of our two weeks in remote and sparsely populated areas of America was a little overwhelming. Neon lights, the noise of slot machines and people everywhere actually felt quite unpleasant. We humans are very adaptable, though, and Allister and I were soon enjoying some great food, some not-so-great gambling and a show. It was a terrific end to a fantastic holiday.

Coming home and going back to work, I really felt like we had moved on. There was and still would be for some time to come those moments of worry, but I think this worry was at a sensible and more acceptable level now. Allister's regular check-ups were those moments when I felt that being a little anxious was ok. I never really understood why Al was never anxious, but

I think he felt so well that he wouldn't allow himself to believe that he wasn't going to get anything but a clean bill of health. The year 2005 concluded with this being the case and it ended what had been overall a fantastic year.

FORTY-SIX

Life Changes A Happy Ending

2006 to 2009

We took a decision in early 2006 to change the oncology consultant that Al was seeing for his check-ups. This was in no way a criticism of the consultant or the care and support she had given both Allister and me during his illness and recovery. She had been wonderful and most importantly she had got him well again, and we both were and always will be forever grateful for that. The problem for us was that when we attended her outpatient clinics, we often weren't seeing her and in fact we were seeing different doctors in her team each time Al had a check-up appointment. Al had private health insurance, but we had never used it for his oncology care because we wanted to stay with the consultant who had got him through his cancer and understood fully his long and complicated history. As we were struggling to actually see her, though, we thought that perhaps seeing an oncologist privately would give us that consistency of care that we wanted.

Allister decided to write her a letter to thank her and to explain our thoughts about potentially changing consultants. She phoned Al and was very understanding. She gave us the name of the only oncologist she said she would be comfortable with transferring Allister to and said she would write to him. It seemed he was the doctor who taught her everything she knew and a renowned expert in lymphoma. Sounded like a good choice to me!

Al contacted his insurers to verify the transfer and then we phoned the new consultant's secretary to make an appointment for his next check-up.

I was at home working a few days later when the phone rang. It was the new consultant on the phone, and he had phoned to say hello to us both. I did think this was a little odd, especially as he was talking to me as if he knew me. I felt I had been caught a bit off guard as I mumbled that I was fine and hoped he was too. The real confusion kicked in when he said, 'It has been a long time since I have seen you and Allister.' The man was clearly mad, I thought. We had never met him before.

It was such a strange moment when he explained that when Allister was treated for lymphoma when he was fifteen, he was a junior doctor and had looked after Allister on several occasions. Here we were twenty years later, and he was going to be his doctor again. Al had come full circle. I did have to explain to him, though, that he was mistaken about meeting me. I hadn't met Allister until I was nineteen and at that time did not attend any of his check-up appointments. I was convinced that he was confused. He was adamant that he had met me and went on to explain why he was right.

Al and I had found out just before our wedding that we couldn't have children. I remember Al going to the hospital to do his little test. I remember the results came back and we found out Al was sterile. What I didn't remember is how we got the results. The doctor on the phone was telling me his side of this story.

When Allister went for a check-up just before we got married, he saw a doctor who asked him how he felt about not being able to have children. This doctor was the doctor on the phone. It was full circle indeed. The doctor told me how he felt when it was apparent that Allister did not know what he was talking about. He said it was a consultation he had never forgotten, but what was worse was the following appointment, when both Allister and I went back for the results. This is how he met me and remembered me so well. It was an odd thing, though. I had and still do not have any recollection of this appointment. The doctor I was chatting to on the phone said it was a horrible experience for him. Firstly, this was because of his original and yet wrong assumption that Allister knew there was a chance that his lymphoma treatment had made him sterile. Secondly, he then had to deliver the news to a very young, soon-to-be-married couple that they definitely couldn't have children. I guess it must have been even worse for me, as I seemed to have blocked this appointment from my memory completely.

With the confusion untangled he confirmed the appointment, which would be in Southampton, and said he looked forward to meeting us both again. This all made for interesting conversation over dinner with Al that evening. Al's memory was obviously better than mine as he remembered both the appointment and the doctor.

I think it was great for the doctor when he met Al again. He had spent a long time reading his notes before the first consultation and could appreciate how remarkable it was that such a fit and healthy person was sitting in his room. It turned out that he was responsible for the development of the treatment that Al had undertaken in 2003. He was a lymphoma guru for sure! Having met us both before, there was a real personal touch to that appointment. Al was examined and had an X-ray and his recent blood tests were reviewed. All was well, of course, but as usual I needed to hear it before I could relax again.

One thing that sticks in my mind quite vividly from that appointment was a feeling of optimism. Allister had been closely monitored since 2003. Monitoring like this can make you feel uneasy as it suggests the disease could rear its ugly head again at any point. It is a mixed feeling, though, as regular check-ups reassure you that nothing will be missed. Whilst I had always felt relief after Allister's previous check-ups, I had never felt such optimism before. This doctor had such a pragmatic approach to the chances of the disease recurring. Yes, it could happen, but if it does then we will just treat it again and get rid of it again was the message he gave. He described it in such a way that I felt that Allister's chances of getting cancer again were no greater than my own, and this, strange as it may sound, was reassuring.

The six-month check-ups became annual check-ups, and in 2008 as we sat chatting to the consultant, he said that the time had come for Allister to be discharged. Now, I am fully aware that I should have been absolutely thrilled at this news. My Al was officially being declared cured. I am afraid I just panicked! How could we possibly cope without the reassurance that the annual check-ups gave us? My panic must have been very evident as the doctor looked at me and tried to reassure me that Al was fine and that he didn't need an annual check-up to confirm that. He went on to say that any worries we had at any time then we only had to pick up the phone and call him. All of this was of course fantastic, but I wasn't having any of it. It was too soon, and I wasn't ready to have my comfort blanket removed.

It was agreed that Al would be booked for another check-up the following year. Al didn't care one way or the other but recognised my need to know that he was still being monitored, even if he thought I was worrying for no reason.

It was a good thing, though, because when we went back in 2009 for that final check-up all I wanted was to hear that word: 'discharged'. I realised that a trip to see an oncologist just gave us a feeling that it wasn't over. Neither of us wanted that feeling anymore. It was time to move on. The final appointment was quick and ended with a lovely chat with the doctor and an acknowledgement that Al really had moved past his illness, and that actually I had too. We shook hands with the doctor and said our goodbyes. I did manage to slip a card with his contact details on into my pocket, though, just in case. Some things had not and will not ever change. Worrying about the most important person in your life is normal, but I do that now without it dominating my every waking moment. There are even times when I don't think about Al at all, but don't tell him that!

Al and I walked across the car park holding hands. We didn't say much. What was there to say? We felt free. That summed up the moment. We drove home, had a cup of tea and carried on living.

The year drifted by until November, when on a very cold night in Covent Garden we reached that moment. It was that moment when our life was to change again, but this time it was for all the right reasons and for reasons that we controlled. It was the night when I uttered the words that were about to change everything.

'If we keep going on these nice holidays every year we are never going to go travelling. No one thinks we will go anyway so are we or not?'

'You're right,' said my husband. 'Let's just do it, let's go next year.'

So, we did!

EPILOGUE

2019

HAVE YOU EVER SEEN THE FILM *SLIDING DOORS*? IF you haven't, then I recommend it. A chance moment of a girl catching or missing a train. The film tells the story of her life if she catches it and how different her life becomes if she doesn't. A cleverly written and thought-provoking film. We can all say we have had moments of *Sliding Doors*. Allister and I cannot help but define our life since 2003 as such. How different would our life have been if Allister had not been so ill?

It is not just about the drive it gave us to go travelling, although that of course is a key moment; it is also about how the trip has changed our life and who we are since we got home.

It is now the summer of 2019. Al still works for Sainsbury's, the company that supported him so well through his long illness. He has in fact recently reached the milestone of thirty years' service. He has a different role now, working in HR, but I'm sure it's not only the many years of experience he has within the company but also those experiences he has had outside of it that mean he has much to offer.

His love of life is always there for everyone to see. Time with me is what he loves the most. How lucky does that make me? Running, hiking, football, motorbikes, gardening, playing snooker, friends, family and so much more are all important parts of his life. How wonderfully normal and yet defined by both his illness and the experience of travelling. He fills every minute of every day, always happy, always positive, always looking forward and luckily always mine. A man defined by his 'sliding door'.

As for me? Well, travelling taught me so much about the value of time. Time with Al is the most important thing to me, and our lifestyle now means I get a lot more of that. I know having time allows so much. Time for yourself, time with those you love, time to enjoy different things with different people and sometimes just time to think.

I no longer work in the corporate world. I work within the wonderful organisation that saved my husband's life. I am forever grateful to the NHS and those people in it that touched our lives during the hardest time we have ever had. I am now a medical secretary. I work part time and have found myself doing a job that is right for me. Would I have made this change had I not gone travelling? No. Would I have gone travelling if Al hadn't been ill? No, I don't think so. *Sliding Doors*.

We returned from our travels in 2011 and some five years later, in 2016, we felt like we had reached a turning point once more. We were often asked if we wanted to go travelling again. Yes, was always the answer, but in a different way at a different time. We were happy with our life but sitting still does not come naturally and so we found ourselves thinking about a change.

We were approaching twenty years in the same house. Was it time to move? We thought so. We didn't move far, only ten minutes further south, but with more space and a great location we knew it was a good decision. We found it quite remarkable how different life felt. Change is definitely a good thing.

Since 2011, our life, as is so often the case for us all, has had both ups and downs. Some very difficult times have been thrown across our path and it has, at times, not always been easy to remain positive. What I do know for sure, though, is that our love for each other is stronger than ever and that our desire to make the most of every minute and enjoy life remains, no matter what challenges come our way.

Travel and adventure, albeit on a smaller scale, still play a very important part in our life and we are making sure that we continue with our love of seeing the greater world.

We travel overseas and travel on home shores. This year we went to Austria for our first skiing holiday together. Never too old! Unsurprisingly, and somewhat annoyingly, Al was a natural. I took the slightly more cautious approach but we both fell in love with it; after all, it's great exercise, stunning scenery and the après-ski is pretty good too! We are hooked and plan for this to be an annual event from now on.

We still of course hide out in Polperro when we can, and we have enjoyed mountain walking holidays in the Lake District and Wales. Scotland's spectacular landscape lures us the most, though. We have travelled to the Isle of Skye several times over the last few years and the beautiful Outer Hebrides in the summer of 2015 was a truly breathtaking adventure.

We both feel something special when we reach the summit of a Scottish mountain. We go back to Scotland time and time again. Why? Because there is always 'one more mountain'.

ACKNOWLEDGEMENTS

WHEN I STARTED WRITING *ONE MORE MOUNTAIN*, I had no idea how hard it would be. Without the unfailing support and encouragement from my husband, Allister, I might never have finished it. I cannot thank him enough for never letting me give up.

I must thank my family and friends for their continual interest and endless enthusiasm about me writing this book. Specifically, thanks to Ony Rogers, who patiently reviewed every page and provided invaluable advice.

One More Mountain is the culmination of many wonderful and extraordinary years with Allister. I wish to thank all my family and friends for the love and support they have given to both of us, through the bad times, the sad times, the good times and the great times. They know who they are.